EMOTIONAL WELLNESS

More OSHO Books

Transforming fear,
anger, and jealousy into
creative energy

EMOTIONAL WELLNESS

Harmony Books
New York

Copyright © 2007 by Osho International Foundation, Switzerland

All rights reserved.
Published in the United States by Harmony Books, an imprint of the
Crown Publishing Group, a division of Random House, Inc., New York.

Harmony Books is a registered trademark and the Harmony Books
colophon is a trademark of Random House, Inc.

OSHO is a registered trademark of Osho International Foundation,
used with permission/license.

The material in this book is selected from various discourses by Osho
given to a live audience. All of the Osho discourses have been published
in full as books and are also available as original audio recordings.
Audio recordings and the complete text archive can be found via the
online Osho Library at www.osho.com.

ISBN: 978-0-307-33788-7

Printed in the United States of America

CONTENTS

EMOTIONAL WELLNESS

PART I

Understanding

the Nature

of Emotions

Emotions cannot be permanent. That's why they are called "emotions"—the word comes from "motion," movement. They move; hence, they are "emotions." From one to another you continually change. This moment you are sad, that moment you are happy; this moment you are angry, that moment you are compassionate. This moment you are loving, another moment full of hatred; the morning was beautiful, the evening is ugly. And this goes on. This cannot be your nature, because behind all these changes something is needed like a thread that holds all of them together.

In a garland you see flowers, but you don't see the thread. These emotions are like the flowers of a garland. Sometimes anger flowers, sometimes sadness flowers, sometimes happiness, sometimes pain, sometimes anguish. These are the flowers, and your whole life is the garland. There must be a thread; otherwise you would have fallen apart long ago. You continue as an entity—so what is the thread, the polestar? What is permanent in you?

FIRST THINGS FIRST

The Mechanics of the Mind

Your emotions, your sentiments, your thoughts—the whole paraphernalia of the mind—are manipulated by the outside. Scientifically, it has become more clear now, but even without scientific investigation the mystics have been saying exactly the same thing for thousands of years—that all these things your mind is filled with are not yours; you are beyond them. You get identified with them, and that's the only problem.

For example, somebody insults you and you become angry. You think you are becoming angry, but scientifically speaking the other person's insult is only functioning as a remote control. The person who has insulted you is managing your behavior. Your anger is in his hands; you are behaving like a puppet.

Now scientists are able to put electrodes in the brain at certain centers, and it is almost unbelievable. The mystics have been talking about it for thousands of years, but only recently has science discovered that there are hundreds of centers in the brain controlling all your behavior. An electrode can be put at a particular center—for example, the center for anger. Nobody insults you, nobody humiliates you, nobody says anything to you; you are sitting silently, happily, and somebody pushes a button on a remote control and you become angry! It is a very strange feeling because you cannot see the reason anywhere, why you are becoming angry. Perhaps you will rationalize it somehow. You see a man passing by in the hallway and you remember that he insulted you—you will find some rationalization just to console yourself that you are not going mad. Sitting silently . . . and suddenly feeling so angry without any provocation?

And the same remote controller can work to make you happy. Sitting in your chair you start giggling, and you look all around— if somebody is watching you he will think you are going crazy! Nobody has said anything, nothing has happened, nobody has slipped on a banana peel, so why are you giggling? You will rationalize it, you will try to find some rational grounds for giggling. And the strangest thing is that the next time the same button is pushed and you giggle, you will again come up with the same rationale, the same consolation, the same explanation— not even the rationalization is yours! It is almost like a gramophone record.

When I was reading about the scientific investigations into these centers, I was reminded of my student days. I was a competitor in an inter-university debate; all the universities of the country were participating. The Sanskrit University of Varanasi was also participating, but naturally the students from Sanskrit

University were feeling a little inferior compared with competitors from other universities. They knew ancient scriptures, they knew Sanskrit poetry, drama, but they were not familiar with the contemporary world of art, literature, philosophy, or logic. And the inferiority complex works in very strange ways. . . .

After I had spoken, the next person was the representative from Sanskrit University. And just to impress the audience and to hide his inferiority complex, he started his speech with a quotation from Bertrand Russell—he had memorized it, and Sanskrit students are more capable of memorizing things than anybody else. But his stage fright was such . . . he knew nothing about Bertrand Russell, he knew nothing about what he was quoting. It would have been better to have quoted something from Sanskrit, because he would have been more at ease.

In the middle he stopped—just in the middle of a sentence. And I was sitting by his side, because I had just finished. There was silence, and he was perspiring, and just to help him, I said, "Start again"—because what else to do? He was simply stuck. I said, "If you cannot go ahead, start again; perhaps it may come back to you."

So he started again: "Brothers and sisters . . ." and at exactly the same point he got stuck again. Now it became a joke. The whole hall was shouting, "Again!" and he was in such a difficult situation. Neither could he go ahead nor could he keep standing there silent; it would look too idiotic. So he had to start again. But he would start at the very beginning, "Brothers and sisters . . ."

For the whole fifteen minutes we heard only that portion—beginning with "Brothers and sisters . . ." and going up to the point where he got stuck, again and again. When his time was finished he came and sat next to me. He said, "You destroyed my whole thing!"

I said, "I was trying to help you."

He said, "This is help?"

I said, "You were going to be in difficulty anyway. This way at least everybody enjoyed it—except you, that I can understand. But you should rejoice that you made so many people happy! And why did you choose that quotation? When I was saying to you, 'Start again' there was no need to start over from the very beginning—you could have dropped that quotation, there was no need."

But I came to know through reading the scientific research that the speech center is exactly like a gramophone record, but with one thing very strange and special. The moment the needle is taken away from the record you can put the needle back at the spot where you took it from, and go on from there. But in the speech center, when the needle is taken away and put back again, the center instantly goes back to the very beginning.

If this happens, can you say you are the master of what you are saying? Are you the master of what you are feeling? Certainly there are no electrodes implanted in you, but biologically exactly the same work is going on.

You see a certain type of woman, and immediately your mind reacts: "How beautiful!" This is nothing but the remote control. That woman functioned like a remote control attached to an electrode, and your speech center simply went into its recorded speech: "How beautiful!"

The mind is a mechanism. It is not you. It records things from outside, and then reacts to outside situations according to those recordings. That's the only difference between a Hindu and a Mohammedan and a Christian and a Jew—they just have different gramophone records. But inside, it is one humanity. When you play a gramophone record . . . it may be in Hebrew, it may be in Sanskrit, it may be in Persian, it may be in Arabic, but it is the same machine that plays the record. To the machine it does not matter whether it plays Hebrew or Sanskrit.

All your religions, all your political ideas, all your cultural attitudes are nothing but recordings. And in certain situations, certain recordings are provoked.

There is a beautiful incident in the life of one of the wisest kings of India, Raja Dhoj. He was very much interested in wise people. His whole treasury was open only for one purpose—to gather together all the wise people of the country, whatever the cost. His capital was Ujjain, and he had thirty of the country's most famous people in his court. It was the most precious court in the whole country.

One of the greatest poets of the world, Kalidas, was one of the members of the court of Raja Dhoj. One day a man appeared at the court saying that he spoke thirty languages with the same fluency, the same accuracy and accent as any native person could, and he had come to make a challenge: "Hearing that you have in your court the wisest people of the country, here are one thousand gold pieces. Anybody who can recognize my mother tongue, these one thousand gold pieces are his. And if he cannot recognize it, then he will have to give me one thousand gold pieces."

There were great scholars there—and everybody knows that whatever you do, you can never speak any language the way you can speak your own mother tongue, because every other language has to be learned by effort. Only the mother tongue is spontaneous—you don't even learn it, really. It is a result of your whole situation that you simply start speaking it. It has a spontaneity. That's why even the Germans, who call their country "fatherland"—most countries call their land "the motherland"—but even the Germans don't call their language the "father tongue." Every language is called a mother tongue because the child starts learning from the mother. And anyway the father never has the chance to speak in the house! It is always the mother who is speaking; the father is listening.

Many in the court of Raja Dhoj took the challenge. The man spoke in thirty languages—a few pieces in one language, a few pieces in another language—and it was really hard! He was certainly a master artist. He was speaking each language the way only a native can speak his own mother tongue. All of the thirty great scholars lost the contest. The contest continued for thirty days, and every day one person took the challenge and lost it. They would guess, and the man would say, "No, this is not my mother tongue."

On the thirty-first day . . . King Dhoj had been continually saying to Kalidas, "Why don't you take up the challenge? Because a poet knows language in a more delicate way, with all its nuances, more than anybody else." But Kalidas remained silent. He had been watching for thirty days, trying to determine which language the man spoke with more ease, with more spontaneity, with more joy. But he had not been able to find any difference, the man spoke all the languages in exactly the same way.

On the thirty-first day, Kalidas asked King Dhoj and all the wise people to stand outside in front of the hall. There was a long row of steps, and the man was coming up; as he came up to the last step, Kalidas pushed him down. And as he fell rolling down the steps, anger came up—he shouted.

Kalidas said, "This is your mother tongue!" Because in anger you cannot remember, and the man had not been expecting this tactic to be used in the contest. And that actually was his mother tongue. Deepest in his mind, the recording was of the mother tongue.

One of my professors used to say—he had lived all over the world, teaching in different universities—"Only in two situations in life have I been in difficulty in other countries, and those are when I was fighting or falling in love. In those times, one needs one's mother tongue. However beautifully you express your love in another language, it is not the same, it seems superficial.

And when you are angry and fighting in somebody else's language, you cannot have that same joy . . ." He said, "Those are two very significant situations—fighting and loving—and mostly they are together with the same person! With a person you are in love, and with that same person you have to fight."

And he was right to say that everything in a language that you have learned remains superficial—you can neither sing a beautiful song nor can you use the real four-letter words of your own language. In both cases, it remains lukewarm.

The mind certainly is a mechanism for recording experiences from the outside, and reacting and responding accordingly. It is not you. But unfortunately the psychologists think the mind is all, and beyond mind there is nothing. That means you are nothing but a collection of impressions from the outside; you don't have any soul of your own. Even the very idea of the soul is given by the outside.

This is where the mystics differ. They will agree absolutely with the contemporary scientific research about the mind. But it is not right about the human being's totality. Beyond the mind, there is an awareness that is not given by the outside, and is not just an idea—and there is no experiment up to now that has found any center in the brain that corresponds to awareness.

The whole work of meditation is to make you aware of all that is mind, and disidentify yourself from it. When the mind is angry, you can realize that it is simply a gramophone record. When the mind is sad, you can simply remember that it is only a gramophone record. A certain situation is pressing the remote control and you feel sad, you feel angry, you feel frustrated, you feel worried, you feel tense—all these things are coming from the outside and the mind is responding to them. But you are the watcher, you are not the actor. It is not your reaction.

Hence the whole art of meditation is to learn awareness, alertness, consciousness. While you are feeling angry, don't repress it; let it be there. Just become aware. See it as if it is some object outside you. Slowly go on cutting your identifications with the mind. Then you have found your real individuality, your being, your soul.

Finding this awareness is enlightenment—you have become luminous. You are no longer in darkness, and you are no longer just a puppet in the hands of the mind. You are a master, not a servant. Now the mind cannot react automatically, autonomously, the way it used to do before. It needs your permission. If somebody insults you and you don't want to be angry, then you don't become angry.

Gautam Buddha used to say to his disciples, "To be angry is so stupid that it is inconceivable that intelligent human beings go on doing it. Somebody else is doing something and you are getting angry? He may be doing something wrong, he may be saying something wrong, he may be making some effort to humiliate you, to insult you—but that is his freedom. If you react, you are a slave. If you say to the person, 'It is your joy to insult me, it is my joy not to be angry,' you are behaving like a master."

Unless this master becomes crystal clear in you, crystallized, you don't have any soul. You are just a phonograph record, and as you grow older your recording goes on expanding. You become more knowledgeable, and people think you are becoming wiser— you are simply becoming a donkey loaded with books.

Wisdom consists only of one thing—not of knowing many things but of knowing only one thing, and that is your awareness and its separation from the mind.

Just try watching in small things, and you will be surprised. People go on doing the same things every day. They go on deciding to do something, and they go on repenting because they have not done it; it becomes a routine. Nothing you do is new. The things that have been giving you misery, sadness, worries, wounds, and you don't want to do anymore—somehow mechanically you go on doing these things again and again as if you are helpless. And you will remain helpless unless you create a separation between mind and awareness.

That very separation is the greatest revolution that can happen to a human being. And from that very moment your life is a life of celebration—because you need not do anything that harms you, you need not do anything that makes you miserable. Now you can do and act on only that which makes you more joyous, fulfills you, gives you contentment, makes your life a work of art, a beauty.

But this is possible only if the master in you is awake. Right now the master is fast asleep, and the servant is playing the role of master. And the servant is not even your servant; the servant is created by the outside world. It belongs to the outside world; it follows the outside world and its laws.

This is the whole tragedy of human life: you are asleep and the outside world is dominating you, creating your mind according to its own needs—and the mind is a puppet. Once your awareness becomes a flame, it burns up the whole slavery that the mind has created. And there is no blissfulness more precious than freedom, than being a master of your own destiny.

The mind is not your friend. Either the mind is pretending to be the master or it has to be put into its right place as a servant—but the mind is not your friend. And the struggle for freedom, for bliss, for truth is not with the world; it is a fight with this puppet mind. It is very simple.

Kahlil Gibran has a beautiful story. The farmers in the villages, to protect their cultivated crops, create a false man, a scarecrow. It is just a stick tied to another stick; it looks almost like a cross. And then they put some clothes on it, and perhaps a mud pot in place of the head. That's enough to make birds and animals afraid that somebody may be standing there. The clothing and the two hands make them think somebody is watching. For the animals it is enough; they keep away from the farm.

Gibran says: Once I asked such a scarecrow, "I can understand the farmer who made you—he needs you. I can understand the poor animals—they don't have great intelligence to see that you are bogus. But in the rain, in the sun, in the hot summer, in the cold winter, you remain standing here: for what?"

And the scarecrow said, "You don't know my joy. Just to make those animals afraid is such a joy that it is worth suffering rain, suffering sun, suffering heat, winter, everything. I am making thousands of animals afraid! I know I am bogus, there is nothing inside me, but I don't care about that. My joy is in making others afraid."

I want to ask you: Would you like to be just like this bogus man—nothing inside, making somebody afraid, making some- body happy, making somebody humiliated, making somebody re- spectful? Is your life only for others? Will you ever look inside? Is there anybody in the house or not? Are you interested in the search to find the master of the house?

The master is there—perhaps asleep, but he can be awak- ened. And once the master is awakened within you, your whole life takes new colors, new rainbows, new flowers, new music, new dances. For the first time you become alive.

The door opens into reality not through the mind but through the heart.

The greatest problem that modern man is facing is that the mind is trained too much and the heart is completely ne- glected—not only neglected, but condemned, too. Feelings are not allowed, feelings are repressed. The man of feeling is thought to be weak; the man of feeling is thought to be childish, imma- ture. The man of feeling is thought to be not contemporary— primitive. There are so many condemnations of feeling and of the heart that naturally one becomes afraid of feelings. One starts learning how to cut off feelings and slowly the heart is simply by-passed; one goes directly to the head. Slowly the heart becomes nothing but an organ that pumps the blood, purifies the blood, and that's all.

In the history of humankind, for the first time the heart has been reduced to something utterly physiological—it is not. Hidden behind the physiology of the heart is the true heart—but that true heart is not part of the physical body, so science cannot discover it. You will have to learn about it from the poets, painters, musicians, sculptors. And finally, the secret key is kept by the mystics. But once you know that there is an inner chamber of your being—absolutely uncontaminated by education, society, culture; utterly free from Christianity, Hinduism, Islam, completely unpolluted by all that has been happening to modern human beings, still virgin—once you have contacted that source of your being, your life is lived on a different plane.

That plane is divine. To live in the mind is the human plane, to live below the mind is the animal plane. To live beyond the mind, in the heart, is the divine plane. And with the heart we are connected with the whole. That is our connection.

All the meditations that I have devised are meant for a single purpose: to throw you from your head into your heart, somehow to pull you out of the mire of the head into the freedom of the heart, somehow to make you aware that you are not just the head.

The head is a beautiful mechanism; use it, but don't be used by it. It has to serve your feelings. Once thinking serves feelings, everything is balanced. A great tranquility and a great joy arise in your being, and not from anything outside but from your own inner sources. It wells up, it transforms you, and not only you—it makes you so luminous that whosoever comes in contact with you will have a little taste of something unknown.

REPRESSION AND CONTROL

The Roots of Emotional Conditioning

Every child is born feeling the whole universe, not knowing his separation from it. It is by slow education that we teach him to feel separate. We give him a name, we give him an identity, we give him qualities, we give him ambitions—we create a personality around him. Slowly, slowly, the personality becomes thicker through upbringing, education, religious teaching. And as the personality becomes thicker the child starts forgetting who he used to be in his mother's womb—because there, the child was not a doctor or an engineer. There he had no name; there he was not separate from existence. He was absolutely together with the mother, and beyond the mother there was nothing. The womb was all, the child's whole universe.

The child in the mother's womb never worries, "What will happen tomorrow?" He has no money, no bank account, no business. He is utterly unemployed, with no qualifications. He does not know when night comes, when day comes, when seasons change; he simply lives in utter innocence, in deep trust that everything will be okay, as it has been before. If it is okay today it will be okay tomorrow. He does not "think" this way, it is just an intrinsic feeling; there are no words because he does not know words. He knows only feelings, moods, and is always in a jubilant mood, rejoicing—absolute freedom without any responsibility.

Why does every child coming out of the womb give so much pain to the mother? Why is every child born crying? If you try to look deeply into these small matters, they may reveal to you great secrets of life. The child resists getting out of the womb because the womb has been his home. He does not know any calendar; nine months are almost an eternity—it feels like forever. Ever since he has known that he is, he has always been in the womb. Now suddenly his home is being taken away. He is being thrown out, expelled, and he resists with all the power he has. He clings to the womb; that is the problem. The mother wants him to be born sooner, because the longer he remains inside the more pain she has to suffer. But the child clings, and he is always born crying—every child, without exception.

Only about one man, Lao Tzu, is it said that he was born laughing. It is possible; he was an exceptional man, crazy from the very beginning. Not knowing exactly what to do, that this is the time to cry, he laughed. And he remained that way his whole life, just doing wrong things at wrong times. The story of his whole life's strangeness begins with the laughter. Everybody was shocked because no child has ever done that. But that is the only exception—which may be simply a myth, which may be just a retrospective idea. Seeing Lao Tzu's whole life, the people who wrote about him must have thought that his beginning could not be the same as everybody else's; it must have been a little crazy. His whole life he was crazy and surely his beginning must have been consistent with his life. Perhaps it is only a myth. But even historically, if he did laugh it is an exception, not the rule.

Why is every child born crying? Because his home is being taken away, his world is being destroyed—suddenly he finds himself in a strange world amongst strange people. And he continues to cry because every day his freedom becomes less and less, and his responsibility becomes more and more weighty. Finally he finds there is no freedom left but only duties to be fulfilled, responsibilities to be carried out; he becomes a beast of burden. Seeing this with the clarity of innocent eyes, if he cries you cannot condemn him.

The psychologists say the search for truth, for God, for paradise, is really based on the experience of the child in the womb. He cannot forget it. Even if he forgets it in his conscious mind, it goes on resounding in his unconscious. He is searching again for those beautiful days of total relaxation with no responsibility, and all the freedom of the world available.

There are people who have found it. My word for it is "enlightenment." You can choose any word, but the basic meaning remains the same. One finds that the whole universe is just like a mother's womb to you. You can trust, you can relax, you can enjoy, you can sing, you can dance. You have an immortal life and a universal consciousness.

But people are afraid to relax. People are afraid to trust. People are afraid of tears. People are afraid of anything out of the ordinary, beyond the mundane. They resist, and in their resistance they dig their own graves and they never come to the juicy moments and ecstatic experiences that are their birthright—they only have to claim them.

A man living in Los Angeles goes to see a psychiatrist. He introduces himself as Napoleon Bonaparte, even though his file card shows his name to be Hymie Goldberg. "So what seems to be the problem?" asked the doctor.

"Well, Doc, actually everything is great. My army is strong, my palace is magnificent, and my country is prospering. My only problem is Josephine, my wife."

"Ah," says the doctor, "and what is her problem?"

Throwing his hands up in despair, the man says, "She thinks she is Mrs. Goldberg."

In his tensions, in his anxieties, his problems, man loses himself in the crowd and becomes someone else. Deep down he knows that he is not the role he is playing; he is somebody else. And this creates a tremendous psychological split in him. He cannot play the role correctly, because he knows it is not his authentic being—and he cannot find his authentic being, either. He has to play the role because the role gives him his livelihood, his wife, his children, his power, his respectability, everything. He cannot risk it all, so he goes on playing the role of Napoleon Bonaparte. Slowly, slowly he starts believing it himself. He has to believe it; otherwise, it will be difficult to play the part. The best actor is the one who forgets his individuality and becomes one with his acting; then his crying is authentic, his love is authentic, then whatever he says is not just the prompted role, it comes from his very heart—it looks almost real. When you have to play a part, you have to be deeply involved in it. You have to become it.

Everybody is playing some part, knowing perfectly well that this is not what he or she is supposed to be. This creates a rift, an anxiety, and that anxiety destroys all your possibilities of relaxing, of trusting, of loving, of having any communion with anybody—a friend, a beloved. You become isolated. You become, with your own actions, self-exiled, and then you suffer.

So much suffering in the world is not natural; it is a very unnatural state of affairs. One can accept once in a while somebody suffering, but blissfulness should be natural and universal.

Why is it so difficult and scary to show your real feelings and just be yourself?

It is difficult to show your feelings and just be yourself because for thousands of years you have been told to repress your feelings. It has become part of your collective unconscious. For thousands of years you have been told not to be yourself. Be Jesus, be Buddha, be Krishna, but never be yourself. Be somebody else. Down the ages you have been taught so continuously, so persistently, that it has gone into your blood, into your bones, into your very marrow.

A deep self-rejection has become part of you. All the priests have been condemning you. They have been telling you that you are sinners, you are born in sin. Your only hope is that Jesus can save you, or Krishna can save you, but there is no hope as far as you are concerned—you cannot save yourself, somebody else will save you. You are doomed; you can only pray to Jesus, to Krishna, to save you. As far as you are concerned you are just worthless; you are just dust and nothing more. You have no value, you have been reduced to ugly things, to disgusting beings. It is because of this that one finds it very difficult and scary to show one's true feelings. You have been taught to be a hypocrite.

Hypocrisy pays, and whatever pays seems to be valuable. They say honesty is the best policy—but remember, the best "policy." Even honesty has become only a policy, because it pays. If it does not pay, then? Then dishonesty is the best policy. The whole thing depends on what works, what pays, what makes you richer or more respectable, what makes you more comfortable, safer, more secure, what gives you more nourishment for the ego—that's the best policy. It may be honesty, it may be dishonesty; whatever it is, use it as a means—it is not an end.

Religion also has become a good policy. It is a kind of insurance for the other world. You are preparing for the other world by being virtuous, by going to church, by donating to the poor. You are opening a bank account in paradise, so when you go there you will be received with great joy, angels shouting "Alleluia!" and dancing, playing on their harps. How big a bank account you have there will depend on how many virtuous deeds you have done. Religion too has become business, and your reality is repressed.

And the repressed people have been respected so much. You call them saints; they are really schizophrenic. They should be treated. They need therapy, and you worship them! Out of a hundred saints, if even one turns out to be a real saint, that will be a miracle. Ninety-nine are just hocus-pocus, pretenders, deceivers. And I am not saying they are trying to deceive you; they are deceiving themselves, too. They are repressed people.

I have known many mahatmas in India, respected by the masses like anything. I have been very intimate with these people and in their privacy they have opened their hearts to me. They are uglier than you will find ordinary people.

I used to visit prisoners to teach them how to meditate, and I was surprised in the beginning that the prisoners—even those who have been sentenced for their whole lives—are far more innocent than your saints, far better people than your saints, far simpler, far more innocent. Your saints are cunning, clever. Your saints have only one quality, and that is that they are able to repress themselves. They go on repressing, and then naturally they become split. Then they have two kinds of lives: one that they live at the front door, and the other that they live at the back door; one that they live as a showpiece, and the other— the real one— that they don't show to anybody. They are afraid even to see it themselves.

And that's the case with you too, on a smaller scale, of course, because you are not a saint. Your illness is not yet incurable; it can be cured. It is not yet so acute, it is not yet chronic. Your illness is just like the common cold; it can disappear easily.

But everybody is influenced by these so-called saints, who are really insane people. They have repressed their sex, they have repressed their greed, they have repressed their anger, and they are boiling within themselves. Their inner life is nightmarish. There is no peace, no silence. All their smiles are painted.

Hindu scriptures are full of stories that whenever a great saint reaches very close to attaining enlightenment, beautiful women come from the gods to disturb him. I have not yet been able to find out why the gods should be interested in disturbing these poor fellows. Some ascetic, fasting for years, repressing himself, standing on his head, torturing himself . . . he has not done any harm to anybody except himself. Why should the gods be so interested in distracting him? They should really help him! But they send beautiful women, naked, and those women dance around and make obscene gestures to the poor fellow. Naturally he becomes a victim, he is seduced, and he falls from grace—as if the gods are against anyone who is reaching close to enlightenment. This seems so ridiculous! They should help, but rather than helping they come to destroy.

But those stories should not be understood literally; they are symbolic, they are metaphors, and they are very meaningful. Had Sigmund Freud come across those stories he would have utterly enjoyed them. They would have been a treasure for him, they would have supported his theories of psychoanalysis as nothing else.

Nobody was coming; those repressed people were projecting. These were their desires, repressed desires—repressed so long that now they had become so powerful, even with open eyes these people were dreaming.

In India, if a woman is sitting down somewhere, the saints are taught not to sit in that place for a certain length of time after the woman has left, because that space vibrates with danger. Do you see the foolishness of it all? And these have been the teachers of humanity. These are the people who have made you scared of your own feelings—because you cannot accept those feelings. You reject them, hence the fear.

Accept them. Nothing is wrong in your feelings, and nothing is wrong with you! What is needed is not repression or destruction, you have to learn the art of creating harmony in your energies. You have to become an orchestra. Yes, if you don't know how to play on musical instruments you will create noise, you will drive your neighbors mad. But if you know the art of playing on the instruments, you can create beautiful music, you can create celestial music. You can bring something of the beyond to the earth.

Life is also a great instrument. You have to learn how to play upon it. Nothing has to be cut, destroyed, repressed, rejected. All that existence has given to you is beautiful. If you have not been able to use it beautifully, it simply shows that you are not yet artful enough. We have all taken our lives for granted, and that is wrong. We are given only a raw possibility. We have been given only a *potential* for life; we have to learn how to actualize it.

All possible resources have to be used, so that you can learn to use your anger in such a way that it becomes compassion, to use your sex in such a way that it becomes love, to use your greed in such a way that it becomes sharing. Every energy that you have can become its polar opposite, because the polar opposite is always contained in it.

Your body contains the soul, matter contains mind. The world contains paradise, dust contains the divine. You have to discover it, and the first step toward discovery is to accept yourself, rejoice in being yourself. You are not to be a Jesus, no. You are not to be a

Buddha or anybody else. You have to be just yourself. Existence does not want carbon copies; it loves your uniqueness. And you can offer yourself to life only as a unique phenomenon. You can be accepted as an offering, but only as a unique phenomenon. An imitation Jesus, Krishna, Christ, Buddha, Mohammed—these won't do. Imitators are bound to be rejected.

Be yourself, authentically yourself. Respect yourself. Love yourself. And then start watching all kinds of energies in you— you are a vast universe! And slowly, as you become more conscious, you will be able to put things right, into their right places. You are topsy-turvy, that is true, but nothing is wrong with you. You are not a sinner; with a little rearrangement you will become a beautiful phenomenon.

> Can you talk more about repression and how we can get free of it? What is it, exactly, and if it's so much better not to repress, why do we keep doing it?

Repression is to live a life that you were not meant to live. Repression is to do things that you never wanted to do. Repression is to be the person that you are not; repression is a way to destroy yourself. Repression is suicide—very slow, of course, but a very certain, slow poisoning. Expression is life; repression is suicide.

When you live a repressed life, you live not at all. Life is expression, creativity, joy. When you live the way existence wanted you to live, you live the natural way.

Don't be afraid of the priests. Listen to your instincts, listen to your body, listen to your heart, listen to your intelligence. Depend on yourself, go wherever your spontaneity takes you, and you will never be at a loss. And going spontaneously with your natural life, one day you are bound to arrive at the doors of the divine.

Your nature is the divine within you. The pull of that nature is the pull of life within you. Don't listen to the poisoners; listen to the pull of nature. Yes, nature is not enough—there is a higher nature too—but the higher comes through the lower. The lotus grows out of the mud. Through the body grows the soul, through sex grows transcendence.

Remember, through food grows consciousness. In the East we have said, "*Annam brahm*," food is God. What type of assertion is this that food is God? The lowest is linked with the highest, the shallowest is linked with the deepest.

The priests have been teaching you to repress the lower. And they are very logical, only they have forgotten one thing—that life is illogical. They are very logical and it appeals to you. That's why you have listened down the ages and followed them. It appeals to your reason that if you want to attain the higher, you shouldn't listen to the lower. It looks logical. If you want to go high, then don't go low—it is very rational. The only trouble is that life is not rational.

Just the other day one of the therapists here was talking to me. In his group workshop sometimes he comes to moments when the whole group falls silent—out of nowhere, out of the blue. And those few moments of silence are of tremendous beauty. He was saying, "They are so mysterious, those moments. We are not managing them, we don't think about them, they simply come sometimes. But when they come, the whole group immediately feels the presence of something higher, something greater than everybody, something mysterious. And everybody falls silent in those moments." And his logical mind said, "Perhaps it will be good if I do the whole workshop in silence." He must have started thinking, "If those few moments, far and few between, are so beautiful, then why not do the whole thing in silence?"

I said to him, "There you go—you are being logical, and life is not logical. If you remain silent throughout the whole process, those moments will never come again."

There is a polarity in life. The whole day you work hard, you chop wood, then in the night you go into your deepest sleep. Now you can think logically; you can be mathematical about it. The next morning you can think, "The whole day I worked so much and was tired, but still I could come to such a deep sleep. If I practice resting the whole day long, I will go into an even deeper sleep." The next day you simply recline in your easy chair, you practice resting. Do you think you are going to have a good sleep? You will lose even your ordinary sleep! That's how people who don't do much in the day can suffer from insomnia.

Life is not logical, nature is not logical. Nature gives sleep to the beggars who have been working the whole day, moving from one place to another in the hot summer, begging. Nature gives a good sleep to laborers, to stonecutters, woodcutters. The whole day they have been working hard and getting tired. Out of that tiredness, they fall into deep sleep.

This is the polarity. The more you are exhausted energy-wise the more is your need for sleep, because you can only get more energy from deep sleep. If you exhaust your energy, you create a situation in which you will fall into deep sleep. If you don't work at all, then there is no need. You have not used even the energy that was given you, so what is the point of giving you any more? Energy is given to those who use it.

Now this therapist was being logical. He thought, "If we do the whole process in silence . . ." But then even those few moments of silence will be missed and the whole group will start chattering inside. Of course, on the outside they will remain silent, but their minds will go crazy inside. Right now they are working hard, they are expressing their emotions, catharting, bringing everything up, throwing everything out—they become exhausted. Then come a few moments when they are so exhausted that there is nothing else to throw out. In that moment, suddenly, there is a contact; silence descends.

Out of work is rest. Out of expression is silence. This is how life works. Its ways are very irrational. If you really want to be secure, you will have to live a life of insecurity. If you really want to be alive, you will have to be ready to die at any moment. This is the illogic of life! If you want to be authentically true, then you will have to risk. Repression is a way to avoid the risk.

For example, you have been taught never to be angry, and you think that a person who is never angry is bound to be very loving. You are wrong. A person who is never angry will not be able to love either. They go together; they come in the same package. A person who really loves will sometimes be really angry. But that anger is beautiful—it is out of love! The energy is hot, and you will not feel hurt by the person's anger. In fact, you will feel grateful that the person was angry. Have you watched it? If you love somebody and you do something, and the person is really angry, frankly angry, you feel grateful because he loved you so much that he can afford anger. Otherwise why? When you don't want to give the other person the energy of your anger, you remain polite. When you don't want to give anything, you don't want to take any risks, you go on smiling. It doesn't matter.

If your child is going to jump into the abyss, will you remain un-angry? Will you not shout? Will your energy not be boiling? Will you go on smiling? It is not possible!

There is a story:

Once it happened in Solomon's court that two women came fighting over a child. Both were claiming that the child belonged to them. It was very difficult. How to decide? The child was so small that he could not say anything.

Solomon looked, and he said, "One thing I will do—I will cut the child in two and divide the child. That is the only way possible. I have to be just and fair. There is no proof either way that the child belongs to A or to B. So I, as the king, have decided—cut the child in two and give each woman half."

The woman who was holding the child continued to smile, she was happy. But the other woman became simply crazy, as if she would kill the king! She said, "What are you saying? Have you gone mad?" She was in a rage. She was no longer an ordinary woman, she was anger incarnate, she was on fire! And she finally said, "If this is justice, then I give up my claim. Let the child remain with the other woman. The child belongs to her, he is not my child!" Angry, yet with tears flowing down her face. And the king said, "The child belongs to you. You take it. The other woman is just bogus, false."

When you love, you can be angry. When you love you can afford it. If you love yourself—and that is a must in life, otherwise you will miss your life—you will never be repressive, you will be expressive of whatsoever life gives. You will be expressing it: its joys, its sadness, its peaks, its lows, its days, its nights.

But you have been brought up to become bogus, you have been brought up in such a way as to become a hypocrite. When you feel angry you go on smiling a painted smile. When you are in a rage, you repress the rage. You are never true to what is within you.

It happened . . .

> Joe and his little daughter, Midge, took a trip to an amusement park. En route they stopped for a huge meal. At the park they came to a hotdog stand, and Midge explained "Daddy, I want—" Joe cut her short and stuffed her with popcorn.
>
> When they came to the ice cream vendor, little Midge once more shouted, "Daddy, I want—" Joe interrupted

*her again, and this time he said, "You want, you want! I
know what you want—ice cream?"*

"No, Daddy," she pleaded, "I want to throw up."

That's what she wanted from the very beginning. But who listens?

Repression is not listening to your nature. Repression is a trick to destroy you.

> *Twelve skinheads walk into a pub wearing their Levi's jackets and all their equipment. They walk up to the bartender and say, "Thirteen pints of bitter, please."*
>
> *"But there are only twelve of you."*
>
> *"Look, we want thirteen pints of bitter."*
>
> *So he gives them the beer and they all sit down. There's a little old fellow sitting in a corner and the skinhead leader walks over to him and says "Here you are, dad, here's a pint of beer for you."*
>
> *The little fellow says, "Thank you, thank you. You are generous, son."*
>
> *"It's all right, we don't mind helping cripples."*
>
> *"But I'm not a cripple."*
>
> *"You will be if you don't buy the next round."*

That's what repression is; it is a trick to cripple you. It is a trick to destroy you, it is a trick to weaken you. It is a trick to put you against yourself. It is a way of creating conflict within you, and whenever a man is in conflict with himself, of course he is very weak.

The society has played a great game—it has put everybody against himself, so you are continuously fighting within yourself. You don't have any energy to do anything else. Can't you observe it happening in you? Continuously fighting. The society has divided you into a split person, it has made you schizophrenic and it has confused you. You have become driftwood. You don't know who you are, you don't know where you are going, you don't know what you are doing here. You don't know why you are here in the first place. It has really confused you. And out of this confusion are born great leaders—Adolf Hitler, Mao Zedong, Josef Stalin. Out of this confusion arises the Pope, and a thousand and one things arise. But you are destroyed.

Be expressive. But remember, expression does not mean irresponsibility. Be expressive intelligently, and no harm will happen to anybody because of you. A person who cannot harm himself will never harm anybody else. And a person who harms himself or herself is dangerous in a way. If you are not even in love with yourself, you are dangerous; you can harm anybody. In fact, you *will* harm.

When you are sad, when you are depressed, you will create other people around you who are sad and depressed. When you are happy, you would like to create a happy society, because happiness can exist only in a happy world. If you are living joyfully, you would like everybody to be joyful; that is true religiousness. Out of your own joy, you bless the whole of existence.

But repression makes you false. It is not through repression that anger, sex, greed are destroyed, no. They are still there, just the labels are changed. They go into the unconscious and they start working from there. They go underground. And, of course, when they are underground they are more powerful. The whole psychoanalytic movement tries to bring what is underground to the surface. Once it becomes conscious, you can be freed of it.

> *A Frenchman was staying in England, and a friend asked him how he was getting on. He said he was doing very well, except for one thing. "When I go to a party, the hostess, she does not tell me where is the pissoir."*

"Ah, Georges, that's just our English prudery. Actually, she will say, 'Do you want to wash your hands?' And that means the same thing."

The Frenchman made a mental note of this, and the next time he went to a party, sure enough the hostess asked him, "Good evening, Mr. Du Pont, do you want to wash your hands?"

"No, thank you, Madame," said Georges. "I have just washed them up against the tree in the front garden."

That's what happens; just the names change. You become confused, you don't know what is what. Everything is there—just the labels change, and that creates a sort of insane humanity.

Your parents and your society have destroyed you, and you are destroying your children. Now, this is a vicious circle. Somebody has to come out of the vicious circle.

If you understand me rightly, then my effort is to bring you out of the vicious circle. Don't be angry at your parents; they could not do better than they have done. But now become more conscious, and don't do the same thing to your children. Make them more expressive, teach them more expression. Help them, so that they become more authentic, so that they can bring out whatsoever is inside them. And they will be tremendously grateful forever, because there will be no conflict within them. They will be in one piece; they will not be in fragments. They will not be confused, they will know what they want.

And when you know exactly what you want, you can work for it. When you don't know what you really want, how can you work for it? Then anybody who takes hold of you, anybody who gives you any ideas, you start following. Some leader comes who can convince you argumentatively, and you start following him. You have followed many people, and they have all destroyed you.

Follow your nature.

Each generation destroys the next generation. Unless somebody becomes very alert, aware, the destruction is bound to happen.

> You talk about being "natural." But isn't it true that human nature, if left on its own to express itself, is precisely the problem? If we didn't have rules and norms of behavior, like those supplied by our religions, wouldn't our emotions and impulses always be getting us into trouble?

The first thing to understand is that up to now humanity has lived under a curse, and the curse is that we have never been allowed to trust our nature. We have always been told, "Trust your nature and you will go wrong." Mistrust, restrict, control—don't go according to your feeling. We have been told that human nature is somehow basically evil. This is stupid; this is foolish and poisonous. Human nature is not evil, human nature is divine. And if the evil has arisen, it has arisen because of restrictions. Now let me explain it to you.

You never see animals going to war. Of course there are fights sometimes, but they are individual fights—not world wars with all the crows of the East fighting with all the crows of the West, or all the dogs of India fighting all the dogs of Pakistan. Dogs are not so foolish, neither are crows. Yes, sometimes they fight, and there is nothing wrong in it. If their freedom is violated they fight, but the fight is individual. It is not a world war.

Now what have you done? You have repressed humanity and you have not allowed individuals to be angry sometimes—which is natural. The ultimate, total result is that everybody goes on gathering his anger, goes on repressing his anger, and then one day everybody is so full of poison that it explodes in a world war.

Every ten years a great war is needed. And who is responsible for these wars? Your so-called saints and moralists, do-gooders, the people who have never allowed you to be natural.

Have you ever seen dogs killing other dogs? Yes, they fight sometimes—but just fight. Man is the only animal who kills other men. Crows don't organize wars to kill other crows, lions don't kill other lions. Man is the only species of animal that kills its own kind. What has happened to man? Has he fallen lower than the animals? Then who is responsible? Only one thing is missing from the animals, and that is that they don't have saints and moralists, Christian and Hindu and Mohammedan. They don't have temples, mosques, Bibles, and Vedas, that's all. That is the only difference.

There are still a few primitive societies where, down through the ages, murder has never happened because nobody has poisoned their minds with morality, nobody has trained them to be moral. They are natural people. When you are natural you function harmoniously. Sometimes you become angry, but that is natural—and it is momentary.

A person who never becomes angry and goes on controlling his anger is very dangerous. Beware of him; he can kill you. If your husband never becomes angry, report him to the police! A husband who sometimes becomes angry is just a natural human being; there is no need to be fearful about it. A husband who never becomes angry will one day suddenly jump and suffocate you—and he will do it as if he is possessed by something. Murderers have always been telling the courts, "I committed the crime, but I was possessed." Who possessed them? Their own unconscious, repressed unconscious, exploded.

Have you noted a simple fact? If you have a picture of a beautiful bitch and bring it to a dog, he will not be interested at all. Dogs are not playboys. Not that they don't love bitches, they love them tremendously, but they will not be interested in a picture, in pornography. To create pornography you need saints. First repress the sexual instinct, the natural instinct, and tell people that it is wrong and evil. When they repress their sexual instinct, the repressed instinct finds outlets.

Now it is difficult to go and enjoy watching beautiful women passing down the road. So what to do? Lock yourself in your room and look at *Playboy* magazine. That is safer; nobody comes to know about it. You can hide your *Playboy* magazine inside the Bible and pretend you are reading the Bible.

Only man is pornographic. No other animal is pornographic. These are simple facts.

And who has made man pornographic? Primitives are not interested in pornography—still are not. Women are naked and move about naked and without any fear. So what type of civilization do you say you are living in? A woman cannot walk down the street without being pinched on the bottom, without being treated inhumanly. A woman cannot walk in the night alone—and this is civilization? People are just obsessed with sex twenty-four hours a day.

Who has given this obsession to man? Animals are sexual but not obsessed; they are natural. When sex becomes an obsession it takes perverted forms, and these perverted forms are rooted in the moralizers and their teachings.

The so-called religious people have never trusted human nature. They talk about trust, but they have never trusted life. They trust rules, laws; they never trust love. They talk about God, but the talk is just empty talk. They trust in the police, in the courts. They trust in hellfire. They trust in creating fear and in creating greed. If you are saintly and good and moral, you will have heaven and all the pleasures of paradise. Or, if you are not moral, then you will suffer hellfire—eternally, remember, forever and forever. These things are rooted in fear and greed. These people have been manipulating the human mind through fear and greed.

I trust you and I trust your nature. I trust animal nature. If nature is allowed its own course, yes, there will be a little anger sometimes and there will be a little flaring up, too, but nothing is wrong in it. It is human and it is beautiful. But there will be no war.

Psychologists say all your weapons are phallic. Because you could not penetrate a woman's body, you penetrate somebody's body with a sword. The sword is a phallic symbol. It is beautiful to love a woman, but to penetrate somebody's body with a sword is ugly. But this is how things have been.

You have lived with rules and with norms, and what has happened? Look at the state of humanity today. It is a neurotic earth, a great madhouse. This is what has happened out of your norms, your idealism, perfectionism, morality. Out of all your commandments this has happened—the whole earth has turned into a neurotic campground, a big madhouse. And still you are afraid of hellfire, and still you go on. This is a vicious circle.

It is as if you make a person fast, and when he fasts of course he becomes hungry and he starts looking obsessively for food. Then, seeing that he has become obsessed with food, you put him in chains because otherwise he will break into somebody's kitchen. Now, you say that if he is not put in chains he is dangerous; he can break into somebody's kitchen. He cannot be relied upon so you put him in chains, and you continue forcing him to fast. And then you become more and more afraid because he is going mad. This is a vicious circle! In the first place, why has he become so obsessed with food? Your insisting too much on fasting has created this illness.

Fasting is not natural. Yes, sometimes it happens in animals, but they don't "believe in" fasting, they don't have a philosophy of fasting. Sometimes it happens. One day the dog feels sick and he will not eat. This is natural. He simply does not eat because he does not *feel* like eating. He moves with his feeling; it is not that he is following a rule. Nobody has taught him to fast. In fact he will go and eat grass and vomit; the grass helps him to vomit, and he will vomit. Nobody has taught him. And he will not eat unless the desire to eat arises again. He moves with nature. When he feels like eating, he eats; when he does not feel like eating, he does not eat. This is what I would call real life.

Sometimes when you feel like not eating, don't eat—I am not against fasting, I am against the philosophy of fasting. Don't make a rule that every Sunday you have to fast. That is foolish, because how can you decide that every Sunday you will not feel like eating? Sometimes it may be Friday when you don't feel like eating. Then what will you do? You will force yourself to eat because it is Friday.

When you feel like eating, eat. When you don't feel like eating, don't eat. Move with your feeling, and by and by you will be in tune with your nature.

To be in tune with nature is to be religious, to me. My definition of religion is to be in tune with nature. And that is the meaning of the Indian word *dharma*; it means "nature," intrinsic nature. Trust nature and don't violate it.

But you have been taught to violate your nature, so people who have lived starved lives think that religion has to be of the cemetery, it has to be negative. Men and women holding hands in a religious place? This is dangerous. We cannot trust men, we cannot trust women. This is dangerous, it is playing with fire. One has to create restrictions, build Great Walls of China around people and their expressions.

No, I trust nature. I don't trust your laws. Your laws have corrupted the whole of humanity. Enough is enough! The time has come when all the old, rotten religions have to be burned completely and a totally new concept of religiousness has to arise, life-affirmative: a religion of love and not of law, a religion of nature and not of discipline, a religion of totality and not of perfection, a religion of feeling and not of thinking. The heart should become the master, and then things will settle on their own.

If you can trust nature, by and by you become quiet, silent, happy, joyful, celebrating—because nature is celebrating. Nature is a celebration. Look all around. Can you see any flower that looks like your saints? Can you see any rainbow that looks like your saints? Or any cloud, bird singing, the light reflecting in the river, the stars? The world is celebrating. The world is not sad, the world is a song, an utterly beautiful song, and the dance continues.

Become part of this dance and trust your nature. If you trust your nature, by and by you will come closer to the cosmic nature. That is the only way. You are part of the cosmic, and when you trust yourself you have trusted the cosmic in you. Through that goes the way. From that small thread, you can reach to the very goal. Trusting yourself, you have trusted life itself. Not trusting yourself, you have distrusted the existence that has brought you here.

I am not saying there will always be flowers and flowers in your life. No, there are thorns, but they too are good. And I am not saying that your life will always be sweet. It will many times be very bitter, but that's how life grows: through dialectics. I am not saying you will always be good. Sometimes you will be very bad, but one thing will be certain: when you are bad you will be authentically bad, and when you are good you will be authentically good. One can trust, one can rely upon you. When you are angry, one can rely on it that your anger is not false, not cold; it is hot and alive. And when you love, one can rely upon you that it is alive and warm.

Remember, a person who cannot be angry cannot be loving. The roses grow only with the thorns. If you cannot be hotly angry in some moment, you cannot be hotly in love—because you cannot be hot, you cannot be warm, you remain frozen. And if you have repressed anger too much, you are always afraid to move into love, because who knows?

A man came to me and he said he could not move into deep orgasm while making love. A perfectly healthy young man—what has gone wrong with him? He cannot move into orgasm, or at the most the orgasm remains only local, it does not spread all over his body. And a local orgasm is not of much significance. When the orgasm is total, and every fiber of your being throbs with new life, you are refreshed, rejuvenated, and for a moment you become part of the whole, part of the tremendous creativity that surrounds you. You lose yourself. You are no longer an ego, you melt. You don't have any boundaries then.

I inquired about his anger. He said, "But why are you asking about anger, because my question is about love. I cannot love deeply." I said, "Forget about love. First we have to think about anger, because if you cannot love deeply that means you cannot be angry deeply." He was surprised, but that's how it turned out to be. From his very childhood he had been brought up in a very religious family and he had always been told not to be angry, to control his anger. He had learned to control. He had become so efficient that he did not even know that he was controlling. He had *really* become a controller, so much so that now the control had become unconscious. He was a very controlled person. Everybody respected him; in the society he would succeed everywhere. He was a success, but in his inner life he was a failure. He could not even love.

I told him, "You start by being angry, because my understanding is that when you come to a peak in your orgasm you cannot allow it because, if you allow it, you are afraid that maybe with it the repressed anger will also be allowed."

He said, "What are you saying? I always dream that I have killed my woman. I dream that I kill her, suffocate her while making love to her. And I am afraid that if I lose control I will not be able to resist the temptation to suffocate and kill her."

Now the anger has become a great force inside him. He is so afraid to decontrol, how can he love? It is impossible. And if you miss love you will miss everything that is valuable in life.

This repressive society, this repressive civilization has failed utterly. Yet you are not aware.

I have heard a beautiful story:

> In the days when Khrushchev was important in the Soviet Union, he often admitted that Stalin treated him occasionally like a court jester or clown and ordered him, "Dance the gopak." And, Khrushchev admitted, "I danced." When he said this, somebody in the crowd would always cry out, "Why did you let him make a fool of you?" And Khrushchev would demand, "Who asked that question? Stand up!"
>
> Inevitably, nobody answered, and after the appropriate pause, Khrushchev would conclude, "That, comrades, is why I danced."

Just because of the fear that Stalin can kill you. Stalin is death, and your priests have been death, representatives of death, not of life. Your priests have been in conspiracy with death and they have crippled life. Your priests talk about God, but it seems they are partners with the devil. It is a great conspiracy, and they have destroyed the whole human mind. They have uprooted you from your feelings; they have made you stuck in your head. Now you don't know how you feel. That's why you cannot trust your feelings and you have always to look to somebody to tell you what to do.

In your childhood the parents go on telling you to do this and don't do that. Then in school it is the teacher; then in the university it is the professor. Then in the society it is the boss, the politician, the leader. Everywhere you are being told what to do and what not to do. And you are always seeking somebody to dominate you so that you can become dependent, because you don't know how to get commandments from your own heart, from your own being. You always depend on some authority outside.

This is ugly, this is miserable, this should not be.

People come to me and they say, "Osho, tell us exactly what we have to do." But why can't you listen to your own heart? You have life bubbling inside you. The spring is there, the source is there. Go in. I can tell you how to go in, I can teach you the devices for how to go in, but take your commandments from there. The Bible is there inside you: the real book, the real knowledge. Get your instructions from there, and once you start getting your instructions from your innermost core you will be free and happy. A free person is happy; an unfree person is never happy. You are not meant to be slaves.

> If I start getting into my feelings—for instance, anger—then my whole body starts to shake uncontrollably. I feel I'm some kind of an emotional spastic, vibrating all over the place! It doesn't feel like a problem, but I'm not sure.

No, it is not a problem. It is good. In fact, everybody should behave that way. If the body is not repressed, that will be the natural functioning of the body.

When the mind is filled with emotion, the body must correspond to it; emotion must be parallel with the body motion. If the emotion is there and the body is not moving with it, that means that there is a certain suppression of the body. But the body has been suppressed for centuries. People have been taught to make love without moving the body; to make love as if the whole body is immobile and love is only a local affair. Women have been taught to remain still, almost dead, corpse-like, because if the woman starts moving, the man will become afraid.

Because of that fear, man has forced woman to remain quiet while he makes love. Otherwise the woman is going to be in ecstatic movement, almost frenzied, she will almost go mad. She will jump and dance, and she will create an orgy and the whole neighborhood will know! The man becomes afraid.

And the fear is even deeper than the fear of the neighborhood. The fear is that if the woman is really moving, no man can satisfy her—no man, because naturally there is a limitation to a man's energy. A man can have only one orgasm, and women can have multiple orgasms: six, nine, twelve. So a man will become almost impotent with any woman. Any man, however potent, will always prove impotent if the woman starts moving.

For centuries women completely forgot about orgasm. In some cultures even the word has disappeared. It is just within the past few decades that the word has been revived again. There are languages into which the word *orgasm* cannot be translated. In Hindi it cannot be translated, there is no parallel word. Just think how the body has been crippled!

When you feel fear, the body has to tremble. It is just as if the wind is blowing and the leaves are trembling. When the fear is blowing, your body has to tremble. That's the natural function of the body to move with the emotion. The word "emotion" means movement. It must correspond with a body movement; otherwise, it is not emotion.

So this is a trick of controlling the emotion: if you control the body the emotion will be controlled. For example, if tears are coming in the eyes and you force them not to come, in that very effort you will see that crying and weeping have disappeared inside.

William James had a theory about emotions. The theory is very famous, the James-Lange theory. Ordinarily we think that a person feels afraid, and then runs in fear. James and Lange hypothesized that just the reverse is the case: a person runs, that's why he feels afraid. They said that if you stop running the fear will stop—don't run, and suddenly you will see that the fear has disappeared. And they are right in a way, fifty percent right, because body and mind are fifty-fifty; they balance. When you make love, your mind starts creating a fantasy and your body starts moving. If both the mind and body are running naturally they will function together. If somehow the body has been crippled they will not run together.

So whether you feel fear or you feel love or you feel anger, the body has to move with it. Each emotion has to correspond with a movement of the body. And that's a natural function, so don't create a problem out of it. Enjoy it, allow it: not even a subtle repression. For example, if you feel your hand shaking and the mind says to stop it, that it doesn't look good, that you are not a coward, so why are you trembling—if you stop it you will be forcing something unnatural on yourself.

So this is my suggestion: that you cooperate with it, and by and by you will see that the body will have a very subtle and graceful movement with every emotion. While making love, go completely wild. Love should not be a local thing—not only the genital organs should be involved, your totality should be involved. You should not only have a sexual orgasm, a spiritual orgasm is needed. Your totality has to be stirred, has to be madly ecstatic, has to come to a peak and relax. In fact, if you really make love you will be in a sort of madness and you will not know where you are going and what is happening. It will be almost as if you are stoned, drugged.

Love is the greatest drug there is. The chemistry is inner, that's all—otherwise it is a drug. If you have been really mad in love, then after it you will fall into a deep sleep, the deepest that you can attain, as if dead; the whole mind stops. And when you come back to consciousness, you will feel a resurrection.

Each lovemaking has to be a crucifixion and a resurrection. Then it is so satisfying that there is no need to repeat the experience daily. People are repeating too much what they call lovemaking because they are never satisfied.

In India, the most ancient text about sex, Vatsyayana's *Kama Sutra*, says that if you make really wild love, once a year is enough! It will look almost impossible for the modern mind— once a year? And these were not people who were suppressing in any way. Vatsyayana is the first sexologist of the world, and the first who brought meditation to sex, the first who came to realize its deepest centers. He is right. If the affair really goes to the extreme, once a year is almost enough. It will satisfy you so deeply that the afterglow will continue for months.

So don't make a problem out of it. Just be natural and let things happen.

BIG BOYS DON'T CRY,
NICE GIRLS DON'T SHOUT

Varieties of Emotional Expression

Love, compassion, sympathy, kindness—all these great qualities have a flavor of the feminine. And there are male qualities, qualities of the warrior, courage. They are hard qualities; one has to be like steel. Because men's qualities have developed through war, and female qualities have developed at home with the husband and children, she has lived in a totally different world. Men have lived continuously fighting; in three thousand years there have been five thousand wars on the earth—as if killing is their only profession.

The world has lived in two parts. The man has made his world, while the woman has lived in a shadow and has created her own world in that shadow. It is very unfortunate—because a man or a woman, to be complete, to be whole, must have all the qualities together. Both men and women should be as soft as a rose petal and as hard as a sword, both together, so that whatever the opportunity and whenever the situation demands it they can respond. If the situation needs you to be a sword, you are ready; if the situation needs you to be just a rose petal, you are ready. This flexibility to move between the rose petal and the sword will make your life richer—and not only between those two qualities but amongst all the qualities.

Man and woman are two parts of one whole; their world should also be one whole, and they should share all the qualities without any distinction. No quality should be stamped as feminine or masculine.

When you make somebody "masculine" that person loses great things in his life. He becomes juiceless, he becomes stale, hard, almost dead. And the woman who completely forgets how to be hard, how to be a rebel, is bound to become a slave because she has only soft qualities. Now roses cannot fight with swords, they will be crushed and killed and destroyed.

A total human being has not been born yet. There have been men and there have been women, but there have not been human beings. My whole approach is to bring the whole human being to the earth—with all the beautiful qualities of women and with all the courageous, rebellious, adventurous qualities of men. And they should all be part of one whole.

But from the very beginning we start training children. A small boy, if he wants to play with dolls like girls do, we immediately stop him: "Be ashamed of yourself; you are a boy, you are a man, don't be girlish." And if a girl tries to climb a tree we stop her immediately: "This is not ladylike, climbing a tree, this is for the boys, rough. You just come down!" From the very beginning we start dividing men and women into parts. Both suffer because climbing a tree has a joy of its own, no woman should miss it. To be on top of a tree when the wind is strong, in the sun, with the birds singing . . . if you have not been to that point, you have missed something. And just because you are a girl? Strange: to be adventurous, to climb the mountains, to swim the oceans, should not be prevented just because you are a girl, because that thrill is something spiritual.

A boy should not be prevented when he wants to cry. He is prevented, he cannot bring tears—tears are only for girls: "You are a man; behave like a man!" And tears are such a beautiful experience. In deep sadness or in great joy, whenever something is overflowing, tears give expression to it. And if tears are repressed, at the same time whatever they were going to express, the deep sadness or the great joy, is also repressed. And remember perfectly well that nature has not created any difference. It has given men and women the same tear glands, of equal size. But if you are a man and you are crying, then everybody condemns you: "You are behaving like a woman."

You should say, "What can I do? Nature itself has given me tear glands. Nature is behaving like a woman. It is not my responsibility, I am simply enjoying my nature. Tears are my right."

All qualities should be available to everybody.

There are men who become incapable of love because they are trained for certain qualities: "You have to be hard, you have to be competitive. You are not to show emotions, you must not be sentimental." Now, how do you expect a man who is not emotional, not sentimental, who is not allowed to feel . . . how can you expect him to love? And when he misses love, his life becomes miserable. And the same is happening on both sides.

I would like all distinctions to disappear. Everybody should be allowed everything that is naturally possible to the person, whether man or woman. And we would have a richer world consisting of richer people.

A man thinks, a woman feels, and feeling is irrational. A man finds it hard to imagine, but a woman is very easily capable of imagining anything. Her center of functioning is feeling, emotion, sentiments; her eyes are continuously filled with dreams. These dreams can be useful in poetry, in drama, but these dreams cannot be of any help; on the contrary, they are great hindrances on the path of truth.

Truth is not your imagination, it is not your feeling. Truth is your being.

But the woman is very easily persuaded by her imagination—it is not her fault, it is her nature. These are some of the differences between men and women. Men are basically skeptical, doubtful about everything, suspicious; hence they are more capable of scientific research. For a woman it is more difficult to be a scientist. But as far as imagination is concerned, if she is allowed—and she has not been allowed for centuries—then no painter can compete with her, no poet can compete with her, no musician can go higher than she can go, no dancer can come even close to her. She can prove of tremendous help in creating a beautiful planet. She can fill it with songs, dances, and love.

But unfortunately man has not allowed her freedom to stand on her own and contribute to life. Half of humanity has been deprived of contributing.

It is my understanding that this has been done out of fear. Man is afraid of woman's imagination. He is afraid because once she is allowed freedom to be creative, the man will not be able to compete with her. His sense of superiority, his ego, is in danger. Because of this fear that his superiority will be destroyed, that all his great poets will look like pygmies and all his great painters will look amateurish, it is better not to allow the woman education, the opportunity to express her feelings and her heart.

But as far as the ultimate truth is concerned, man's problem is his reason and woman's problem is her feeling. Both are barriers to enlightenment. The man has to drop his reasoning; the woman has to drop her feeling. Both are at an equal distance from enlightenment. Man's distance is of reasoning, of the mind; woman's distance is of feeling, of the heart—but the distance is equal. Man has to drop his logic and woman has to drop her emotions. Both have to drop something that is obstructing the path.

> **Before enlightenment, is there any hope for communication between men and women? My wife is very much against reason. She calls all my attempts at reasoning "rationalization." What is reasoning, and what is rationalization? Isn't there a difference?**

I can understand your trouble. Reason is male, emotion is female—hence the difficulty of communication between a man and a woman, between husband and wife. They are always shouting at each other but the message never reaches to the other because their ways of understanding things are totally different.

In fact, because the ways are different, that's why they are interested in each other, attracted to each other. They are polar opposites, like the positive and negative charges in electricity. They are pulled together. But because they are opposite, communication is very difficult, almost impossible.

The man always talks from the head and the woman always talks from the heart. Now these are two different languages, as if you speak Chinese and I speak German, and there is no communication.

They were having a quarrel and the husband said,
"Let's not quarrel, my dear, let's discuss the thing sensibly."

> "No," said the angry wife. "Every time we discuss
> something sensibly, I lose!"

If the woman is ready to lose, only then can she talk rationally, sensibly. And every woman knows that a reasonable discussion is not the way to win. She will be defeated, because the male mind is an expert in reasoning. So rather than being logical, she starts crying—now you are defeated. You love the woman and she is crying . . . now what is the point of arguing with her? You say, "Okay, you are right." She has learned that tears work far better. And it is not a question of what is right; it is a question of who wins.

If you really want to communicate with your woman, or a woman wants to communicate with her man, the only way is that both should step aside from reason and emotion. Both should become more meditative. Meditation is neither reason nor emotion; it is going beyond, it is going beyond the polarity. It is transcendental. Meditation takes you beyond reasoning and beyond emotions; it is neither of the head nor of the heart. And the only possibility of any communion, of any communication between man and woman, is meditation. Otherwise, there is no possibility.

The woman will call your reason rationalization. And what do you call it when the woman starts being emotional? You call it sentimentality. These are condemnatory words. *Rationalization* is a condemnatory word, and when you call the woman's emotion "sentimentality," that is a condemnatory word. But you feel right in yourself, and the woman feels right in herself. These are just different ways of thinking. No one is right and no one is wrong— because *all* ways of thinking are wrong! A state of no-thought is right. A state of no-emotion is right.

So when you love a woman and the woman loves you deeply, there is communion, because in that love there is meditation.

But that what you generally call love comes and goes. You are not yet capable enough of containing it forever, so the honeymoon disappears soon. When you first fall in love, everything goes well. You both agree with each other, never is there any argument—so understanding of each other, so compassionate toward each other, so sympathetic! But after the honeymoon is over, then small things . . . so small that when you want to talk about them you feel embarrassed.

It happens almost every day that a couple comes to see me. They have been fighting, on the verge of separation, and I ask, "What is the matter?" And the man says to the woman, "You say it," and she says, "No, you say it." The fact is that both are embarrassed because the matter is nothing, trivial. Just a small thing: maybe the quarrel has started because the woman wanted to buy a dress, and the man didn't like the color, and he said, "I am not going anywhere with you wearing that dress!" How stupid—stupid of both, but it can trigger a great argument. Then they start bringing other things into it, greater things, and all their differences immediately surface. Daggers are drawn; they have made a mountain out of a molehill. And they go on condemning each other: "You are wrong—all your reasoning is just a rationalization."

And I am not saying that all your reasoning is reasoning: ninety-nine percent of it *is* rationalization. And I am not saying that all the emotion of women is emotion: ninety-nine percent *is* sentimentality. Mind is very tricky, whether it is male or female. Mind is very cunning.

> *A man of fifty married a woman of thirty. The marriage caused quite a bit of talk in their circles. When someone asked the newly married man about the difference in age, he replied, "It's not bad at all. When she looks at me she feels ten years older and when I look at her I feel ten years younger. So really, we're both forty!"*

This is a rationalization. A rationalization is a way of hiding things. It is a clever way, very clever. You can rationalize about anything and you can pretend that it is reasoning. It is not. Reasoning has to be objective, without any prejudice on your part.

Once a man came to me. He had written many books, and he was the head of a department in a university for paranormal, or parapsychological, research work. He came to me and he said, "I am trying to prove that reincarnation is a scientific truth."

I said to him, "Until you have proved it, don't say anything about it, because that shows a prejudice. You have already accepted the idea that it is a scientific truth, and now all that is needed is to prove it. This is not being objective or scientific. This is not being rational. Deep down you are a Hindu and you accept the theory; if you were a Mohammedan, you would be trying to prove scientifically that there is no reincarnation. Neither the Hindu nor the Mohammedan mind is a scientist. The Mohammedan does not believe in reincarnation, so he tries to prove his belief with the help of science. You are trying to prove your belief with the help of science. This is rationalization."

A man of pure reason has no belief, no prejudice, no *a priori* idea. He simply goes into inquiry with no judgment, no conclusions. The inquiry will decide what the conclusion is. It will be decided by the inquiry itself. If you have even a lurking desire to prove something, you *will* prove it, but you have destroyed its scientific objectivity. It is no longer reason, it is rationalization.

And the same is the case with emotion. Emotion is a purity, sentimentality is a trick. You have learned a trick. The woman knows that if she cries, she will be the winner of an argument. Now, sometimes the tears are not coming at all, because crying is not so easily manipulated. But she tries to bring it, she acts, she pretends. Those tears are false. Even if they are flowing through the eyes, they are false because they are not arising out of the situation, really, they are being brought.

Sentimentality is emotion created, manipulated cunningly. Rationality is one thing; rationalization is a manipulation of reason, just as sentimentality is a manipulation of emotion. If you are rational, *really* rational, you will become a scientist. If you are really emotional, you will become a poet. These are beautiful things. But still, a real dialogue will be difficult. With rationalization and sentimentality it is impossible; with reason and emotion it is a little easier—still there will be difficulties, but there will be compassion and an effort to understand each other. The rational man will try to understand the woman's viewpoint rationally; and the woman will try to understand the man's viewpoint—emotionally, of course, but compassion will be there.

The first step is to drop all rationalizations and all sentimentalities. The second step is to drop reason and emotion, too. And then in that state of ecstasy, of meditation, there is communion. And that communion is prayerfulness, in that communion when you say "thou" there is no woman, there is just godliness; there is no man, there is godliness.

A therapist once told me that we can get stuck in our feelings just as much as in the mind and that feelings too have to be dropped or gone beyond. I often wonder about this, as my feelings are usually my guide in life and also, I feel things very intensely. Would you please comment?

There are three centers from which all your actions come: the head, the heart, and the being. The head is the most superficial. It has to think about things—even if you fall in love the head thinks about it: Am I really in love? And if it decides that, yes, it seems you are in love, the head is going to say to the other person, "I think I am in love with you." But thinking is the base.

Men function mostly from the head. It has its utility; it has created all the sciences, all the technologies—and all the nuclear weapons, and perhaps is bringing a global suicide soon. The woman functions from the heart. She cannot say, "I think I love you." It has never been heard in the whole history of humanity! She simply says, "I love you," and thinking plays no part. The heart is enough unto itself; it does not need any help from the head.

If one has to choose between the head and the heart, one should choose the heart, because all the beautiful values of life belong to the heart. The head is a good mechanic, technician, but you cannot live your life joyously just by being a mechanic, a technician, a scientist. The head has no capacity for joy, for blissfulness, for silence, for innocence, for beauty, for love, for all that makes the life rich: it is the heart that has this capacity.

But what the therapist said to you was not wrong. You can get stuck in your heart, in your feelings too, just as people get stuck in their thoughts. But perhaps the therapist was himself not aware that there is a deeper center than the heart, and that is the being, which has all the qualities of the heart and still more qualities, more riches, more treasures. Blissfulness, silence, serenity, centeredness, rootedness, sensitivity, awareness . . . a certain insight into the godliness of existence.

First drop from your head to your heart. But don't stop there; it is only an overnight stay, a *caravanserai*. You can have a little rest there, but it is not the goal. Drop from the heart into the being. And this is the secret of meditation, that wherever you are, in the head or in the heart, it doesn't matter; meditation brings you from the head or from the heart to the being. Meditation is the way to your own center of existence, where there is no question of getting stuck. You *are* it. Who is going to get stuck in what? There are not two things, only you—you and your absolute glory.

But the questioner is a woman, and naturally afraid. Her feelings are her guide in life, and she feels things very intensely. But it is easier to reach to the being from the heart than from the head. You will not lose guidance; in fact, you will not need it at all. You will be so full of light, so full of clarity. . . . Guidance is needed by the blind. You will have new eyes to see even that which is not visible to your ordinary eyes. And you will be able to feel new experiences, which are not available even to the heart.

So there is nothing to be worried about. Your worry is simply natural because feelings are your guide, and you feel intensely; you are concerned that if you drop them, who will guide you? Then how will you feel things intensely? You don't know that there is still a deeper center in you where guidance is not needed at all, where *you* are the guide and where your intensity becomes total, one hundred percent. And not only about those things that you have felt in the heart, but about universal experiences of enlightenment, of awakening. You will not be a loser; you need not worry at all.

But a woman, after all, is a woman.

> I have heard that a group of women decided to improve their intellectual acuity. No more talk of mates or children or sons-in-law, but only politics and social questions—Poland, El Salvador, Afghanistan, the bomb. Then one asked, "And what about Red China?"
>
> "I love it, I love it!" said Sarah. "Especially on a nice white tablecloth!"

The woman has her own way of feeling and thinking and looking at things. You are worried: how can you drop your feelings? You need not drop them. Simply learn the art of meditation and they will drop by themselves, just like dry leaves dropping from the trees. When the wind blows strong . . . just yesterday I was sitting on my porch, and the wind was blowing strong and the dry leaves were showering like rain.

When meditation deepens in you, your thoughts and your feelings all start disappearing. Meditation makes you a silent pool without any ripples, so silent that it looks like a mirror; you can see your face. And it takes nothing from your intelligence or from your feelings; it only makes everything more authentic, more real, more total, more pure. Intelligence reaches to its highest peak, just as love reaches to its highest peak.

To know your being and to be centered in your being is to have found the meaning of life. You have found the purpose for which you have come here on this planet. The intention of existence is revealed to you.

> **According to my girlfriend, I isolate myself too much and don't give her enough energy. I do feel I'm more the calm and quiet type—at least outside of my relationship! But at the center of myself I have very strong emotions, both of anger and of love.**

To be calm and quiet is your way. Don't force any activity on yourself; that will be a violation of your nature. One has always to listen to one's own being, to one's own heart. You can become very active, outgoing, but it will always be a strain on you; it will never be fulfilling. You don't have a male type of mind, you have a very feminine energy. Your nature expresses itself through passivity, not through activity. Any activity will become feverish for you, will be destructive. So only the essential is to be done. You have to remain calm, collected, and centered. The less of the periphery, the better it will be for you.

Emotions are of two types—the active emotions, which can only be fulfilled through great activity, and the passive emotions, which cannot be fulfilled through activity, which can only be fulfilled through happenings. You cannot be a great lover, you can only be a great receiver of love. It will be a gift to you; you cannot create it, you cannot "do" it. You can only allow it to happen. The activity that is possible for you is that of allowing, but you cannot approach life in an active way. You have to wait. Wait till life comes and knocks at your door.

Your life is going to be that of awaiting—not of search, not of an active search, of an intense desire, of an intense thirst, but that of waiting just like a woman. A woman never takes the initiative in love. She waits for her man to take the initiative. She does not even say, "I love you," she waits for the man to say it. Then she accepts or rejects, but she never takes the initiative. And whenever a woman takes the initiative she is more of the male type, and she will need a feminine type of man.

And always remember, when I talk about male and female I don't just mean the physiological aspect; that is very superficial. People differ in their innermost core. Many men are feminine and many women are male, and because we don't understand it much complexity arises.

For example, if you meet a real woman—and by "real woman" I mean one who is physiologically woman and intrinsically also a woman—you will not be satisfied by her because it will be almost like a homosexual relationship to you. You need a very active woman, almost male. Only then will you feel a certain deep love for her. That's what your girlfriend is doing for you; that's why you feel that she brings much life to you, because she brings the neglected part of you. She becomes your activity, which you cannot become; she complements you.

So the first thing is that you are not to think about active approaches to truth or life. You have to remain passive: passive, yet alert. I'm not saying passive and drugged, I'm not saying passive and asleep. No, I'm saying passive and alert—not going anywhere, not doing anything; just watching whatsoever happens, allowing it and watching it. Be in a deep let-go but fully aware. That awareness has to be your only activity.

And the second thing is that even when you are in love, don't "try" in any way. Because that is the natural tendency in the man's mind; when he is in love he wants to prove to the woman that he is very active, very aggressive, very male. If you do that you will be going against your nature and you will be deceiving the woman; she will never be happy with it. You have to be yourself. Only then is some deep relationship and intimacy possible.

Only truth satisfies. So it is for your girlfriend to decide. She has fallen in love with a monk—what to do? You should have really been in a monastery, but you are in the world, and she has caught hold of you!

Simply remain whatsoever you are. All falsities one day or other are exposed. Simply relax and be yourself, because people love the truth, never postures. Don't make empty gestures. It will be good for your health, it will be good for your inner peace, it will be good for your growth. And it will be good for the other person to understand you and to settle this way or that.

> I can't express my needs, and I've never been able to. I cover them over with manners, and rationalizations, and generalizations. It feels so phony when I try to say what I'm feeling!

Feelings cannot be expressed. If you only live in your head you will feel you are authentic, because the head can express itself easily. All the ways of expression are invented by the head; they are head ways of speaking. But when you start *feeling* something, this problem will arise automatically. You will feel inauthentic, phony, because whatever you can express will not be the thing you are feeling, and what you are feeling will not be expressed.

It is not inauthentic—you just have to recognize the fact that feelings cannot be expressed. All expression is very inadequate for feelings.

So no need to be sad about it, no need to be worried about it. Just remember that feelings cannot be expressed the way thoughts can. Language is created by thought, for thoughts, so it is perfectly okay with thoughts. Feelings are a different world altogether. Just remember that feelings cannot be expressed adequately, and there is no need to be worried about it.

It is not that you are inauthentic. For the first time in many years you have felt feelings; hence the problem. It is not that you are inauthentic, it is just that you have remained so long in the head. For the first time the heart is opening, a new world is opening for which you have no language, so in that world you feel almost uneducated, illiterate. It happens to everybody, because all literacy is in the head. When the heart opens you suddenly feel illiterate. But by and by the heart will find its own way.

It will never be as adequate as the head, never be as clear, as skillful, as the head. It will never be as efficient either, but it will find its own ways. That's how you love a person—you just hold hands, because whatever you can say looks so stupid that now you are trying to say something through body language. Or you hug the person. You are saying, "I cannot say it, I can only be it"—a hug is a way of being. Or you cry and the tears come down from your eyes; you are so full of joy that words are inadequate. Or you dance, you sing a song. . . . But these are all indirect ways.

They will come by and by; don't be worried. You will just have to learn a new language, a new grammar, a new semantics. You cannot do anything about it. You just have to go deeper into it, you have to become more foolish, that's all. The mind will say that you are getting more and more foolish; but you have to become a little madder! And the heart finds its own ways; they are utterly different from the ways of the head.

Right now your heart is opening for the first time, so you will feel this difference. Your head is developed, intelligent, skillful; your heart is absolutely new. The disparity will create the feeling that you are being phony—you are not!

Just enjoy the heart and its feelings. Be more in the body and say things through the body, through actions. And small things are so expressive, mm? You may not be able to say something to your woman but you can give her a flower. Or just the way you look at her, the way you are charmed by her, the way your eyes have a glint is enough. Women are very understanding about that. In fact, if you talk too much, that is all junk. A woman doesn't see what you are saying, she sees what you are *feeling*. That is one of the problems: the man thinks, "I am talking such beautiful things, I am being so loving, I am saying such great things," and the woman is simply uninterested! She knows when you are talking but your heart is not in it. Sometimes you are silent and the woman understands. In the way you look at her, or you hold her hand, or just sit in simple silence where not a single word is uttered, something is communicated.

The woman is still intuitive. She is still more natural than man, wilder than man; that's her beauty. And that is the hope for humanity, that at least half of humanity is still wild, uncivilized. There is hope that the other half will also fall back into un-civilization, will become uncultured again.

Isn't there a kind of courage in the feminine willingness to expose and express the more tender emotions? Can you say something more about the courage and wisdom of the heart, as opposed to the

adventurous and scientific qualities of the mind?

The way of the heart is beautiful but dangerous. The way of the mind is ordinary but safe.

The man has chosen the safest and the most shortcut way of life. The woman has chosen the most beautiful, but the most mountainous, dangerous path of emotions, sentiments, moods. And because up to now the world has been ruled by men, women have suffered immensely. The woman has not been able to fit with the society that men have created because the society is created according to reason and logic.

The woman wants a world of the heart, and in the society created by man there is no place for the heart. Men have to learn to be more heartful, because reason has led the whole of humanity toward a global suicide. Reason has destroyed the harmony of nature, the ecology. Reason has given beautiful machines but it has destroyed the beautiful humanity. A little more heart is needed in everything.

As far as I am concerned, the way to your innermost being is closer from the heart than from the mind. Mind is a shortcut if you are going outward, and the heart is a very long way. If you are going inward, the whole thing changes into its opposite: the heart is the shortcut to the being, and the mind is the longest way you can think of.

That's why I am all for love, because from love it is very easy to take you to meditation, to take you to the eternity of your life, to take you to your godliness; it is very difficult from the head. First one has to come to the heart, and only then one can move toward the being.

My emphasis on love has a basic spiritual reason. From the heart the woman can immediately move . . . and the man can move toward the heart without any difficulty. He has just been wrongly trained; it is only a conditioning. He has been told to be hard, to be strong, to be manly, and all this is nonsense. No man cries and lets his sadness or his joy flow through his tears because he has been told since he was a child that tears are for women, it is girlish. Men never cry and weep.

But what is the purpose of those tears? They are needed! They are a tremendously significant language. There are moments when you cannot say anything but your tears can show it. You may be so full of joy that tears come to your eyes. Tears are always the symbol of overflowing experience. You may be so sad that words cannot contain it; tears help you. It is one of the reasons why women go mad less than men, because they are ready to weep and cry and throw things any moment; temporarily, they can go mad every day. A man goes on accumulating, and then one day he explodes—wholesale! Women go mad retail—and that is a wiser way, to be finished with it every day. Why collect?

Men commit suicide more than women. It is a little strange; women *talk* of committing suicide more than men, but they rarely do it. Men almost never talk about committing suicide but they actually commit suicide more, almost twice as often. The man goes on repressing, goes on showing a certain face, which is fake. And there is a limit to everything; a point comes where he cannot hold it anymore and everything falls apart.

Men have to be taught to be more heartful, because from the heart opens the way to being. You cannot bypass the heart. The woman is in a better position; she can go directly toward the being from the heart. But instead of recognizing this immense quality in women, men have been condemning women. Perhaps there is a reason; perhaps they have been aware of some superiority in women, the superiority of love.

No logic can be higher than love, and no mind can be higher than the heart. But the mind can be very murderous, the mind can be very violent, and that's what the mind has done for centuries. Men have been beating women, repressing women, condemning women. And as a result men have been deprived of raising their own consciousness. They could also have learned the art of moving upward; they could also have moved on the same path. Hence, I always say that the liberation of women is also the liberation of men. It is even *more* the liberation of men than the liberation of women.

Yes, women have more love . . . but they should also be made aware of the other side of the coin. The male part of the mind has logic, and the woman's side is illogical; it is not dangerous, it is just a mistake, it can be corrected. That's why the way of the heart is beautiful, but dangerous. The other side of love is hate; the other side of love is jealousy. So if a woman gets caught in hate and jealousy, all the beauty of love dies and she is left only with poison in her hands. She will poison herself and she will poison everybody who is around.

To be loving, one has to be more alert, because you can fall into the ditch of hate, which is just very close by. Every peak of love is very close to the dark valley of hate; it is surrounding the peak from everywhere and you can slip into it very easily. Perhaps that is the reason many women decide not to love. Perhaps that is the reason men have decided to live in the head and forget all about the heart . . . because the heart is so sensitive. It feels hurt very easily; its moods change just like the weather.

One who really wants to learn the art of love has to remember all of these things, and has to save love from falling into all these ditches of hatred, jealousy. Otherwise, going to the being will become impossible—even more impossible than it is from the head.

The woman has to drop jealousy, she has to drop hatred. The man has to drop logic and be a little more loving. Logic can be used; it is utilitarian. In scientific work it is useful, but not in human relationships. The man has to be careful that logic does not become his only way, that it remains just an instrument he uses and puts aside. The woman has to be aware that she does not fall into hatred, into jealousy, into anger, because they will destroy her most precious treasure of love. And both have to move deeper into love. The deeper they move in love the closer they will reach to the being.

Being is not very far away. It is the deepest part of love, a love that is absolutely pure, unconditional. A love that is absolutely alert, aware, conscious, immediately turns into a tremendous revolution; it opens the doors of the innermost shrine of being. And to reach to your very center is to gain all that life can give to you: all the fragrance, all the beauty, all the joy, all the benedictions.

EMOTIONS AND THE BODY

Your body is not simply physical. In your muscles, in the structure of your body, many other things have entered through suppression. If you suppress anger, the poison goes into the body. It goes into the muscles, it goes into the blood. If you suppress anything it is not only a mental phenomenon, it is also physical, because you are not really divided. You are not body "and" mind; you are bodymind, psychosomatic. You are both together. So whatever is done with the body affects the mind and whatever is done with the mind affects the body. Body and mind are two aspects of the same entity.

For instance, if you get angry, what happens to the body? Whenever you get angry, certain poisons are released into the blood. Without those poisons you will not get mad enough to be angry. You have particular glands in your body, and those glands release certain chemicals. Now, this is scientific, it is not just a philosophy. Your blood becomes poisoned. That is why, when you are angry, you can do things that you cannot do ordinarily. Because you are angry, you can push a big rock—you cannot do it ordinarily. You cannot even believe afterward that you could have pushed this rock, or thrown it, or lifted it. When you are back to normal again you will not be capable of lifting it because you are not the same. Certain chemicals were circulating in the blood; you were in a state of emergency; your total energy was brought to your action.

But when an animal gets angry, he just gets angry. He has no morality about it, no teaching about it; he simply gets angry and the anger is released. When you get angry, you get angry in a way similar to any animal, but then there is society, morality, etiquette, and thousands of things. You have to push the anger down. You have to show that you are not angry, you have to smile a painted smile. You create a smile, and you push the anger down. What is happening to the body? The body was ready to fight—either to fight or escape from the danger, either to face it or fly from it. The body was ready to *do* something; anger is just a readiness to do something. The body was going to be violent, aggressive.

If you could be violent and aggressive, then the energy would be released. But you cannot be: it is not convenient, so you push it down. Then what will happen to all those muscles that were ready to be aggressive? They will become crippled. The energy pushes them to be aggressive, and you push them back down in order not to be aggressive. There will be a conflict. In your muscles, in your blood, in your body tissues there will be conflict. They are ready to express something and you are pushing them not to express. You are suppressing them. Then your body becomes crippled.

This happens with every emotion and it goes on day after day, for years. Then your body becomes crippled all over. All the nerves become crippled; they are not flowing, they are not liquid, they are not alive. They have become dead, they have been poisoned, and they have become all tangled up. They are not natural.

Look at any animal and see the grace of the body. What happens to the human body? Why is it not so graceful? Every animal is so graceful—why is the human body not so graceful? What has happened to it? You have done something with it. You have crushed it, and the natural spontaneity of its flow has gone. It has become stagnant. In every part of your body there is poison. In every muscle of your body there is suppressed anger, suppressed sexuality, suppressed greed, jealousy, hatred. Everything is suppressed there. Your body is really diseased.

Psychologists say that we have created an armor around the body and that armor is the problem. If you are allowed total expression when you get angry, what will you do? When you get angry, you start crushing your teeth together; you want to do something with your nails and with your hands, because that's how your animal heritage would deal with it. You want to do something with your hands, to destroy something. If you don't do anything, your fingers will become crippled; they will lose their grace, their beauty. They will not be alive limbs. And the poison is there, so when you shake hands with someone there really is no touch, no life, because your hands are dead.

You can feel it. Touch a small child's hand: a subtle difference is there. If a child is not feeling like giving you his hand, then it is all right; he will withdraw. He will not give you a dead hand, he will simply withdraw. But if he wants to give you his hand, then you will feel as if his hand is melting into your hand. The warmth, the flow—as if the whole child has come to the hand. The very touch, and he expresses all the love that it is possible to express.

But the same child, when grown up, will shake hands as if the hand is just a dead instrument. He will not come into it, he will not flow through it. This has happened because there are blocks. Anger is blocked, and really, before your hand becomes alive again to express love, it will have to pass through agony, it will have to pass through a deep expression of anger. If the anger is not released, that anger is blocking your energy and love cannot flow.

Your whole body has become blocked, not only your hands. So you can embrace someone, you can take someone close to your chest, but that is not synonymous with taking someone close to your heart. These are two different things. You can hold someone near your chest—this is a physical phenomenon. But if you have an armor around your heart, a blocking of emotions, then the person remains as distant as he ever was; no intimacy is possible. But if you *really* take a person near and there is no armor, no wall between you and the person, then your heart will melt into the other's heart. There will be a meeting, a communion.

When your body has again become receptive and there is no block, no poisons around it, you will always have a subtle feeling of joy wrapped around you. Whatsoever you are doing or not doing, you will always feel a subtle vibration of joy around your body. Really, joy only means that your body is in a symphony, nothing else—that your body is in a musical rhythm, nothing else. Joy is not pleasure; pleasure is that which has to be derived from something else. Joy is just to be yourself: alive, fully vibrant, vital. A feeling of a subtle music around your body and within your body, a symphony—that is joy. You can be joyful when your body is flowing, when it is a riverlike flow.

? I've noticed that when I feel angry or sad or anxious, there is a corresponding physical sensation in my stomach, or my solar plexus. Sometimes if I'm very upset, this feeling is so strong that I have difficulty sleeping, or I don't feel like eating. Can you talk about this?

Everybody is carrying much rubbish in the stomach, because that is the only space in the body where you can suppress things. There is no other space. If you want to suppress anything it has to be suppressed in the stomach. You want to cry—your wife has died, your beloved has died, your friend has died—but it doesn't look good. It looks as if you are a weakling, crying for the loss of someone, and you suppress it. Where will you put that crying? Naturally, you have to suppress it in the stomach. That is the only space available in the body, the only hollow place where you can store things.

If you suppress in the stomach . . . And everybody has suppressed many sorts of emotions—love, sexuality, anger, sadness, weeping, and even laughter. You cannot have a good belly laugh—it looks rude, looks vulgar. In many cultures to have a good belly laugh means you are not cultured. So, you have suppressed everything. And because of this suppression you cannot breathe deeply, you have to breathe shallowly. If you breathe deeply then those wounds of suppression would release their energy. You are afraid. Everybody is afraid to allow themselves to breathe into the stomach.

Every child, when he or she is born, breathes into the belly. Look at a child sleeping: the belly goes up and down, never the chest. No child breathes from the chest; they breathe from the belly. They are completely free now, nothing is suppressed. Their stomachs are empty of suppression, and that emptiness has a beauty in the body.

Once the stomach has too much suppression in it, the body is divided in two parts, the lower and the higher. Then you are not one; you are two. The lower part is the discarded part. The unity is lost; a duality has entered into your being. Now you cannot be beautiful, you cannot be graceful. You are carrying two bodies instead of one, and there will always remain a gap between the two. You cannot walk beautifully; somehow you have to carry your legs. In fact, if the body is one, your legs will carry you. If the body is divided in two then you have to carry your legs. You have to drag your body; it is like a burden. You cannot enjoy a good walk, you cannot enjoy a good swim, you cannot enjoy a fast run, because the body is not one. For all these movements, and to enjoy them, the body needs to be reunited. A unison has to be created again; the stomach will have to be cleansed completely.

For the cleansing of the stomach, very deep breathing is needed, because when you inhale deeply and exhale deeply, the stomach throws all that it is carrying. In exhalations, the stomach releases itself. Hence the importance of deep breathing. The emphasis should be on the exhalation so that everything that the stomach has been unnecessarily carrying is released.

And when the stomach is not carrying emotions inside, if you have had constipation it will suddenly disappear. When you are suppressing emotions in the stomach, there will be constipation because the stomach is not free to move. You are deeply controlling it; you can't allow it freedom. So if emotions are suppressed, there will be constipation. Constipation is more a mental disease than a physical one; it belongs to the mind more than it belongs to the body.

But remember, I am not dividing mind and body in two. They are two aspects of the same phenomenon. Mind and body are not two things; your body is a psychosomatic phenomenon. Mind is the subtlest part of the body, and body is the grossest part of the mind. And they affect each other; they run parallel. If you are suppressing something in the mind, the body will start a journey of suppression. If the mind releases everything, the body also releases everything. That's why I emphasize catharsis very much in the meditations that I have developed. Catharsis is a cleansing process.

In India we call the solar plexus *manipura*; it is the center of all your sentiments, emotions. We go on repressing our emotions in the *manipura*. The word means "the diamond"—life is valuable because of sentiments, emotions, laughter, crying, tears, and smiles. Life is valuable because of all these things; these are the glory of life—hence the third chakra, the third energy center, is called *manipura*, the diamond chakra.

Only the human being is capable of having this precious diamond. Animals cannot laugh; naturally, they cannot cry either. Tears are a certain dimension that is available to man only. The beauty of tears, the beauty of laughter, the poetry of tears, and the poetry of laughter are available only to human beings. All other animals exist with only two chakras or centers: the *muladhar*, or sex center, the center of life, and *svadhisthan*, the hara, or the center where life leaves the body. Animals are born and they die; between the two events there is nothing much. If you are also born and you die, and only that, you are an animal: you are not human yet. And many millions of people exist only with these two chakras; they never go beyond them.

We have been taught to repress our feelings, we have been taught not to be sensitive. We have been taught that feeling does not pay: Be practical, be hard. Don't be soft, don't be vulnerable, otherwise you will be exploited. Be hard! At least show that you are hard, at least pretend that you are dangerous, that you are not a soft being. Create fear around you. Don't laugh, because if you laugh you cannot create fear in others. Don't weep; if you weep you show that you are afraid. Don't show your human limitations. Pretend that you are perfect.

Repress the third center and you become a soldier, not a man but a soldier: an army man, a false man. Much work is done in Tantra to relax this third center. Emotions have to be relieved, relaxed. When you feel like crying you have to cry; when you feel like laughing you have to laugh. You have to drop this nonsense of repression; you have to learn expression, because only through your sentiments, your emotions, your sensitivity, do you come to that vibration through which communication is possible.

Have you not seen it? You can say as much as you want and nothing is said; but a tear rolls down on your cheek and everything is said. A tear can say much more. You can talk for hours and it won't do, but a tear can say all. You can go on saying, "I am very happy, this and that . . ." but your face can show just the opposite. A little laughter, a real authentic laughter, and you need not say anything—the laughter says all. When you see your friend, your face beams, flashes with joy.

The third center has to be made more and more available. It is against thinking, so if you allow the third center you will relax in your tense mind more easily. Be authentic, sensitive; touch more, feel more, laugh more, cry more. And remember, you cannot do more than is needed; you cannot exaggerate. You cannot even bring a single tear more than is needed, and you cannot laugh more than is needed. So don't be afraid, and don't be miserly.

As I have begun to meditate, I notice that my body and the feelings I have toward it are changing a lot. The way I walk, the way I look at myself when taking a shower, the way I feel in my body—everything seems so different to me that I can barely recognize

**it! Does the body follow the mind, and is
my mind being influenced by my heart?**

Man is not a machine but an organism, and the difference between the two is very significant to understand. The machine has
parts, the organism has members. You can take the parts apart;
nothing dies. You can put the parts together again and the machine starts functioning. But in an organism, if you take the
members apart, something dies. You can put them together again,
but the organism will not be alive again. The organism is a living
unity; everything is connected with everything else.

Whatever happens to you, in the body or in the mind or in
the heart or in your awareness, is going to change everything in
the whole organism. You are going to be affected as a whole. The
members of the organic unity are not just parts put together;
there is something more.

A machine is simply a sum total of its parts. An organism is
something more than the sum total of its parts—and that "more"
is your soul, which penetrates everything in you. So every change,
wherever it happens, is going to ring bells all over your being.

That's why there are different systems. For example, yoga is
one of the most prominent systems for those who are working for
self-realization. But almost its whole function is with the body,
the body postures. It is a tremendous research; the people who
have created it have done an almost impossible job. They have
found in what postures your mind takes a certain attitude, your
heart takes a certain rhythm, your awareness becomes more
acute or less acute. They have developed all the body postures in
such a way that just working on the body, not touching anything
else, they will change your total being.

But it is long, tedious, difficult work, because the body is an
absolutely unconscious part of your being. To train it, and in
strange postures that are not natural, is bound to be a difficult

job. And because the people who developed the system of yoga found that life is too short to work on all the postures of the body, to change the whole inner being, they were the first people in the world to think of lengthening the human life span so that they could accomplish the task in one life.

The difficulty with the body is that you may have worked your whole life—sixty years, seventy years—and you may have come to a certain state, but this body will die. And when you get a new body, you will have to start from scratch; you cannot start from where you had stopped in the past life. This was such a great difficulty in the yoga system that yogis started looking at how to lengthen the body's life span.

For example, everybody knows about the lotus posture in which you see Buddha sitting. That is the most famous posture. It has been found now that gravitation has the least effect on you if sit in the lotus posture with your spine absolutely straight and the whole body relaxed. And it is gravitation that kills you; the more you are affected by gravitation, the more you are pulled toward the grave. It became perfectly clear when Einstein declared that if we can create vehicles that move at the speed of light, then the people who travel in those vehicles will not age— not at all. If they leave the earth and come back after fifty years, their contemporaries will be dead. Perhaps one or two may still be alive, on their deathbeds, but the space travelers will come back exactly the same age as when they left.

His idea was that at the speed of light, aging stops. But that is only a hypothesis; there is no experiment to prove it. It is difficult to create a vehicle that will move with the speed of light, because at that speed everything will burn up. There is no metal, there is no material out of which you can make the vehicle, so it seems to be impossible.

But Einstein was not aware of the yoga explanation. The yoga explanation is that the person would come back to the earth the same age because he has been out of the field of gravitation; that's why he cannot age. And that seems to be far more practical, far more scientific, not just a hypothesis. Thousands of yogis have lived longer than anybody else. Just sitting in that posture, gravitation has the least effect on them.

But the reason yogis became interested in methods to lengthen life was not out of their lust for life itself, but because they had chosen a very slow vehicle of transformation: the body. But, through the body people have reached to enlightenment. They have not done anything but learn and practice certain body postures. In a certain posture the mind functions in a certain way. In one posture the mind stops functioning, in another posture you become very alert, and so on.

You can see this happening in ordinary life also. With every mood, emotion, thought, your body takes a certain posture. If you are just watchful you will see that there is a relationship, and the relationship is such that you cannot change it. For example, a person like me—if you tie down both my hands I cannot speak! I simply cannot speak, I will simply be at a loss for what to do, because my hands are so deeply connected with my expressions.

And you must know that each hand is connected to one hemisphere of the mind, the left hand with the right hemisphere, the right hand with the left hemisphere. They are extensions of your mind. So whenever I speak, I am speaking through two mediums: through words and through hands. Each gesture of the hand helps me give expression to a certain idea. If my hands are tied down, it is impossible for me to say anything. I have tried it, and I suddenly find speaking absolutely difficult. I want to say something, and I say something else. The whole reason is that the rhythm with my hands is disturbed.

From the lowest to the highest in you, everything is connected. Yoga has worked on the body; it is a long, arduous process and perhaps has no future unless science joins hands with it and helps it. Then perhaps it may have an explosion. Yoga is one of the most ancient sciences developed by man. It is at least five thousand years old. If science is not going to join hands with it, then yoga is asking too much. Modern man cannot afford that much time; shorter ways have to be found.

If you are working with the mind, that is a shorter way than the body and the work is easier, because with the mind nothing much has to be done, only awareness, only watchfulness. No psychoanalysis—that is again prolonging the process unnecessarily. Yoga at least comes to an end. Psychoanalysis never comes to an end because the mind goes on creating new garbage every day; it is very productive. You go on sorting out dreams and it goes on creating new dreams. It is so clever that it can manage a dream in which you see that you are sleeping and having a dream, and in the dream you have fallen asleep and are again having a dream. It can be very complicated. And analyzing all this rubbish helps a little bit, gives a little relief, but it is an unending process.

Those who have really worked with the mind have worked with watchfulness, witnessing; and as you witness the mind, the mind slowly starts becoming silent, stops its gibberish, becomes calm and quiet. And as the mind becomes calm and quiet your body will go through changes, amazing changes—and that's what is happening to the questioner. You will see that the body is behaving in new ways; it has never behaved like this. It is walking differently, its gestures have changed. When your mind becomes calm and quiet, your body also starts becoming calm and quiet; there is a certain stillness in the body, a certain aliveness that you had never felt before. You have been in the body but you have never been in such deep touch with it, because the mind was continuously keeping you engaged. The mind was a barrier, so your awareness was never bridged with your body.

Now that the mind is silent, the awareness for the first time becomes alert about the body. So a buddha has his own gestures;

his walk is different, his look is different. Everything is different because now there is no mind. The body is now not following the mind; mind is not in the way. Now it is following awareness, the innermost quality of your being.

So when changes start happening in the body, watch them and rejoice. Be more alert and more changes will happen. Be more conscious and you will see that even the body starts having a consciousness of its own. And as you are becoming more alert and more aware, you will feel more loving toward your body, more compassionate toward your body; you will feel more close, more intimate, a kind of new friendship arising. Up to now you have simply used it. You have never said even a thank-you to your body, and it has been serving you in every possible way. So it is a good experience. Let it become more intense and help it. And the only way to help is to become more alert.

FROM HEAD TO HEART TO BEING

A Journey Back to the Center

Society does not want you to be a person of the heart. Society needs heads, not hearts.

Once when I was visiting a university in Varanasi, I was talking to one of the most famous scholars in India at that time, Dr. Hajari Prasad Dwivedi. He was presiding at the meeting I was going to address, and he was the head of the faculty of arts. I asked him, "Have you ever wondered why you are called the head, and not the heart?"

He said, "You ask strange questions"—he was an old man, and now he is dead. He said, "In my whole life nobody ever asked, 'Why are you called the head and not the heart?'" But he considered it;

he said, "There is something significant in your question. You make me also wonder why people are not called the heart of the philosophy department, for example. That would be more authentic, more essential; but they are called the head."

Society is divided between heads and hands. Have you noticed that laborers are called hands? Poor people working with their hands, manual workers, are called "hands," and there are people above them who are called "heads." But the heart is completely missing; nobody is called the "heart."

It is immensely significant when you start feeling a stirring in your heart, because your heart is far more valuable than your head. Your head is all borrowed, it has nothing of its own. But your heart is still yours. Your heart is not Christian or Hindu, your heart is still existential. It has not been corrupted and polluted. Your heart is still original.

It is a great quantum leap from the head to the heart. One step more, from the heart to being, and you have arrived home; the pilgrimage is over.

Nobody can move directly from the head to the being. They are strangers; they are not at all connected with each other. They have not even been introduced! Neither your being knows anything about the head nor does your head know anything about the being. They live in the same house but they are absolute strangers. Because their functioning is so different, they never come across each other; they never encounter each other.

The heart is the bridge. Part of the heart knows the head, and part of the heart knows the being. The heart is a midway station. When you are moving toward your being, the heart is going to be an overnight stay.

From the heart you will be able to see something of the being—but not from the head; hence, philosophers never turn into mystics. Poets turn into mystics, are transformed . . . painters, sculptors, dancers, musicians, singers are closer to the being.

But our whole society is dominated by the head, because the head is capable of earning money. It is very efficient; machines are always more efficient. It is capable of fulfilling all your ambitions. The head is nurtured by your educational systems and your whole energy starts moving there and bypassing the heart.

The heart is the most significant thing because it is the gateway to your being, to your eternal life source. I would like all the universities of the world to make people aware of the heart, to make them more aesthetic, more sensitive: sensitive to all that surrounds us, the immense beauty, the immense joy.

But the heart cannot fulfill your egoistic desires; that is the problem. It can give you a tremendous experience of love, an alchemical change. It can bring the best in you to its clearest and purest form. But it will not create money, power, prestige—and they have become the goals.

Go on slipping from your head to your heart, and then just take a little greater risk and slip from the heart to the being. That is the very foundation of your life.

There is a beautiful story by Turgenev, *The Fool.*

Once in a town there was a man who was condemned by the whole crowd as the greatest idiot who had ever lived. Obviously, he was continuously in difficulty. Whatever he said, people would start laughing—even if he was saying something beautiful and true. But because it was known that he was an idiot, a fool, people thought whatever he did and said was bound to be idiotic. He might be quoting sages, but still people would laugh at him.

He went to a wise old man and told him that he felt like committing suicide, that he could not live anymore. "This constant condemnation is too much—I cannot bear it any longer. Either help me find a way out of it, or I am going to kill myself."

The old wise man laughed. He said, "There is not much of a problem, don't be worried. Do only one thing, and come back to see me after seven days: start saying no to everything. Start questioning each and every thing. If somebody says, 'Look—look at the sunset, how beautiful it is!' ask immediately, 'Where is there any beauty? I don't see any—prove it! What is beauty? There is no beauty in the world, it is all nonsense!' Insist on proofs; say, 'Prove where beauty is. Let me see it, let me touch it. Give me a definition.' If somebody says, 'The music is ecstatic,' immediately jump into it and ask, 'What is ecstasy? What is music? Define your terms clearly. I don't believe in any ecstasy, it is all foolishness, all illusion. And music is nothing but noise.'

"Do this with everything, and after seven days come to me. Be negative, ask questions that cannot be answered: What is beauty, what is love, what is ecstasy? What is life, what is death, what is God?" After seven days the fool came back to the wise man and he was followed by many, many people. He had been garlanded and was beautifully dressed. The wise man asked, "What happened?"

And the fool said, "It was magic! Now the whole city thinks I am the wisest man in the world. Everybody thinks I am a great philosopher, a great thinker. I have silenced everybody; people have become afraid of me. In my presence they remain silent because whatsoever they say I immediately turn it into a question and I become absolutely negative. Your trick worked!"

The wise man asked, "Who are these people who are following you?"

He said, "These are my disciples. They want to learn from me what wisdom is!"

This is how it is. The mind lives in the no, it is a no-sayer; its nourishment comes from saying no to each and every thing. The mind is basically atheistic, negative. There is nothing like a positive mind.

The heart is positive. Just as mind says no, the heart says yes. Of course, it is better to say yes than to say no, because one cannot really live by saying no. The more you say no, the more you become shrunken, closed. The more you say no, the less alive you are. People may think you are a great thinker, but you are shrinking and dying; slowly you are committing suicide.

If you say no to love, you are less than you were before; if you say no to beauty, you are less than you were before. And if you go on saying no to each and every thing, chunk by chunk you are disappearing. Ultimately a very empty life is left, meaningless, with no significance, with no joy, with no dance, with no celebration.

That's what has happened to the modern mind. The modern man has said more nos than ever before. Hence the questions: What is the meaning of life? Why are we alive at all? Why go on living? We have said no to God, we have said no to the beyond, we have said no to all for which man has lived down the ages. We have proved to our heart's content that all the values man has lived for are worthless. But now we are in difficulty, in deep anguish. Life has become more and more impossible for us. We go on living only because we are cowards; otherwise we have destroyed all the reasons to live. We go on living because we cannot commit suicide. We are afraid of death, hence we go on living. We live out of fear, not out of love.

It is better to be positive, because the more positive you are the more you are moving toward the heart. The heart knows no negative language. The heart never asks, "What is beauty?" It enjoys it, and in enjoying it, it knows what it is. It cannot define it, it cannot explain itself, because the experience is such that it is inexplicable, inexpressible. Language is not adequate, no symbols help. The heart knows what love is, but don't ask. The mind knows only questions and the heart knows only answers. The mind goes on asking but it cannot answer.

Hence philosophy has no answers, only questions and questions and questions. Each question becomes, slowly, a thousand and one questions. The heart has no questions—this is one of the mysteries of life—it has all the answers. But the mind will not listen to the heart; there is no communion between the two, no communication, because the heart knows only the language of silence. No other language is known by the heart, no other language is understood by the heart—and the mind knows nothing of silence. The mind is all noise, a tale told by an idiot, full of fury and noise, signifying nothing.

The heart knows what significance is. The heart knows the glory of life, the tremendous joy of sheer existence. The heart is capable of celebrating, but it never asks. Hence the mind thinks the heart is blind. The mind is full of doubts, the heart is full of trust; they are polar opposites.

That's why it is said that it is better to be positive than to be negative. But remember: the positive is joined with the negative, two sides of the same phenomenon.

I am not here to teach you the ways of the heart—yes, I use them, but only as a device to bring you out of your mind. I use the heart as a vehicle to take you to the other shore; I use the heart as a boat. Once you have reached the other shore, the boat has to be left behind; you are not expected to carry the boat on your head.

The goal is to go beyond duality. The goal is to go beyond no and yes both, because your yes can have meaning only in the context of no; it cannot be free of the no. If it is free of the no, what meaning will it have? Your yes can exist only with the no, remember; and your no can also exist only with the yes. They are polar opposites, but they help each other in a subtle way. There is a conspiracy: They are holding hands. They are supporting each other, because they cannot exist separately. Yes has meaning only because of the no; no has meaning only because of the yes. And you have to go beyond this conspiracy, you have to go beyond this duality.

I am not teaching you a positive way of living and I am not teaching you a negative way of living. I am teaching you the way of transcendence. All dualities have to be dropped—the duality of mind and heart, the duality of matter and mind, the duality of thinking and emotion, the duality of the positive and the negative, the duality of male and female, yin and yang, day and night, summer and winter, life and death—*all* dualities. Duality as such has to be dropped, because *you* are beyond duality.

The moment you start moving away from both yes and no, you will have your first glimpses of the ultimate. Hence the ultimate remains absolutely inexpressible; you cannot say no, you cannot say yes.

But if you are going to choose between the negative and the positive, then I will say choose the positive because it is easier to slip out of the yes than to slip out of the no. No does not have much space in it; it is a dark prison cell. Yes is wider; it is more open, more vulnerable. To move from no, you will find it very difficult. You don't have much space; you are enclosed in it from every side, and all the doors and all the windows are closed. No is a closed space. To live in the negative is the most stupid thing a person can do, but millions are living in the negative. Modern man particularly is living in the negative. He is repeating the story of Turgenev, because living in the negative he feels great; his ego feels satisfied.

Ego is a prison cell created by the bricks of nos; negativity is its food. So if you have to choose between the negative and the positive, choose the positive. At least you will have a little wider scope; a few windows and doors will be open, the wind and the sun and the rain will be available to you. You will have a few glimpses of the open sky outside and the stars and the moon. And sometimes the fragrance of flowers will start coming to you, and sometimes you will be thrilled by the joy of just being alive. And it is easier to move from the yes to the beyond.

From the no come to the yes, and from the yes go to the beyond. The beyond is neither positive nor negative: the beyond is godliness, the beyond is enlightenment.

> **Will it ever be possible that we can function from a blend of both head and heart, or must the two always remain totally divorced? Do we have to make a conscious choice for one way or the other?**

It all depends on you, because both are mechanisms. You are neither the head nor the heart. You can move through the head, you can move through the heart. Of course you will reach different places because the directions of the head and the heart are diametrically opposite.

The head will go round and round thinking, brooding, philosophizing; it knows only words, logic, argument. But it is very infertile; you cannot get anything out of the head as far as truth is concerned, because truth needs no logic, no argument, no philosophical research. Truth is so simple; the head makes it so complex. Down through the centuries philosophers have been seeking and searching for the truth through the head. None of them have found anything, but they have created great systems of thought. I have looked into all those systems and there is no conclusion.

The heart is also a mechanism, different from the head. You can call the head the logical instrument and the heart the emotional instrument. Out of the head all the philosophies, all the theologies are created; out of the heart come all kinds of devotion, prayer, sentimentality. But the heart also goes round and round in emotions.

The word "emotion" is good. Watch: it consists of motion, movement. So the heart moves, but the heart is blind. It moves fast, quick, because there is no reason to wait. It does not have to think, so it jumps into anything. But truth is not to be found by any emotionality. Emotion is as much a barrier as logic. The logic is the male in you, and the heart is the female in you. But truth has nothing to do with male and female. Truth is your consciousness. You can watch the head thinking, you can watch the heart throbbing with emotion. They can be in a certain relationship. . . .

Ordinarily, the society has arranged that the head should be the master and the heart should be the servant, because society is the creation of the male mind and psychology. The heart is feminine. And just as man has kept the woman a slave, the head has kept the heart a slave. We can reverse the situation; the heart can become the master and the head can become the servant. If we have to choose between the two, if we are forced to choose between the two, then it is better that the heart become the master and the head become the servant.

There are things that the heart is incapable of, and exactly the same is true about the head. The head cannot love, it cannot feel, it is insensitive. The heart cannot be rational, reasonable. For the whole past they have been in conflict. That conflict only represents the conflict and struggle between men and women. If you are talking to your wife, you must know—it is impossible to talk, it is impossible to argue, it is impossible to come to a fair decision because the woman functions through the heart. She jumps from one thing to another without bothering about whether there is any relationship between the two. She cannot argue but she can cry. She cannot be rational but she can scream. She cannot be cooperative in coming to a conclusion. The heart cannot understand the language of the head.

The difference is not much as far as physiology is concerned; the heart and the head are just a few inches apart from each other. But as far as their existential qualities are concerned, they are poles apart.

My way has been described as that of the heart, but it is not true. The heart will give you all kinds of imaginings, hallucinations, illusions, sweet dreams, but it cannot give you the truth. The truth is behind both; it is in your consciousness, which is neither head nor heart. Just because the consciousness is separate from both, it can use both in harmony.

The head is dangerous in certain fields, because it has eyes but it has no legs: it is crippled. The heart can function in certain dimensions. It has no eyes but it has legs; it is blind but it can move tremendously, with great speed—of course, not knowing where it is going! It is not just a coincidence that in all the languages of the world love is called blind. It is not love that is blind, it is the heart that has no eyes.

As your meditation becomes deeper, as your identification with the head and the heart starts falling away, you find yourself becoming a triangle. And your reality is in the third force in you, the consciousness. Consciousness can manage very easily, because the heart and the head *both* belong to it.

I have told the story of a blind beggar and a crippled beggar who lived in the forest outside a village. Of course they were competitors to each other, enemies; begging is a business. But one day the forest was on fire. The cripple had no way to escape, because he could not move on his own. He had eyes to see which way they could run to get out of the fire, but what use is that if you don't have legs? The blind man had legs and could move fast and get out of the fire, but how was he going to find the places where the fire had not reached yet?

Both were going to die in the forest, burned alive. It was in such an emergency that they forgot their competition, immediately dropped their antagonism—that was the only way to survive. The blind man took the cripple on his shoulders and they found the way out of the fire. One was seeing, and the other was moving accordingly.

Something like this has to happen within you; the head has the eyes, and the heart has the guts to move into anything. You have to create a synthesis between the two. And the synthesis, I have to emphasize, should be that the heart remains the master and the head becomes the servant.

You have as a servant a great asset: your reasoning. You cannot be fooled, you cannot be cheated and exploited. The heart has all feminine qualities: love, beauty, grace. The head is barbarous. The heart is far more civilized, far more innocent.

A conscious person uses the head as a servant and the heart as the master. And this is so simple for a man of consciousness to do. Once you are unidentified with head or heart, and you are simply a witness of both, you can see which qualities should be higher, which qualities should be the goal. And the head as a servant can bring those qualities, but it needs to be commanded and ordered. Right now, and for centuries, just the opposite has been happening: the servant has become the master. And the real master is so polite, such a gentleman, that he has not fought back; he has accepted the slavery voluntarily. The madness on the earth is the result.

We have to change the very alchemy of man.

We have to rearrange the whole inside of man, and the most basic revolution will come when the heart decides the values. It cannot decide for war, it cannot go for nuclear weapons, it cannot be death-oriented. The heart is life's juice. Once the head is in the service of the heart, it has to do what the heart decides. And the head is immensely capable of doing anything; just right guidance is needed. Otherwise, it is going to go berserk, it is going to be mad. For the head there are no values. For the head there is no meaning in anything. For the head there is no love, no beauty, no grace—only reasoning.

But this miracle is possible only by disidentifying yourself from both. Watch the thoughts, because in your watching them, they disappear. Then watch your emotions, sentimentalities; by your watching, they also disappear. Then your heart is as innocent as that of a child, and your head is as great a genius as Albert Einstein, Bertrand Russell, Aristotle.

But the trouble is far bigger than you can conceive. It is a male-dominated society; the man has been creating all the rules of the game, the woman has just been following. And the conditioning has gone so deep, because it has been going on for millions of years.

If the revolution happens in the individual and the heart is re-enthroned, given its right place as the master, and the head given its right place as a great servant, this will affect your whole social structure. There is a possibility, but the possibility has a basic condition to be fulfilled: you become more conscious, a witness, a watcher of all that goes on inside you. The watcher becomes immediately free from identification. Because he can see the emotions, it is an absolute certainty that "I am not the emotions." He can see the thoughts; the simple conclusion is "I am not my thought process."

"Then who am I?"—a pure watcher, a witness, and you reach to the ultimate possibility of intelligence in you. You become a conscious human being. Amongst the whole world sleeping, you become awake, and once you are awake there is no problem. Your very awakening will start shifting things to their right places. The head has to be dethroned, and the heart has to be crowned again. This change amongst many people will bring a new society, a new kind of human being in the world. It will change so many things, you cannot conceive.

Science will have a totally different flavor. It will not serve death anymore, it will not make weapons that are going to kill the whole of life on the earth. It will make life richer, discover energies that can make man more fulfilled, that can make man live in comfort, in luxury, because the values will have completely changed. It will still be mind functioning, but under the direction of the heart.

My way is the way of meditation. I have to use language, unfortunately. That's why I say my way is the way of meditation—neither of head nor of heart, but of a growing consciousness that is above both mind and heart.

This is the key to open the doors for a new human being to arrive on the earth.

> After listening to you talk about thinking, feeling, and being, and having to let go of the one in order to reach the next, the question arises in me, "Does this mean I will have to let go of love, too?" Is love a feeling of the being that will always be there? Can you please say something about feeling, love, and being?

I can say much, but first I want to ask you, do you know what love is, that you are afraid love will be lost? People go on imagining things. . . .

In a court there was a case. Two friends, old friends, had beaten each other very badly. They were brought into the court. The judge could not believe it. It was a small town, and everybody knew that these two persons were always together and they were great friends. He asked, "What happened? What caused the fight?"

One said to the other, "You tell it." The other said, "No, you tell it."

The judge said, "Anybody can tell it, it's not a question of etiquette, of who should tell it first. But let me know." But both were silent. The judge, to be hard on them, said, "Speak! Or I will throw you both into jail."

Then one of the men said, "It is so embarrassing . . . In fact, we both were sitting on the sands by the side of the river, and my friend said that he was going to purchase a cow. I said, 'You drop that idea, because your cow might enter my farm fields and trample the crops, and that will be the end of our friendship. I will kill the cow.'

"My friend said, 'You have some nerve! I am perfectly free to purchase one cow or ten cows. And cows are cows—sometimes they may enter your field, and then we'll see what happens. If you can kill my cow, I can burn your whole crop!'"

And so it went, one thing led to another. Finally, the man who had the farm had drawn a picture of the farm on the sand with his finger and said, "This is my farm. Let your cow enter into it and I will show you what happens."

And the man said, "Your Honor, this man, with his fingers, brought five cows into my field, and said to me, 'Now what do you want to do?' Then we started beating each other; there was no cow, there was no farm. So I could not beat his cows and he could not burn my farm. We are very embarrassed, that's why we were each insisting, 'You tell the judge what happened.'"

The judge said, "This is sheer stupidity! He has not purchased the cow yet; your farm is empty, you have not sown the seed—and you both have fractures?"

You ask me, "When the mind is transcended, when emotions, sentiments, feelings, are transcended, will I have to lose my love too?" Do you actually have it? First purchase the cow!

I know you don't have it, because if you had, the question would not have arisen. That's why I am saying with such certainty that you don't have it.

Still, your question is significant.

There are three layers of the human individual: the physiology, the body; the psychology, the mind; and the being, the eternal self. Love can exist on all three planes, but its qualities will be different. On the plane of physiology, the body, it is simply sexuality. You can call it love because the word "love" seems poetic, beautiful, but ninety-nine percent of people are calling their sex "love." Sex is biological, physiological. Your chemistry, your hormones—everything material is involved in it.

You fall in love with a woman or a man. Can you describe exactly why this person attracted you? Certainly you cannot see the self of the person; you have not seen your own self yet. You cannot see the person's psychology either, because to read somebody's mind is not an easy job. So what have you found? Something in your physiology, in your chemistry, in your hormones, is attracted to the other person's hormones, physiology, chemistry. This is not a love affair; this is a chemical affair.

Just think: the woman you have fallen in love with goes to a doctor and gets her sex changed, starts growing a beard and mustache—will you still love her? Nothing has changed, only the chemistry and hormones. So where has your love gone?

Only one percent of people know a little bit deeper. Poets, painters, musicians, dancers, singers have a sensitivity that they can feel beyond the body. They can feel the beauties of the mind, the sensitivities of the heart, because they live on that plane themselves.

Remember it as a ground rule: wherever you live, you cannot see beyond that. If you live in your body, if you think you are only your body, you can be attracted only to somebody's body. This is the physiological stage of love. But a musician, a painter, a poet lives on a different plane. He does not think, he feels. And because he lives in his heart, he can feel the other person's heart. That is ordinarily called love. It is rare. I am saying only one percent perhaps, once in a while.

Why are many more people not moving to the second plane? Because it is tremendously beautiful . . . but there is a problem. Anything very beautiful is also very delicate. It is not hardware; it is made of very fragile glass. And once a mirror has fallen and broken, then there is no way to put it back together. People are afraid to get so much involved that they reach to the delicate layers of love, because at that stage love is tremendously beautiful but also tremendously changing. Sentiments are not stones, they are like rose flowers. It is better to have a plastic rose flower, because it will be there always, and every day you can give it a shower and it will be fresh. You can put some French perfume on it. If its color fades you can paint it again. Plastic is one of the most indestructible things in the world. It is stable, permanent; hence, people stop at the physiological. It is superficial, but it is stable.

Poets, artists, are known to fall in love almost every day. Their love is like a rose flower. While it is there it is so fragrant, so alive, dancing in the wind, in the rain, in the sun, asserting its beauty. But by the evening it may be gone, and you cannot do anything to prevent it. The deeper love of the heart is just like a breeze that comes into your room, brings its freshness, coolness, and then is gone. You cannot catch hold of the wind in your fist. Very few people are so courageous as to live with a moment-to-moment, changing life. Hence, they have decided to fall into a love on which they can depend.

I don't know which kind of love you know—most probably the first kind, perhaps the second kind. And you are afraid that if you reach your being, what will happen to your love?

Certainly it will be gone, but you will not be a loser. A new kind of love will arise, which arises only perhaps to one person in millions. That love can only be called lovingness.

The first love should be called sex. The second love should be called love. The third should be called lovingness: a quality, unaddressed, not possessive and not allowing anybody else to possess you. That loving quality is such a radical revolution that even to conceive of it is very difficult.

At the point of being, you simply have a fragrance of lovingness. But don't be afraid. Your concern is right; what you think of as love will be gone. But what will come in its place is immense, infinite. You will be able to love without being attached. You will be able to love many people, because to love one person is to keep yourself poor. That one person can give a certain experience of love, but to love many people . . . you will be amazed that every person gives you a new feeling, a new song, a new ecstasy.

It is for that reason that I am against marriage. People can live together their whole life if they want, but it should not be a legal necessity. People should be moving, having as many experiences of love as possible. They should not be possessive. Possessiveness destroys love. And they should not be possessed, because that again destroys your love.

All human beings are worthy of being loved. There is no need to be tethered to one person for your whole life. That is one of the reasons why all the people around the world look so bored. Why can't they laugh, why can't they dance? They are chained with invisible chains: marriage, family, husband, wife, children. They are burdened with all kinds of duties, responsibilities, sacrifices. And you want them to smile and laugh and dance and rejoice? You are asking the impossible.

Make people's love free, make people nonpossessive. But this can happen only if in your meditation you discover your being. It is nothing to practice. I am not saying to you, "Tonight you go to some other woman or some other man just as a practice." You will not get anything, and you may lose your partner, and in the morning you will look silly. It is not a question of practicing, it is a question of discovering your being.

With the discovery of being follows the quality of impersonal lovingness. Then you simply love, and it goes on spreading. First it is human beings, then soon it is animals, birds, trees, mountains, stars. A day comes when this whole existence is your beloved. That is our potential, and anybody who is not achieving it is wasting his life.

Yes, you will have to lose a few things, but they are worthless. You will be gaining so much that you will never think again of what you have lost.

A pure, impersonal lovingness that can penetrate into anybody's being: that is the outcome of meditativeness, of silence, of diving deep within your own being. I am simply trying to persuade you. Don't be afraid of losing what you have.

My function is basically to persuade you by and by to move from the physiology to the psychology—move from the mind to the heart. Then move from the heart to the being. From the being opens the door of the ultimate being of existence. It is impossible to describe it. It can only be pointed at—a finger pointing to the moon.

But don't be worried. You will be losing only your poverty, your misery. You will not be losing anything that is valuable.

PART II

Emotional Wellness:
Reclaiming Our
Inner Harmony

When you use your energy as awareness, that brings you close to the very center of existence. Your thinking takes you a little far away, and your expression takes you even further away. In turning back from expression to thinking, and from thinking to nonthinking—just pure awareness—you are closest to your own center and to the center of existence itself.

In emotions, in thoughts, in expressions, the energy is moving toward the periphery, the circumference. And the closer you are to the circumference, the farther away you are from yourself.

Drop backward step by step. It is a journey to the source, and the source is all that you need to experience . . . because it is not only your source, it is the source of the stars and the moon and the sun. It is the source of all.

BEGIN WITH ACCEPTANCE

The greatest desire in the world is for inner transformation. The desire for money is nothing, the desire for more power, prestige, is nothing; the greatest desire is the so-called spiritual desire. And once you are caught in that desire you will remain miserable forever. Transformation is possible, but not by desiring it. Transformation is possible only by relaxing into that which is, whatsoever is. Unconditionally accepting yourself brings transformation.

We will have to go deeper into this phenomenon, because this is at the heart of everybody's situation.

Man is in misery, man is in anguish; hence, everybody is searching for a state of bliss, a state of unity with existence. Man feels alienated, uprooted. Hence, the desire is natural to get roots into existence again, to be green again, to be blossoming again.

These few things have to be meditated upon. First, to establish that perfect unity with existence, consciousness must first unify itself. And that is only possible when we reject nothing that is experientially real. This is the first thing to be understood.

You feel fear—now the fear is an existential reality, an experiential reality; it is there! You can reject it, but by rejecting it you will be repressing it. By repressing it you will create a wound in your being. You feel cowardice—you can manage not to look at it but it is a fact, a reality. Just by not looking at it, it is not going to disappear. You are behaving like an ostrich. Seeing the enemy, seeing the danger of death, the ostrich hides its head in the sand. But hiding his head in the sand, closing his eyes, does not make the enemy disappear. In fact the ostrich becomes more vulnerable to the enemy. Thinking that now there is no enemy because nobody is seen, thinking that *seeing* the enemy is what makes it real, now the ostrich is relieved of the fear. But in fact he is more in danger; the enemy is more powerful because it has not been noticed.

Something can be done if the ostrich does not hide his head. But that's what people are doing. You see cowardice, you try not to notice it, but it is a fact! By not noticing it, you have created a part of your being that you will not be able to see. You have divided yourself into segments. Now one day there is something else—anger—and you don't want to accept that there is anger in you. You stop looking at it. Then some other day there is greed, and so on and so forth. And whatever you stop looking at remains, but now you go on shrinking. Many more parts of your being become separate from you—you have separated them on your own. And the more fragmentary you are, the more miserable you will be.

The first step toward bliss is to be one. That's what all the mystics have been insisting again and again: to be one is so blissful, to be many is to be in hell. So whatever is experientially real, accept it. You cannot do anything by denying it. By denying it you create the problem, and the problem becomes more complex.

It is simple: you feel you are a coward, so what? So, "I am a coward." Just see the point! If you can accept cowardice you have already become brave. Only a brave person can accept the fact of being a coward; no coward can do that. You are already on the way to transformation. So the first thing is that nothing that is experienced as a fact has to be denied reality.

Second, in order to accomplish that, consciousness must first disidentify from all the fixed ideas with which it has identified itself. If your mind holds onto its ideas about who you are, holds onto some fixed and enduring concept of what you are, there will be no space in you for any reality that contradicts its ideas. If you have a certain idea of how you should be, then you cannot accept the experiential truths of your being. If you have the idea that you have to be brave, that bravery is valuable, then it is difficult to accept your cowardice. If you have the idea that you have to be a buddha-like person, compassionate, absolutely compassionate, then you cannot accept your anger. It is the ideal that creates the problem.

If you don't have any ideals then there is no problem at all. You are a coward, so you are a coward! Because there is no ideal of being brave, you don't condemn the fact—you don't reject it, you don't repress it, you don't throw it into the basement of your being so that there is no need for you to ever look at it.

Anything that you throw into your unconscious will go on functioning from there, it will go on creating problems for you. It is like a disease that you have pushed inward. It was coming to the surface, and from the surface there was a possibility that it might have disappeared. If a wound comes to the surface it is good, it is on the way to being healed—because it is only on the surface that it will be in contact with fresh air and the sun, and can be healed. If you force it inward, if you don't allow it to come to the surface, then it is going to become a cancer. Even a small disease, repressed, can become a dangerous disease.

No disease should ever be repressed. But the repression is natural if you have some ideal. Any ideal will do. If you have the ideal of being a celibate, then sex becomes the problem. You can't watch it. If you don't have the ideal of becoming a celibate, then sex is not rejected. Then there is no division between you and your sexuality. Then there is communion, and that communion brings joy.

Self-communion is the base of all joy.

So the second thing to remember is, don't carry ideals. Just think, if you have an ideal that you have to have three eyes, a problem immediately arises because you have only two eyes, and your ideal says if you don't have three, something is missing. Now you hanker for the third. You have created an impossible problem for yourself! It will not be solved. At the most you can paint a third eye on your forehead. But the painted third eye is just a painted third eye; it is hypocrisy.

Ideals create hypocrisy in people. Look at the absurdity: people have the ideal of not being hypocrites, and hypocrisy comes through ideals. If all ideals disappear there will be no hypocrisy. How can hypocrisy exist? It is the shadow of having ideals. The bigger the ideal the bigger the hypocrisy. In India you will find more hypocrites than anywhere in the world, because India has lived for centuries with great ideals. Strange, berserk ideals . . .

For example, a Jaina monk cannot be satisfied unless he is capable, like the mythological stories of Mahavira, of eating only once in a while. It is said that in twelve years Mahavira ate for a total of only one year. That means after twelve days he would eat for one day, and then for twelve more days he would be fasting. Now, if this is your ideal you are going to remain in great misery. If this is not your ideal then there is no problem.

See it—the problem arises from the ideal. Now, a Christian monk is not plagued by this ideal, he has no problem with fasting. But the Jaina monk is continuously suffering because he cannot attain the ideal; he falls short.

If you are really pure—this is the Jaina idea—your body will not perspire. Now you have a stupid idea there! The body will continue to perspire, and you will continue to suffer.

The more ideals you have the more will be your suffering and the more will be your hypocrisy, because if you cannot fulfill the ideals, then at least you have to pretend. That's how hypocrisy comes in. The world will not be hypocritical at all if we accept experiential facts without any judgment. Whatever is, is. If we live with the is-ness of existence and not with the "oughts" and the "shoulds," how can hypocrisy arise?

Just the other day, somebody asked me, "Are you not a hypocrite? Because you live comfortably, you live in a beautiful house, you move in a beautiful car, you live like a king." Now, he does not understand what the word "hypocrisy" means. It is my whole teaching to live as beautifully as possible. I am not a hypocrite; in fact I am living the way I am teaching. If I were teaching to live in poverty and living in a palace, that would be hypocrisy. But I am not teaching to live in poverty; poverty is not my goal. I live naturally; and it is very natural to live in comfort and convenience. It is simply stupid, if comfort is available, not to live in it. If it is not available, that is another thing. Then whatever is available, live in it comfortably; manage to live in it comfortably.

I have lived in many kinds of situations but I have always lived comfortably. When I was a student I used to walk to the university, four miles every day, but I loved it! I walked those four miles every day with great comfort; I enjoyed it. When I was a teacher I used to go on a bicycle to the university; I enjoyed that too. Whatsoever has been the situation, whether I have had a bicycle or a Mercedes-Benz, it doesn't make any difference. I have lived in comfort. Comfort is an attitude of mind; it is an approach toward life. I have lived in very poor houses. When I became a teacher in the university I started by living in one single room with no windows, no ventilation. The rent was just twenty rupees per month. But I loved it, I enjoyed it, it was not a problem at all. Whatever the moment allows, I have squeezed the moment to its totality. I have drunk fully of the moment, I have never repented, and I have never desired something else. If something else started happening I enjoyed that too. You can never say to me that I am a hypocrite. It is impossible for me to be a hypocrite, because I have no ideals to fulfill, no "oughts," no "shoulds." The "is" is all that is, and I live in it.

So the second thing to remember is, don't have certain ideas about yourself. People are carrying so many ideas of how they should be. If you have the idea to be a brave man then it looks ugly to be a coward. But cowardice is a fact, and the ideal is just an ideal, a fantasy of the mind.

Sacrifice fantasies to reality, drop all ideals, and then life starts becoming integrated. All the rejected fragments start coming back home and the repressed starts surfacing. For the first time you start feeling a kind of togetherness; you are no longer falling apart.

For example, if I think of myself as a "kind" person, I won't be able to allow myself to recognize and accept angry feelings when they arise. "Kind" people don't get angry. So to bring about a unity in my consciousness, I have to see that I am only the moment-to-moment, experiential reality. Some moments I am angry, some moments I am sad. Some moments I am jealous, some moments I am joyful. Moment to moment, whatever happens is accepted.

Then you become one. And this oneness is the most fundamental thing to understand.

My purpose here, my function here, is to take all ideals away from you. You come with ideals; you would like me to enhance your ideals, you would like me to support you and help you to become that which you want to become. That may be your motivation in coming here, but that is not my work. My work is just the opposite: to help you to accept that which is already the case and to forget all about your fantasies. I want you to become more realistic and pragmatic. I want to give you roots in the earth—and you are hankering for the sky and you have completely forgotten the earth.

Yes, the sky is also available, but only to those whose roots have gone deep into the earth. If a tree wants to rise high in the sky and whisper with the clouds and play with the winds and have some communion with the stars, then the tree will have to send deeper and deeper roots into the earth. The first thing is sending roots into the earth, the second thing happens of its own accord. The deeper the roots go the higher the tree goes; there is no need to do anything else.

My effort is to send your roots deep into the soil of truth. And the truth is that which you *are*. Then suddenly things will start happening. You will start rising. The ideals that you have always tried for and have never been able to achieve will start happening of their own accord.

If a person can accept reality as it is, in that very acceptance, all tension disappears. Anguish, anxiety, despair—they all simply evaporate. And when there is no anxiety, no tension, no fragmentariness, no division, no schizophrenia, then suddenly there is joy. Then suddenly there is love, then suddenly there is compassion. These are not ideals; these are very natural phenomena. All that is needed is to remove the ideals, because those ideals are functioning as blocks. The more idealistic a person is, the more blocked.

Yes, cowardice gives you pain, fear gives you pain, anger gives you pain; these are negative emotions. But peace can be attained only by accepting and absorbing the painful, not by rejecting it. By rejecting it you will become smaller and smaller and smaller, and you will have less and less power. And you will be in a constant inner war, a civil war in which one hand will fight with the other, in which you will simply dissipate your energy.

A very fundamental thing to be remembered is that only communion with psychological pain opens the door for its liberation and transcendence: *only communion with psychological pain*. All that is painful has to be accepted; a dialogue has to be created with it. It is you. There is no other way to go beyond it. The only way is to absorb it.

And it has tremendous potential. Anger is energy, fear is energy, so is cowardice. All that happens to you has great momentum, a great quantity of energy hidden in it. Once you accept it, that energy becomes yours. You become stronger, you become wider, you start becoming more spacious. You have a bigger inner world then.

Psychological pain ends only by accepting the pain in its totality. Psychological pain does not exist just because of the presence of something you call "painful." The pain is produced by your interpretation of the reality. Try to understand it: psychological pain is your own creation. Cowardice is not painful, only your idea that cowardice is wrong, your interpretation that cowardice should not be there. You have a certain ego and that ego goes on condemning cowardice. It is because of that condemnation and interpretation that pain arises. The cowardice *is* there, so it becomes a wound. You cannot accept it, and you cannot destroy it by rejecting it. Nothing is destroyed by being rejected; sooner or later you will have to cope with it. Again and again it will erupt, again and again it will disrupt your peace.

You are recoiling from the facts of cowardice, fear, anger, and sadness. Don't recoil. Recoiling from a fact creates pain. Watch it inside yourself, become a lab of great experimentation. Just see: you are feeling fear, it is dark and you are alone, and for miles there is nobody. You are lost in a jungle, sitting under a tree on a dark night and lions are roaring—fear is there. Now there are two possibilities. One is to reject it, hold yourself tight so you don't start trembling because of the fear. Then the fear becomes a painful thing—it is there, and it hurts! Even when you are holding yourself very tight, it is there and it hurts.

The second is, enjoy it. Tremble, let it become a meditation. It is natural; lions are roaring, the night is dark, danger is so close by, and death can happen any moment. Enjoy it, let the trembling become a dance. Once you accept it, then trembling *is* a dance. Cooperate with the trembling and you will be surprised: if you cooperate with the trembling, if you *become* the trembling, all pain disappears.

In fact, if you allow yourself to tremble, instead of pain you will find a great upsurge of energy arising in you. That's exactly what the body wanted to do. Why in fear does trembling arise? Trembling triggers a chemical process, it releases energy, it prepares you to fight or take flight. It gives you a great, sudden upsurge of energy—it is an emergency measure. When you start trembling you start warming up.

That's why when it is cold you tremble. There is no fear, so why do you tremble when it is cold? The body automatically trembles in the cold so that it becomes warm. It is a kind of natural exercise of the body. The inner tissues start trembling to become warmed up so they can face the cold. And if you repress trembling when you are feeling cold it will become painful.

That is exactly the case when you are in fear. The body is trying to prepare. It is releasing chemicals into the blood, it is preparing you to face some danger. Maybe you will need to have a fight, or maybe you will have to run away and take flight. Either response will need energy.

See the beauty of fear, see the alchemical work of fear; it is simply trying to prepare you for the situation so that you can accept the challenge. But rather than accepting the challenge, rather than understanding fear, you start rejecting it. You say, "You are such a great person and you are trembling? Remember that there is no death, that the soul is immortal. An immortal soul, and trembling? Remember that death cannot destroy you, fire cannot burn you, weapons cannot penetrate you. Remember it, don't tremble, keep control of yourself."

Now you are creating a contradiction. Your natural process is that of fear, and you are bringing in unnatural ideas to contradict fear. You are bringing ideals to interfere in the natural process. There will be pain because there will be conflict.

Don't bother whether the soul is immortal or not. Right now, the truth is that fear is there. Listen to this moment, and let this moment take you totally; allow this moment to possess you and then there is no pain. Then, the fear is a subtle dance of energies in you. It prepares you; it is a friend, it is not your enemy. But your interpretations go on doing something wrong to you. The split that you create between the feeling and yourself—the fear, the anger, and yourself—makes you become two. You become the observer and the observed. You say, "I am here, the observer, and there is pain, the observed. I am not the pain." Now this *duality* creates pain.

You are not the observed and you are not the observer, you are both. You are the observer and the observed, both.

Don't say, "I am feeling fear." That is a wrong way of saying it. Don't say, "I am afraid." That too is a wrong way of saying it. Simply say, "I am fear. In this moment, I am fear." Don't create any division.

When you say, "I am feeling fear," you are keeping yourself separate from the feeling. You are there somewhere far away and the feeling is around you. This is the basic disunity. Say, "I am fear," and watch—that's actually the case! When the fear is there, you are fear. It is not that sometimes you feel love. When love is really there, you are love. And when anger is there, you are anger.

This is what Krishnamurti means when he says again and again, "The observer is the observed." The seer is the seen, and the experiencer is the experience. Don't create this division of subject and object. This is the root cause of all misery, of all split.

Simply a choiceless awareness of what is—that is the ultimate key to open the innermost mystery of your being. Don't say it is good, don't say it is bad. When you say something is good, attachment arises, attraction arises. When you say something is bad, repulsion arises. Fear is fear, neither good nor bad. Don't evaluate, just let it be. Let it be so. In that choiceless awareness all psychological pain simply evaporates like dewdrops in the early morning sun, and what is left behind is a pure space, virgin space. This is the "one," the Tao, or you can call it God. This "one" that is left behind when all pain disappears, when you are not divided in any way, when the observer has become the observed: this is the experience of godliness, enlightenment, or whatever you want to call it.

And in this state there is no self as such, because there is no observer/controller/judge. One is only that which arises and changes from moment to moment. Some moments it may be elation, other moments it may be sadness, compassion, destructiveness, fear, loneliness. One should not say, "I am sad," or "I have sadness," but "I am sadness"—because the first two imply a self that is separate from that which is. In reality there is no "self" to whom the feeling is happening. There is only the feeling itself.

Meditate over it: there is only the feeling itself.

There is no self that is feeling fear; that being *is* fear in a certain moment. In certain other moments that being is not fear. But you are not separate from the moment, from that which is arising; there is only the feeling itself. Thus, nothing can be done about what is experientially arising in the moment. There is no-body to "do" anything.

Everything that is, is beautiful—even ugliness. Whatsoever is, is, whether you accept it or not. Your acceptance or rejection makes no difference at all to the facticity of it. That which is, is. If you accept it you have joy arising in you, if you reject it you have pain, but the reality remains the same. You may have pain, psychological pain—that is your creation because you were not able to accept and absorb something that was arising. You rejected truth; in that rejection you became a prisoner. The truth liberates, but you rejected it; hence, you are in chains. Reject truth, and you will remain more and more imprisoned.

The truth remains. Whether you reject it or accept it does not change the fact, it only changes your psychological reality. And there are two possibilities: either pain or joy, either disease or health. If you reject it there will be disease, discomfort, because you are cutting a chunk of your being away from you; it will leave wounds and scars on you. If you accept it, there will be celebration and health and wholeness.

No truth ever binds anybody; that is not the quality of truth. But when you reject it, in your rejection you become closed and you are bottled up. In that rejection you become a cripple, you become paralyzed.

And remember, the very idea of getting free is again an ideal. Freedom is not an ideal, it is a by-product of accepting whosoever you are. Freedom is a by-product; it is not a goal of your endeavor and effort. It is not arrived at by great effort, it happens when you are relaxed. And how can you be relaxed if you cannot accept your cowardice? If you cannot accept your fear, if you cannot accept your love, if you cannot accept your sadness, how can you be relaxed?

Why can't people relax? What is the basic cause of their con-stant, chronic tension? This is the basic cause: down through the centuries, your so-called religions have been teaching you to reject and reject. They have been teaching you to renounce, they have been teaching you that all is wrong. You have to change this, you have to change that, only then will you be acceptable to God. They have created so much rejection that you are not even acceptable to yourself, you are not acceptable to the people you live with, how can you be accepted by God?

Existence already accepts you—that's why you are here. Otherwise you would not be. This is my basic teaching to you. Existence already accepts you. You do not have to earn it, you are already worthy. Relax, enjoy the way nature has made you. If nature has put cowardice in you, then there must be something in it. Trust and accept it. What is wrong in being a coward? What is wrong in being afraid? Only idiots don't feel fear, imbeciles are not afraid. If a snake comes on the path you will jump immediately. Only the imbecile, the stupid, the idiot, will not be afraid of the snake. But if you are intelligent, the more intelligent you are the faster you will jump! This is part of intelligence, it is perfectly good. It helps your life, it protects you.

But stupid ideologies have been given to people and you go on persisting in your old patterns. You don't listen to what I am saying. I am saying, whatsoever you are, unconditionally accept it— and acceptance is the key to transformation.

I am not saying to accept yourself in order to be transformed—otherwise you have not accepted yourself at all, because deep down the desire is for transformation. You say, "Okay, if this brings transformation then I will accept myself." But this is not acceptance; you have missed the whole point. You are still desiring transformation. If I guarantee it to you, and you accept yourself because of the guarantee, where is the acceptance? You are using acceptance as a means; the goal is to be transformed, to be free, to attain to self-realization, to nirvana. Where is the acceptance?

Acceptance has to be unconditional, for no reason at all, without any motivation. Only then does it free you. It brings tremendous joy, it brings great freedom, but the freedom does not come as an end. Acceptance itself is another name for freedom. If you have accepted truly, if you have understood what I mean by acceptance, there is freedom—immediately, instantly.

It is not that first you accept yourself, practice acceptance, and then one day there will be freedom, no. Accept yourself and there is freedom, because psychological pain disappears immediately.

Try it. What I am saying is experimental. You can do it, it is not a question of believing me. You have been fighting with your fear; accept it, and see what happens. Just sit silently and accept it, and say, "I have fear, so I *am* fear." In that very meditative state, "I am fear," freedom starts descending. When the acceptance is total, freedom has arrived.

Sometimes, when dark sides of my mind come up, it really scares me. It is very difficult for me to accept that it is just the polar opposite of the bright ones. I feel dirty and guilty and not worthy. Can you please talk about this?

The basic thing to understand is that you are not the mind, neither the bright one nor the dark one. If you get identified with the beautiful part, then it is impossible to disidentify yourself from the ugly part; they are two sides of the same coin. You can have it whole, or you can throw it away whole, but you cannot divide it.

The whole anxiety of man is that he wants to choose that which looks beautiful, bright. He wants to choose all the silver linings, leaving the dark cloud behind. But he does not know that silver linings cannot exist without the dark cloud. The dark cloud is the background, absolutely necessary for the silver linings to show.

Choosing is anxiety, choosing is creating trouble for yourself. Being choiceless means that the mind is there, and it has a dark side and it has a bright side—so what? What has it to do with you? Why should you be worried about it?

The moment you are not choosing, all worry disappears. A great acceptance arises that this is how the mind has to be, this is the nature of the mind—and it is not your problem, because you are not the mind. If you *were* the mind, there would have been no problem at all. Then who would choose, and who would think of transcending? Who would try to accept and understand acceptance?

You are separate, totally separate. You are only a witness and nothing else. But you are being an observer who gets identified with anything that seems pleasant, and forgets that the unpleasant is coming just behind it as a shadow. You are not troubled by the pleasant side, you rejoice in it. The trouble comes when the polar opposite asserts itself—then you are torn apart.

But you started the whole trouble. Falling from being just a witness, you became identified.

The biblical story of the Fall is just a fiction. The real fall is the fall from being a witness into getting identified with something and losing your witnessing.

Just try once in a while: let the mind be whatever it is. Remember, you are not it. And you are going to have a great surprise. As you become less identified, the mind starts becoming less powerful—because its power comes from your identification. It sucks your blood. But when you start standing aloof and away, the mind starts shrinking.

The day you are completely unidentified with the mind, even for a single moment, there is the revelation. The mind simply dies; it is no longer there. Where it was so full, where it was so continuous—day in, day out, waking, sleeping, it was there—

suddenly it is not there. You look all around and it is emptiness, it is nothingness.

And, along with the disappearance of the mind, the self disappears. Then there is only a certain quality of awareness with no "I" in it. At the most you can call it something similar to "am-ness," but not "I-ness." To be even more exact, it is "is-ness" because even in am-ness some shadow of the "I" is still there. The moment you know its is-ness, it has become universal. With the disappearance of the mind disappears the self. And so many things disappear that were so important to you, so troublesome to you. You were trying to solve them and they were becoming more and more complicated; everything was a problem, an anxiety, and there seemed to be no way out.

I will remind you of the story "The Goose Is Out." It is concerned with the mind and your is-ness.

The master tells the disciple to meditate on a koan:

A small goose is put into a bottle, fed, and nourished. The goose goes on becoming bigger and bigger and bigger, and fills the whole bottle. Now it is too big; it cannot come out of the bottle's mouth—the mouth is too small. And the koan is that you have to bring the goose out without destroying the bottle, and without killing the goose.

Now, it is mind-boggling. What can you do? The goose is too big; you cannot take it out unless you break the bottle, but that is not allowed. Or you can bring it out by killing it; then you don't care whether it comes out alive or dead. That is not allowed either.

Day in, day out, the disciple meditates, finds no way, thinks this way and that way—but in fact there is no way. Tired, utterly exhausted, a sudden revelation . . . suddenly he understands that the master cannot be interested in the bottle and the goose; they must represent something else. The bottle is the mind, you are the goose. And with witnessing, it is possible. Without being in the mind, you can become identified with it so much that you start feeling you are in it! The disciple runs to the master to say that the goose is out. And the master says, "You have understood it. Now keep it out. It has never been in."

If you go on struggling with the goose and the bottle, there is no way for you to solve it. It is the realization that it must represent something else, otherwise the master would not have given it to you. What else can it be? Because the whole function between the master and the disciple, the whole business, is about the mind and awareness.

Awareness is the goose—which is not in the bottle of the mind, but you believe that it is, and you are asking everyone how to get it out. And there are idiots who will help you with techniques to get out of it. I call them idiots because they have not understood the thing at all: the goose is out, has never been in, so the question of bringing it out does not arise.

Mind is just a procession of thoughts passing in front of you on the screen of the brain. You are an observer. But you start getting identified with beautiful things; those are bribes. Once you get caught in the beautiful things you are also caught in the ugly things, because mind cannot exist without duality.

Awareness cannot exist with duality, and mind cannot exist without duality.

Awareness is nondual, and mind is dual. So just watch. I don't teach any solutions, I teach *the* solution: just step back a little and watch. Create a distance between you and your mind. Whether it is good, beautiful, delicious, something that you would like to enjoy closely, or it is ugly—remain as far away as possible, look at it just the way you look at a film. But people get identified even with films. . . .

I have seen people weeping in films, tears coming down—and nothing is happening! It is good that in a movie house it is dark; it saves them from feeling embarrassed. I used to ask my father, "Did you see? The fellow by your side was crying!"

He would say, "The whole hall was crying. The scene was such . . ."

But there was only a screen and nothing else. Nobody was killed, there was no tragedy happening—just a projection of a film, just pictures moving on the screen. And people laugh, and weep, and for three hours they are almost lost. They become part of the movie, they become identified with some character.

My father would say to me, "If you are raising questions about people's reactions then you cannot enjoy the film."

I said, "I can enjoy the film, but I don't want to cry; I don't see any enjoyment in it. I can see it as a film, but I don't want to become a part of it. These people are all becoming a part of it."

My grandfather had an old barber who was an opium addict. For something that was possible to do in five minutes he would take two hours, and he would talk continuously. But they were old friends from their childhood. I can still see my grandfather sitting in the old barber's chair . . . and he was a lovely talker. These opium addicts have a certain quality, a beauty of talking and telling stories about themselves, what is happening day to day; it is true. My grandfather would simply be saying, "Yes, right, that's great . . ."

I said to him one day, "About everything you go on saying, 'Yes, right, it is great.' Sometimes he is talking nonsense, simply irrelevant."

He said, "What do you want? That man is an opium addict." And the barber used a straight razor for shaving. "Now what do you want me to say?—with that man who has a sharp knife in his hand, just on my throat. To say no to him . . . he will kill me! And he knows. He sometimes tells me, 'You never say no. You always say yes, you always say great.' I have told him, 'You should understand that you are always under the influence of opium. It is impossible to talk with you, to discuss with you or to disagree with you. You have a knife on my throat, and you want me to say no to something you have said?'"

I asked my grandfather, "Why don't you change barbers? There are so many other barbers in the village, and this man takes two hours to accomplish a five-minute job. Sometimes he takes half your beard and then he says, 'I am coming back,' and you sit there and he is gone for an hour, because he gets involved in a discussion with somebody and forgets completely that a customer is sitting in his chair. Then he comes back and says, 'My God, so you are still sitting here?'"

My grandfather would say, "What can I do? I cannot go home with half the beard shaved." He would ask the barber where he had been, and the barber would say, "I got in such a good argument with somebody that I completely forgot about you. It is good that that man had to go; otherwise you would have been sitting here the whole day."

Sometimes he wouldn't even close the shop at night. He would simply go home, just forget to stop by the shop to close it. Once in a while a customer would still be sitting in the chair, waiting for him to come back, and he would be home sleeping. Somebody would have to say to the customer, "Now you can go; that barber will not be seen again before tomorrow morning. He has forgotten to close his shop and he has forgotten about you. He is fast asleep in his home."

And if the person got angry . . . Sometimes new people got into his shop, and became angry. He would say, "Calm down. At the most you need not pay me. I have cut only half of the beard; you can just go. I don't want to argue. You need not pay me; I don't ask even half payment."

But nobody can leave with just half the beard shaved—or half the head shaved! You would ask him just to shave the beard and he would start shaving your head, and by the time you noticed, he had already done the job. So he would ask you, "Now what do you want? Because almost one-fourth of the work is done. If you want to keep it this way I can leave it; otherwise I can finish it. But I will not charge for it because if you say that you never wanted it to be cut, then it is my fault and I should take the punishment. I will not charge you."

The man was dangerous! But my grandfather used to say, "He is dangerous but he is lovely and I have become so identified with him that I cannot imagine that if he dies before I do I would be able to go to another barber's shop. I cannot conceive . . . for my whole life he has been my barber. The identity has become so deep that I may stop shaving my beard, but I cannot change my barber."

But fortunately my grandfather died before the opium-addict barber did.

You get identified with anything. People get identified with persons and then they create misery for themselves. They get identified with things, then they get miserable if that thing is missing.

Identification is the root cause of your misery. And every identification is identification with the mind.

Just step aside, let the mind pass.

And soon you will be able to see that there is no problem at all: the goose is out. You don't have to break the bottle, and you don't have to kill the goose either.

> I wonder sometimes if I really want to let go of my problems, to accept them instead of struggling with them. It feels like some part of my identity is so identified with this struggle, the idea of dropping it feels a little scary.

It is true; people cling to their diseases, they cling to their complaints, they cling to all that pinches them. They go on saying,

"These are wounds and we would like them to be healed." But deep down they go on creating the wounds, because if all the wounds are healed, they are afraid they themselves will not be there.

Just watch people—they cling to their illness. They talk about it as if it is something worth talking about. People talk about illness, about their negative moods, more than about anything else. Listen to them and you will see that they are enjoying talking about it. Every evening people come to me and I have to listen—for many years I have been listening and looking at their faces. They are enjoying it! They are martyrs . . . their illness, their anger, their hatred, this problem and that, their greed, ambition. And when you just look, the whole thing is simply crazy—because they are asking to get rid of those things but when you look at their faces, they are enjoying it. If these problems are really gone, what will they enjoy then? If all their illnesses disappear and they are completely whole and healthy, there will be nothing for them to talk about.

People go to psychiatrists, and then they go on talking about it—that they have visited this psychiatrist and that, they have been to this teacher and that. Really they enjoy saying, "All of them, everybody, has failed with me. I am still the same, nobody has been able to change me." As if they are succeeding because they are proving every psychiatrist a failure!

I have heard about one man who was a hypochondriac, continuously talking about his illnesses. And nobody believed him, because he was checked and examined in every possible way and nothing was wrong. But every day he would run to the doctor to say that he was in serious difficulty.

By and by the doctor became aware: whatever the man heard—if there was an advertisement on the TV about some medicine, or a talk about some illness—immediately that illness came to him. If he read about any illness in a magazine, immediately, the next day, he was there at the doctor's office, ill, completely ill. And he came up with all the symptoms. So the doctor said to him, "Don't bother me so much, because I read the same magazines you read and I listen to the same TV program you listen to, and just the next day you are here with the disease."

Said the man, "What do you think? Are you the only doctor in town?"

He stopped going to this doctor, but he would not stop this madness about illness. Then he died, as everybody has to die. Before his death he told his wife to write a few words on his gravestone, and they are still written there. In big letters it is written, "Now do you believe me?"

People feel so happy about their misery. I also wonder sometimes: if all their misery disappears, what will they do? They will be so unoccupied they will simply commit suicide. And it has been my observation that if you help them come out of one misery, the next day they will come back with something else. You help them to come out of that thing, they are again ready with another, as if there is a deep clinging to misery. They are getting something out of it; it is an investment and it is paying.

What is the investment? The investment is that when the shoe is not fitting your foot, when it pinches, you feel more that you exist. When the shoe fits completely, you simply relax. If the shoe fits completely, not only is the foot forgotten, the "I" disappears. There cannot be any "I" with a blissful consciousness—impossible! Only with a miserable mind can the "I" exist; the "I" is nothing but a combination of all your miseries. So if you are really ready to drop the "I," only then will your miseries disappear. Otherwise you will go on creating new miseries. Nobody can help you, because you are on a path that is self-destructive, self-defeating.

So next time you come to me with any problem, just first inquire inside whether you would like it to be solved, because be aware: I can give a solution. Are you really interested in solving it or just talking about it? You feel good talking about it.

Go inward and inquire, and you will see that all your miseries exist because you support them. Without your support nothing can exist. Because you give it energy, it exists; if you don't give it energy it cannot exist.

And who is forcing you to give it energy? Even when you are sad, energy is needed, because without energy you cannot be sad. To make the phenomenon of sadness happen, you have to give energy. That's why after sadness you feel so dissipated, drained. What happened? In your depression you were not doing anything, you were simply sad—why do you feel so dissipated and drained? You would think that you would have come out of your sadness full of energy, but no.

Remember, all negative emotions need energy; they drain you. And all positive emotions and positive attitudes are dynamos of energy; they create more energy, they never drain you. If you are happy, suddenly the whole world flows toward you with energy, the whole world laughs with you. People are right when they say, "When you laugh, the whole world laughs with you. When you weep, you weep alone." It is true, it is absolutely true. When you are positive the whole existence goes on giving you more, because when you are happy the whole of existence is happy with you. You are not a burden, you are a flower; you are not a rock, you are a bird. The whole existence feels happy about you.

When you are like a rock, sitting dead with your sadness, nursing your sadness, nobody is with you. Nobody can be with you. There simply comes a gap between you and life. Then whatever you are doing you have to depend on just your energy source. It will be dissipated. You are wasting your energy, you are being drained by your own nonsense.

But one thing is that when you are sad and negative you will feel the ego more. When you are happy, blissful, ecstatic, you will not feel the ego. When you are happy and ecstatic there is no "I." You are bridged with existence, not broken apart; you are together. When you are sad, angry, greedy, moving just within yourself and enjoying your wounds and looking at them again and again, playing with your wounds, trying to be a martyr, there is a gap between you and existence. You are left alone, and there you will feel the "I." And when you feel that "I," the whole existence feels as if it is inimical to you. Not that it is really inimical; it appears to be. If you feel that everybody is an enemy, you will behave in such a way that everybody has to be the enemy.

When you accept nature and dissolve into it, you move with it. The song of the whole is your song, the whole's dance is your dance. You are no longer apart from it. You don't feel that "I am"—you simply feel "The whole is. I am just a wave, coming and going, arrival and departure, being and nonbeing. I come and go, the whole remains. And I exist because of the whole, the whole exists through me."

Sometimes it takes forms, sometimes it becomes formless— both are beautiful. Sometimes it arises in a body, sometimes it disappears from the body. It has to be so, because life is a rhythm. Sometimes you have to be in the form, then you have to rest from the form. Sometimes you have to be active and moving, a wave, and sometimes you go to the depth and rest, unmoving. Life is a rhythm.

Death is not the enemy. It is just a change of the rhythm, moving to the other. Soon you will be born—alive, younger, fresher. Death is a necessity. You are not dying in death; only all the dust that has gathered around you has to be washed. That is the only way to be rejuvenated. Not only Jesus is resurrected, everything is resurrected in existence.

Just now the almond tree outside my room has dropped all his old leaves, now new leaves have replaced them. This is the way! If the tree clings to the old leaves then it will never be new, and then it will get rotten. Why create a conflict? The old disappears just for the new to come. It makes space, room for the new to come. And the new will always be coming and the old will always be going.

You don't die. Only the old leaf drops, just to make room for the new. Here you die, there you are born; here you disappear, there you appear. From the form to the formless, from the formless to the form; from the body to the no-body, from the no-body to the body; movement, rest; rest, movement—this is the rhythm. If you look at the rhythm you are not worried about anything. You trust.

ANGER, SADNESS, AND DEPRESSION

Branches of the Same Tree

Ordinarily, anger is not bad. Ordinarily, anger is part of natural life; it comes and goes. But if you repress it, then it becomes a problem. Then you go on accumulating it. Then it is not a question of coming and going; it becomes your very being. Then it is not that you are sometimes angry; you remain angry, you remain in rage, and you just wait for somebody to provoke it. Or even a hint of provocation, and you catch fire and you do things for which, later on, you will say, "I did it in spite of myself."

Analyze this expression, "in spite of myself." How can you do anything in spite of yourself? But the expression is exactly right. Repressed anger becomes a temporary madness. Something happens that is beyond your control. If you could have controlled it you would have, but suddenly it was overflowing. Suddenly it was beyond you, you couldn't do anything, you felt helpless— and it came out. Such a person may not be angry, but he moves and lives in anger.

If you look at people . . . stand by the side of the road and just watch, and you will find two types of people. Just go on watching their faces. The whole of humanity is divided into two types of people. One is the sad type, who will look very sad, dragging somehow. Another is the angry type, just bubbling with madness, ready to explode at any excuse.

Anger is active sadness; sadness is inactive anger. They are not two things.

Watch your own behavior. When do you find yourself sad? You find yourself sad only in situations where you cannot be angry. The boss in the office says something and you cannot be angry, you might lose your job. You cannot be angry and you have to go on smiling. Then you become sad. The energy has become inactive.

The husband goes home from work, and with his wife he will find a small excuse, anything irrelevant, and become angry. People enjoy anger; they relish it because at least they feel they are doing something. In sadness you feel that something has been done to you. You have been at the passive end, at the receiving end. Something has been done to you and you were helpless and you could not retort, you could not retaliate, you could not react. In anger, you feel a little better. After a big bout of anger, one feels a little relaxed and that feels good. You are alive! You also can *do* things! Of course you cannot do those things to the boss, but you can do it to your wife.

Then the wife waits for the children to come home—because it is unwise to be angry with the husband, he may divorce her. He is the boss, and the wife depends on him and it is risky to be angry at him. She will wait for the children. They will come home from school, and then she can jump on them and punish them— for their own sake. And what will the children do? They will go into their rooms and they will throw their books, tear them up, or punish their dolls, or their dogs, or torture their cats. They will have to do something. Everybody has to do something, otherwise one becomes sad.

The people you see on the streets who have become sad, so permanently sad that their faces have taken a certain mold, are the people who are so helpless, so far down the rung of the ladder, that they can't find anybody to be angry with. These are the sad people, and higher on the rung you will find the angry people. The higher you go, the angrier are the people you will find. The lower you go, the sadder.

In India you can see that the untouchables, the lowest class, look sad. Then look at the Brahmins; they are angry. A Brahmin is always angry; for any small thing he will go mad. An untouchable is simply sad because there is nobody else below him on whom he can throw his anger.

Anger and sadness are two faces of the same energy, repressed.

Ordinary anger has nothing wrong in it. In fact, people who can become angry and forget all about it the next moment are really very good people. You will always find them friendly, alive, loving, compassionate. But people who are always holding onto their emotions, controlling and controlling, are not good people. They will always try to show that they are holier than you, but you can see anger in their eyes. You can see it in their faces, you can see it in their every gesture—the way they walk, the way they talk, the way they relate with others, you can see it always there, boiling. They are ready to burst any moment. These are the murderers, the criminals, these are the real evildoers.

Anger is human, nothing wrong about it. It is simply a situation in which you are provoked, and you are alive so you respond to it. It is saying that you will not yield; it is saying that this is not a situation you can accept; it is saying that this is a situation in which you want to say no. It is a protest, and nothing is wrong about it.

Look at a child when the child is angry with you. Look at his face! He is so angry and so red that he would like to kill you. He says, "Never again will I talk to you. Finished!" And the next moment he is sitting in your lap again and talking beautifully. He has forgotten. Whatever he has said in a rage, he has not carried it. It has not become luggage in his mind. Yes, in the heat of the moment he was angry and he said something, but now the anger is gone and all that he had said that moment has gone. He has not become committed to it forever, it was a momentary flare-up, a ripple. But he is not frozen in it, he is a flowing phenomenon. The ripple was there, a wave had arisen, now it is no more. He is not going to carry it always and always. Even if you remind him, he will laugh. He will say, "All nonsense!" He will say, "I don't remember. Is it so?" He will say, "Have I really said that? Impossible!" It was a flare-up.

This has to be understood. A person who lives moment to moment is sometimes angry, sometimes happy, sometimes sad. But you can depend on the fact that he will not carry these things forever. A person who is very controlled and does not allow any emotion to arise in his being is dangerous. If you insult him, he does not get angry; he holds it back. By and by he will accumulate so much anger that he is going to do something really nasty.

There is nothing wrong in a momentary flare-up of anger— it is beautiful in a way. It simply shows that you are still alive.

A momentary flare-up simply shows that you are not dead, that you respond to situations and respond authentically. When you feel that the situation is such that anger is needed, anger is there. When you feel that the situation is such that happiness is needed, happiness is there. You move with the situation, you have no prejudice for or against. You have no ideology as such.

I am not against anger, I am against accumulated anger. I am not against sex, I am against accumulated sexuality. Anything that is in the moment is good, anything that is carried from the past is diseased, is illness.

> *In the old days it was called "melancholia." Today it is called "depression," and it is practically an epidemic in the developed countries. Explanations for depression have varied from the chemical to the psychological, but either way it seems to be afflicting more and more people all the time. What is depression? Is it a reaction to a depressing world, a kind of hibernation during "the winter of our discontent"?*

Man has always lived with hope, a future, a paradise somewhere far away. He has never lived in the present, his golden age was always still to come. It kept him enthusiastic because greater things were going to happen; all his longings were going to be fulfilled. There was great joy in anticipation.

He suffered in the present; he was miserable in the present, but all that was completely forgotten in the dreams that were going to be fulfilled tomorrow. Tomorrow has always been life-giving.

But the situation has changed. The old situation was not good because the tomorrow—the fulfillment of his dreams—never became true. He died hoping. Even in his death he was hoping for a future life, but he never actually experienced any rejoicing, any meaning.

But it was tolerable. It was only a question of getting through today: it will pass, and tomorrow is bound to come. The religious prophets, messiahs, saviors were promising people all kinds of pleasures in paradise. The political leaders, the social ideologists, the utopians were promising the same thing—not in paradise but here on earth, somewhere far away in the future when the society goes through a total revolution and there is no poverty, no government, and man is absolutely free and has everything that he needs.

Both were basically fulfilling the same psychological need. To those who were materialistic, the ideological, political, sociological utopians were appealing. To those who were not so materialistic, the religious leaders were appealing. But the object of appeal was exactly the same: all that you can imagine, can dream of, can long for, will be absolutely fulfilled. With those dreams to fall back on, the present miseries seemed to be very small. There was enthusiasm in the world; people were not depressed.

Depression is a contemporary phenomenon and it has come into being because now there is no tomorrow. All political ideologies have failed. There is no possibility that man will ever be equal, no possibility that there will be a time when there will be no government, no possibility that all your dreams will be fulfilled. This has come as a great shock. Simultaneously, man has become more mature. He may go to the church, to the mosque, to the synagogue, to the temple, but they are only social conformities. And he does not want, in such a dark and depressed state, to be left alone; he wants to be with the crowd. But basically he knows there is no paradise; he knows that no savior is going to come.

Hindus have waited five thousand years for Krishna to return. He promised not only that he would come once, he promised that whenever there would be misery, suffering, whenever vice would be more prevalent than virtue, whenever nice and simple and innocent people were being exploited by the cunning and the hypocritical, he would come. He said, "I will make myself a reality in every age to come." But for five thousand years no sign has been seen of him.

Jesus has promised he will come back, and when asked when, he said, "Very soon." Now, I can stretch "very soon," but not for two thousand years; that is too much.

The idea that our misery, our pain, our anguish will be taken away is no longer appealing. The idea that there is a God who cares for us seems to be simply a joke. Looking at the world, it doesn't seem as if there is anybody who cares.

The reality is that man has always lived in poverty. Poverty has one thing beautiful about it: it never destroys your hope, it never goes against your dreams, it always brings enthusiasm for tomorrow. One is hopeful, believing that things will be better: "This dark period is already passing; soon there will be light." But that situation has changed. And remember, the problem of depression is not epidemic in undeveloped countries. In the poor countries, people are still hopeful—it is only in the developed countries, where they have everything they had always longed for. Now paradise will not do anymore, nor can a classless society help anymore. No utopia is going to be better.

They have achieved the goal, and this achievement of the goal is the cause of depression. Now there is no hope. Tomorrow is dark, and the day after tomorrow will be even darker.

All these things that they had dreamed of were very beautiful, but they had never looked at the implications of them. Now that they have them, they have the implications, too. When a man is poor, he has an appetite. A rich man has no appetite, no hunger. And it is better to be poor and have an appetite than to be rich and have no appetite. What are you going to do with all your gold, all your silver, all your dollars? You cannot eat them.

You have everything, but the appetite has disappeared, the hunger and the hope that was driving your struggle all along. You succeeded—and I have said again and again that nothing fails like success. You have reached a place that you wanted to reach, but you were not aware of the by-products. You have millions of dollars but you cannot sleep.

When Alexander was in India he met a naked mystic in the desert. He declared: "I am Alexander the Great!"

The mystic said, "You cannot be."

Alexander said, "What nonsense! I am saying it myself, and you can see my armies all over the place."

The mystic said, "I see your armies, but one who calls himself 'The Great' has not yet reached to greatness—because greatness makes people humble. And that is because it is such a failure, an utter failure."

Alexander was a disciple of Aristotle and he was trained by him in fine logic. He could not listen to all this mystical garbage. He said, "I don't believe all these things. I have conquered the whole world."

The mystic asked him, "If in this desert you are thirsty, and for miles there is no water, and I offer you a glass of water, how much would you be able to give me for it? "

Alexander said, "I would give you half of my kingdom."

The mystic said, "No, I will not sell it for half of the kingdom. Either you can have the kingdom or you can have the glass of water. And you are thirsty and you are dying and there are no possibilities of finding water anywhere—what will you do?"

Alexander said, "Then naturally, I would give you the whole kingdom."

The mystic laughed; he said, "So that is the price of your whole kingdom—just a glass of water! And you think you have conquered the whole world? From today, you should start saying you have conquered a whole glass of water."

When man reaches his most cherished goals, then he becomes aware that there are many things surrounding them. For example, for your whole life you try to earn money, thinking that one day when you have it you will live a relaxed life. But in the meantime you have been tense your whole life, tension has become your discipline—and at the end of life, when you have all the money you ever wanted, you cannot relax. The whole life practicing tension and anguish and worry won't let you relax. You are not a winner, you are a loser. You lose your appetite, you destroy your health, you destroy your sensibility, your sensitivity. You destroy your aesthetic sense, because there is no time for all these things that do not produce dollars.

You are running after dollars—who has time to look at the roses, who has time to look at the birds on the wing? Who has time to look at the beauty of human beings? You postpone all these things so that one day, when you have everything, you will relax and enjoy. But by the time you have everything, you have become a certain kind of disciplined person—who is blind to roses, who is blind to beauty, who cannot enjoy music, who cannot understand dance, who cannot understand poetry, who can only understand dollars. But those dollars give no satisfaction.

This is the cause of depression. That's why it is prevalent only in the developed countries, and among people in the richer classes of the developed countries. In developed countries there are poor people also, but they don't suffer from depression. But you cannot give a rich man any more hope in order to remove his depression, because he has everything, he already has more than you could promise to give him. His condition is really pitiable. He never thought of the implications, he never thought of the by-products, he never thought of what he would lose by spending his whole life gaining money. He never thought that he would lose everything that could make him happy—and it is just because he has always pushed all those things aside. He had no time and the competition was tough and he had to be tough. At the end he finds his heart is dead, his life is meaningless. He doesn't see that there is any possibility in the future of any change, because what more can there be?

Enjoyment is something that has to be nourished. It is a certain discipline, a certain art—how to enjoy. And it takes time to get in contact with the great things in life. But the man who is running after money bypasses everything that is a door to the divine, and by the time he realizes what he has lost, he is at the end of the road and there is nothing ahead of him except death.

His whole life he was miserable. He tolerated it, ignored it in the hope that things were going to change. Now he cannot ignore it and he cannot hope it is going to change, because tomorrow there is only death and nothing else. The whole life's accumulated misery that he has ignored, the suffering he has ignored, explodes in his being.

The richest man, in a way, is the poorest man in the world. To be rich and not to be poor is a great art. To be poor and to be rich is the other side of the art. There are poor people whom you will find immensely rich. They don't have anything, but they are rich. Their richness is not in things but in their being, in their multidimensional experiences. And there are rich people who have everything but are absolutely poor and hollow and empty. Deep inside there is just a graveyard.

It is not a depression of the society, because then it would affect the poor too. It is simply natural law, and people now will have to learn it. Up to now there was no need, because not so many people had reached a point where they had everything, while inside there was complete darkness and ignorance.

The first thing in life is to find meaning in the present moment. The basic flavor of your being should be of love, of rejoicing, of celebration. Then you can do anything; then dollars will not destroy it. But instead you put everything else aside and simply run after dollars, thinking that dollars can purchase everything. Then one day you find they cannot purchase anything, and you have devoted your whole life to dollars.

This is the cause of depression.

And particularly in the West, the depression is going to be very deep. In the East there have been rich people, but there was a certain other dimension available. When the road to richness came to an end they did not remain stuck there; they moved in a new direction. That new direction was in the air, available for centuries.

In the East the poor have learned contentment, so they do not bother about running after ambitions. And the rich have understood that one day you have to renounce it all and go in search of truth, in search of meaning. In the West, at the end the road simply ends. You can go back, but going back will not help your depression. You need a new direction.

Gautam Buddha, Mahavira, and many other mystics of the East were at the peak of richness, and then they saw that it was almost a burden. Something else has to be found before death takes you over—and they were courageous enough to renounce all. Their renunciation has been misunderstood. They renounced it all because they did not want to bother a single second more about money, power, because they had seen the top and there was nothing there. They went to the very highest rung of the ladder and found that it leads nowhere; it is just a ladder leading nowhere. While you are somewhere in the middle, or lower than the middle, you have a hope—because there are still higher rungs to climb. But there comes a point when you are on the highest rung of the ladder, and there is only suicide or madness—or hypocrisy, and you go on smiling till death finishes you. But deep down you know that you have wasted your life.

In the East depression has never been such a problem. The poor learned to enjoy what little they had, and the rich learned that having the whole world at your feet means nothing: you have to go in search of meaning, not money. And they had precedents; they knew that for thousands of years people have gone in search of truth and have found it. There is no need to be in despair, in depression; you just have to move into an unknown dimension. They might have never explored it, but as they started exploring the new dimension, which means a journey inward, a journey to their own self—all that they had lost started returning.

The West needs very urgently a great movement of meditation; otherwise this depression is going to kill people. And these people will be the talented ones because they achieved power, they achieved money, they achieved whatever they wanted. These are the talented people, and they are feeling despair. This is going to be dangerous because the most talented people are no longer enthusiastic about life. The untalented are enthusiastic about life, but they don't even have the talents needed to get power, money, education, respectability. They don't have the talent so they are suffering, feeling handicapped. They are turning into terrorists, they are turning toward unnecessary violence just out of revenge because they cannot do anything else, but they can destroy. And the rich are almost ready to hang themselves from any tree because there is no reason for them to live. Their hearts have stopped beating long ago. They are just corpses—well decorated, well honored, but utterly empty and futile.

The West is really in a far worse condition than the East, although to those who don't understand, it seems that the West is in a better condition than the East because the East is poor. But poverty is not as big a problem as the failure of richness; then a man is *really* poor. An ordinary poor man at least has dreams, hopes. But the rich man has nothing.

What is needed is a great meditation movement reaching to every person.

And in the West these people who are depressed are going to psychoanalysts, therapists, and all kinds of charlatans who are themselves depressed, more depressed than their patients— naturally, because the whole day they are hearing about depression, despair, meaninglessness. And seeing so many talented people in such a bad state, they themselves start losing their spirit. They cannot help; they themselves need help.

If they can see that there are people who are not depressed— but on the contrary, who are immensely joyous—perhaps a hope may be born in them. Now they can have everything and there is no need to worry. They can meditate.

I don't teach renunciation of your wealth or of anything. Let everything be as it is. Just add one thing more to your life. Up to now you have been adding only *things* to your life. Now add something to your being—and that will create the music, that will do the miracle, that will do the magic. That will create a new thrill, a new youth, a new freshness.

It is not unsolvable. The problem is big, but the solution is very simple.

> **I'm not rich, nor do I have everything I need. But still I get lonely, confused, and depressed. Is there something I can do about this kind of depression when it happens?**

If you are depressed, be depressed; don't "do" anything. What can you do? Whatever you do will be done out of depression, so it will create more confusion. You can pray to God, but you will pray so depressingly that you will even make God depressed through your prayers! Don't do that violence to poor God. Your prayer is going to be a depressed prayer. Because you are depressed, whatever you do, the depression will follow. More confusion will be created, more frustration, because you cannot succeed. And when you cannot succeed you will feel more depressed, and this can go on ad infinitum.

It is better to remain with the first depression than to create a second circle and then a third circle. Remain with the first; the original is beautiful. The second will be false, and the third will be a far-off echo. Don't create these. The first is beautiful. You are depressed, so this is how existence is happening to you at this moment. You are depressed, so remain with it. Wait and watch. You cannot be depressed for long because in this world nothing is permanent. This world is a flux. This world cannot change its basic law for you so that you remain depressed forever. Nothing is here forever; everything is moving and changing. Existence is a river; it cannot stop for you, just for you, so that you remain depressed forever. It is moving—it has already moved. If you look at your depression, you will feel that even your depression is not the same the next moment; it is different, it is changing. Just watch, remain with it and don't do anything. This is how transformation happens through nondoing.

Feel depression, taste it deeply, live it, it is your fate—then suddenly you will feel it has disappeared, because one who can accept even depression cannot be depressed. A person, a mind that can accept even depression cannot remain depressed! Depression needs a nonaccepting mind: "This is not good, that is not good; this should not be, that should not be; this must not be like this." Everything is denied, rejected, not accepted. "No" is the basic approach; even happiness will be rejected by such a mind. Such a mind will find something to reject in happiness also. You will feel a doubt about it. You will feel that something has gone wrong. You are happy, so you feel something has gone wrong: "Just by meditating for a few days I have become happy? This is not possible."

A nonaccepting mind will "nonaccept" anything. But if you can accept your loneliness, your depression, your confusion, your sadness, you are transcending already. Acceptance is transcendence. You have taken the very ground away, and then the depression cannot stand.

Try this:

Whatsoever your state of mind, accept it and wait for when the state changes itself. You are not changing anything, you can feel the beauty that comes when your state of mind changes by itself. You can know that it is just like the sun rising in the morning and then setting in the evening. Then again it will rise and again it will set, and it will go on. You need not do anything about it. If you can feel your states of mind changing by themselves, you can remain indifferent. You can remain miles away, as if the mind is going somewhere else. The sun is rising, setting; the depression is coming, the happiness is coming, going, but you are not in it. It goes and comes by itself; the states come and move and go.

With a confused mind, it is better to wait and not to do anything so that the confusion disappears. It will disappear; nothing is permanent in this world. You need only a deep patience. Don't be in a hurry.

I will tell you one story that I have told often. Buddha was traveling through a forest. The day was hot—it was just midday—he felt thirsty, so he said to his disciple Ananda, "Go back. We crossed a little stream. You go back and fetch some water for me."

Ananda went back, but the stream was very small and some carts were passing through it. The water was disturbed and had become dirty. All the dirt that had settled in it had come up, and the water was not drinkable now. So Ananda thought, "I will have to go back empty-handed." He came back and he said to Buddha, "That water has become absolutely dirty and it is not drinkable. Allow me to go ahead. I know there is a river just a few miles away from here, so I will go and fetch water from there."

Buddha said, "No! You go back to the same stream." Because Buddha had said it, Ananda had to do it, but he went back with half a heart. He knew that the water could not be brought back, and time was being unnecessarily wasted, and he was feeling thirsty, too. But when Buddha says it he has to go. Again he went to the stream, and again he came back and he said, "Why did you insist? That water is not drinkable."

Buddha said, "You go again." And because Buddha said it, Ananda had to follow.

The third time he reached the stream, the water was as clear as it had ever been. The dust had flowed away, the dead leaves had gone, and the water was pure again. Then Ananda laughed. He filled the jug with water and he came back dancing. He fell at Buddha's feet and he said, "Your ways of teaching are miraculous. You have taught me a great lesson—that just patience is needed and nothing is permanent."

And this is Buddha's basic teaching: nothing is permanent, everything is fleeting, so why be so worried? Go back to the same stream. By now everything should have changed. Nothing remains the same. Just be patient, go again and again and again. Just a few moments, and the leaves will have gone and the dirt will have settled and the water will be pure again.

Ananda had also asked Buddha, when he was going back for the second time, "You insist that I go, but can I do something to make that water pure?"

Buddha said, "Please don't do anything; otherwise you will make it more impure. And don't enter the stream. Just stay outside of it and wait on the bank. Your entering the stream will create a mess. The stream flows by itself, so allow it to flow."

Nothing is permanent; life is a flux. Heraclitus has said that you cannot step twice in the same river. It is impossible to step twice in the same river because the river has flowed on; everything has changed. And not only has the river flowed on, you have also flowed on. You are also different; you are also a river flowing.

See this impermanency of everything. Don't be in a hurry; don't try to do anything. Just wait! Wait in a total nondoing. And if you can wait, the transformation will be there. This very waiting is a transformation.

> **What makes me depressed is when I start judging myself for being so unaware, for not appreciating how beautiful life is, for getting jealous and angry and acting so stupid in so many ways. It feels like the more aware I am of my own behavior, the more depressed I get! Can you talk about self-condemnation, what it is and where it comes from?**

It is a way to remain the same, it is a trick of the mind; rather than understanding, the energy starts moving into condemnation. And change comes through understanding, not through condemnation. So the mind is very cunning—the moment you start seeing some fact, the mind jumps upon it and starts condemning it. Now the whole energy becomes involved in condemnation. Understanding is forgotten, put aside, and your energy is moving into condemnation—and condemnation cannot help. It can make you depressed, it can make you angry, but depressed and angry, you never change. You remain the same and you move in the same vicious circle again and again.

Understanding is liberating. So when you see a certain fact there is no need to condemn, there is no need to be worried about it. The only need is to look into it deeply and to understand it. If I say something and it hits you—and that's my whole purpose, that it should hit you somewhere—then you have to look at why it hits and where it hits and what is the problem; you have to look into it.

Looking into it, moving around it and looking at it from every angle . . . If you condemn you cannot look, you cannot approach it from all the angles. You have already decided that it is bad; without giving it a chance you have already judged.

Listen to the fact, go into it, contemplate over it, sleep on it—and the more you are able to observe it, the more you will become capable of getting out of it. The ability to understand and the ability to get out of it are just two names for the same phenomenon.

If I understand a certain thing, I am capable of getting out of it, going beyond it. If I don't understand a certain thing, I cannot get out of it.

So the mind goes on doing that to everybody; it is not only with you. Immediately you jump on something and you say, "This is wrong, this should not be in me. I am not worthy, this is wrong and that is wrong," and you become guilty. Now the whole energy is moving into guilt.

My work here is to make you as un-guilty as possible. So whatever you see, don't take it in a personal way. It has nothing to do with you particularly; it is just the way the mind functions. If there is jealousy, if there is possessiveness, if there is anger, this is how the mind works—everybody's mind more or less; the differences are only of degree.

The mind has another mechanism and that is, either it wants to praise or it wants to condemn. It is never in the middle. Through praise you become special and the ego is fulfilled; through condemnation also you become special. Look at the trick! Both ways you become special—either you are a saint, a great saint, or you are the greatest sinner, but in each way the ego is fulfilled. In each way you say one thing, that you are special.

The mind does not want to hear that it is just ordinary—the jealousy, the anger, these problems of relationship and being are ordinary, everyone has them. They are as ordinary as hair. Maybe somebody has more, somebody has less, somebody has black and somebody has red, but that doesn't matter much. They are ordinary; all problems are ordinary. All sins are ordinary and all virtues are ordinary, but the ego wants to feel special. It either says that you are the greatest or you are the worst.

You say to yourself, "You should not be depressed. This is not you, this goes against your image, it is a blemish on you—and you are such a beautiful girl! Why are you depressed?" You judge, you condemn, rather than trying to understand.

Depression means that somehow anger is in you in a negative state. Depression is a negative state of anger. The very word is meaningful—it says something is being *pressed*; that is the meaning of "depressed." You are pressing something inside, and when anger is pressed too much it becomes sadness. Sadness is a negative way of being angry, the feminine way of being angry. If you remove the pressure on it, it will become anger. You must have been angry about certain things, perhaps even from your childhood, but you have not expressed them; hence the depression. Try to understand it!

And the problem is that depression cannot be solved, because it is not the real problem. The real problem is anger—and you go on condemning depression, so you are fighting with shadows.

First look at why you are depressed: look deep into it and you will find anger. Great anger is in you—maybe toward the mother, toward the father, toward the world, toward yourself, that is not the point. You are very angry inside, and from your very childhood you have tried to be smiling, not to be angry because being angry is not good. You have been taught, and you have learned it well. So on the surface you look happy, on the surface you go on smiling—and all those smiles are false. Deep down you are holding great rage. Now, you cannot express it so you are sitting upon it—that is what depression is; then you feel depressed.

Let it flow, let anger come. Once anger comes up your depression will go. Have you not watched and observed that sometimes after real anger one feels so good, so alive?

Do an anger meditation every day . . . twenty minutes a day will do. (See page 270 for a description.) After the third day you will enjoy the exercise so much that you will start looking forward to it. It will give you such great release . . . and you will see that your depression is disappearing. For the first time you will *really* smile. Because with this depression you cannot smile, you can only pretend.

One cannot live without smiles, so one has to pretend—but a pretended smile hurts very much. It does not make you happy; it simply reminds you of how unhappy you are.

But when you have become aware of it, it is good. Whenever something hurts, it helps. People are so ill that whenever something is helpful, it hurts, it touches some wound somewhere. But it is good.

> **Is it really possible to be aware during anger? This feeling is so strong it comes always like thousands of wild horses running. I am really tired of it! Can you help me?**

You have the simplest problem: you are making too much out of it. "Like thousands of wild horses running"—that much anger would have burned you! From where do you bring thousands of wild horses?

I have heard that Mulla Nasruddin was having an interview to be employed on a ship, and there were three officials interviewing him. One officer asked him, "A great cyclone comes, tidal waves, and the ship is almost sinking: what will you do?"

Mulla said, "No problem, I will do what is technically right; I will stop the ship and lower the anchor."

The other officer said, "But then another tidal wave is coming, and the ship is just going to sink. What are you going to do?"

Mulla said, "The same: I will lower another anchor; every ship carries them."

The third officer said, "But then another tidal wave . . ."

And Mulla said, "You are unnecessarily wasting my time. I will do the same—lower another anchor to make the ship stable against the tidal wave."

The first official asked, "From where are you getting all these anchors?"

Mulla said, "It is a strange question. From where are you getting all these tidal waves? From the same source! If you can imagine tidal waves, why can't I imagine anchors? You go on bringing as many tidal waves as you want, and I will go on lowering heavier and heavier anchors."

Anger is a very small thing. If you can just wait and watch, you will not find "thousands of wild horses." If you can find even a small donkey, that will be enough! Just watch it and it will go, slowly. It will enter from one side and will go out the other side. You just have to keep a little patience not to ride on it.

Anger, jealousy, envy, greed, competitiveness . . . all our problems are very small, but our ego magnifies them, makes them as big as it can. The ego cannot do otherwise; its anger has also to be great. With its great anger, and great misery, and great greed, and great ambition, the ego becomes great.

But you are not the ego, you are only a watcher. Just stand by the side and let all the thousands of horses pass—"Let us see how long it takes for them to pass." There is no need to be worried. As they come—they *are* wild—they will go.

But we don't miss the opportunity to ride even a small donkey; we immediately jump on it! You don't need thousands of wild horses, just a small thing and you are full of anger and fire. You will laugh about it later on, at how stupid you were.

If you can watch, without getting involved, as if it is something on the screen in a movie or on TV . . . something is passing by, watch it. You are not supposed to do anything to prevent it, to repress it, to destroy it, to pull out a sword and kill it, because from where will you get the sword? From the same source as the anger is coming. It is all imagination.

Just watch and don't do anything, for or against, and you will be surprised: that which was looking very big becomes very small. But our habit is to exaggerate.

A small boy, not more than three years old, comes home running, and tells his mother, "Mom, a huge lion, roaring, was running after me for miles! But somehow I managed to escape. Many times he came very close. He was just about to attack me when I started running faster."

The mother looked outside the door, where she saw a small dog standing, wagging its tail. She looked at the boy and said, "Tommy, I have told you millions of times not to exaggerate!"

"Millions of times"—our minds are very good at exaggerating. You have small problems, and if you can stop exaggerating and just look, then a poor, small dog is standing outside the door. And there is no need to run for miles; your life is not in danger.

When anger comes to you, it is not going to kill you. It has been with you many times before, and you have survived perfectly well. It is the same anger that you have been through before. Just do one thing new, which you have never done. Instead, every time you get involved with it, fight with it. This time just watch as if it does not belong to you, as if it is somebody else's anger. And you are in for a great surprise: it will disappear within seconds. And when anger disappears without any struggle, it leaves behind it a tremendously beautiful and silent and loving state.

The same energy that could have become a fight with the anger is left within you. Pure energy is delight—I am quoting William Blake—"Energy is delight." Just energy, without any name, without any adjective. But you never allow energy to be pure. Either it is anger, or hate, or love, or greed, or desire. It is always involved in something; you never allow it in its purity.

Every time anything arises in you, is a great chance to experience pure energy. Just watch and the donkey will go. It may raise a little dust, but that dust also settles on its own; you don't have to settle it. You simply wait. Don't move from waiting and watching, and soon you will find yourself surrounded by a pure energy, which has not been used in fighting, in repressing, or in being angry. And energy is certainly delight. Once you know the secret of delight, you will enjoy every emotion.

And every emotion arising in you is a great opportunity. Just watch, and bring a shower of delight into your being. Slowly, slowly all these emotions will disappear; they will not come anymore—they don't come uninvited. Watchfulness, or alertness, or awareness, or consciousness, are all different names of the same phenomenon of witnessing. That is the key word.

> Miss Johnson, the English teacher, said, "Today we are
> going to do definitions. When you define something, you
> say what it is. Now, Wesley, will you define 'unaware'?"
> Wesley replies, "It's the last thing I take off at night!"

We are all living in such a situation! Nobody is conscious; nobody is listening to what is being said.

It is such a strange world. If you are aware, then everywhere miracles are happening. But you don't see miracles because rarely are you aware, very rarely. Most of the time you keep your eyes open; most of the time you don't snore. But that does not mean that you are awake. It simply means that you are pretending to be awake, but deep inside are so many thoughts, so much confusion, so many wild horses . . . how can you see anything? How can you hear anything? So although your eyes are open, they don't see. Although your ears are open, they don't hear.

It is a strange phenomenon that nature made eyes in a different way from ears. You cannot close your ears but you can close your eyes. You have eyelids to close, to open, but what about your ears? Nature never bothered to give little earlids, because she knew you are so involved in the mind, you don't need them. Your ears are always deaf; you don't hear—or you hear only what you want to hear.

I have heard that after the church service one Sunday, a preacher stopped a man who had been snoring loudly during the sermon. He caught hold of him and told him, "It is not right! While I was giving the sermon, you were snoring."

The man said, "I am sorry. Next time I will take care."

The preacher said, "You have to take care, because there were so many people asleep and you were disturbing them all. I am not worried about you listening to my sermon, I am worried about the rest of my congregation, who were all fast asleep. You were snoring so loudly you might have woken them up. I go on repeating the same sermon every Sunday, and if you start keeping them awake it will mean more work for me. I will have to prepare new sermons again and again, and that is unnecessarily tedious. I have been using the same sermon forever and nobody objects, because nobody has heard it."

You go into any church and you will find people fast asleep; it is a place to sleep, to have a little rest from worldly affairs, from the world and its tensions. But people are twenty-four hours asleep as far as spirituality is concerned. And in your sleep you see anger and you see greed, and they become so magnified, so big, that you get caught into their net very easily.

One who has a simple art of watchfulness has a golden key. Then it does not matter whether it is anger, or greed, or sensuality, or lust, or infatuation. It may be any kind of disease, it doesn't matter: the same medicine functions. Just watch, and you will be free of it. And watching, slowly, as the mind becomes more and more without content, one day mind itself disappears. It cannot remain without anger, without fear, without love, without hate—all these are absolute necessities for mind to exist.

By watching, you are not only getting rid of anger, you are getting rid of part of the mind. And one day you are suddenly awake and there is no mind at all. You are just a watcher, a watcher on the hills. That is the most beautiful moment. Only from then your real life begins.

UNDERSTANDING THE ROOTS OF JEALOUSY

What makes you jealous? Possessiveness. Jealousy itself is not the root. You love a woman, you love a man, and you want to possess the person just out of fear that perhaps tomorrow they may move with somebody else. The fear of tomorrow destroys your today, and it is a vicious circle. If every day is destroyed because of the fear of tomorrow, sooner or later the person is going to look for some other partner because you are just a pain in the neck. And when the man starts looking for another woman, or the woman starts moving with another man, you think your jealousy has proved right. In fact it is your jealousy that has created the whole thing.

So the first thing to remember is, don't be bothered about to-morrows. Today is enough! Somebody loves you. Let this be a day of joy, a day of celebration. Be so totally in love today that your to-tality and your love will be enough for the other person not to move away from you. Your jealousy will push the person away; only your love can keep him or her with you. The other's jealousy will push you away; their love can keep you.

Don't think of tomorrow. The moment you think of tomorrow, your living today remains half-hearted. Just live today and forget tomorrow; it will take its own course. And remember one thing, that tomorrow is born out of today. If today has been such a beauty of experience, such a blessing, why be worried about it?

Someday the man you have loved, the woman you have loved, may find somebody else. It is simply human to be happy—but your woman is happy with somebody else. It does not make any difference whether she is happy with you or happy with some-body else, she is happy. And if you love her so much, how can you destroy her happiness?

A real love will be happy even if the partner feels joyous with somebody else. In this situation—when a woman is with some-body else, and you are still happy and you are still grateful to the woman and you tell her, "You have absolute freedom; just be to-tally happy and that is my happiness. With whom you are happy is insignificant, what is significant is your happiness."—my feel-ing is that she cannot remain away from you for long, she will be back. Who can leave such a man?

Your jealousy destroys everything, your possessiveness de-stroys everything. You have to understand what you are gaining out of it. You are burning in the fire, and the more you become jealous and angry and hateful, the more you are pushing the other person far away from you. It is simple arithmetic that it is not going to help; you are destroying the very thing that you want to preserve. It is simply idiotic.

Just try to understand a simple fact: human beings are human beings. Once in a while everybody gets bored being with the same person all the time. Be factual; don't live in fictions. Once in a while, everybody gets fed up; that does not mean your love has stopped, it simply means a little change is needed. It is good for your health, it is good for your partner's health. You both need a little holiday from each other. Why not do it consciously? "We are feeling stuck, so what about having a week's holiday? I love you, you love me; that is such a certainty that there is no fear."

My own observation is that after even a day's holiday you will fall in love with each other on a higher and deeper level, because now you will see how much you love each other. You cannot even see the sadness that comes naturally by living together.

Don't possess each other. Keep the freedom intact so that you don't interfere in each other's private world and you respect the dignity of the other person. Once this is experienced, that once in a while you can go on separate holidays and come back again, there will be no need to be worried. You will be surprised that when your woman comes back to you after living with some other man for seven days, and you come back to your woman after living with some other woman for seven days, you each have learned some new things. You can have another honeymoon again. You are new and fresh, and you have learned new tricks. And it is always good to have fresh experiences, enrichment.

You only need human understanding, intelligence, and jealousy will disappear.

Jealousy is one of the most prevalent areas of psychological ignorance about yourself, about others, and more particularly about relationships. People think they know what love is; they do not know. And their misunderstanding about love creates jealousy. By "love" people mean a certain kind of monopoly, some possessive-ness, without understanding a simple fact of life: that the moment you possess a living being you have killed that person.

Life cannot be possessed. You cannot have it in your fist. If you want to have it, you have to keep your hands open.

But the thing has been going on a wrong path for centuries; it has become ingrained in us so much that we cannot separate love from jealousy. They have become almost one energy.

For example, you feel jealous if your lover goes to another woman. You are disturbed by it now, but I would like to tell you that if you don't feel jealous you will be in much more trouble—then you will think you don't love him, because if you loved him you should have felt jealous. Jealousy and love have become so mixed up.

In fact, they are poles apart. A mind that can be jealous cannot be loving, and vice versa: a mind that is loving cannot be jealous.

What is the disturbance? You have to look at it as if it is not your problem, so that you can stand aside and see the whole fabric of it.

The feeling of jealousy is a by-product of marriage.

In the world of animals, birds, there is no jealousy. Once in a while there is a fight over a love object but a fight is far better than to be jealous, far more natural than to be caught up in jealousy and burn your heart with your own hands.

Marriage is an invented institution, it is not natural; hence nature has not provided you with a mind that can adjust to marriage. But society found it necessary that there should be some kind of legal contract between lovers, because love itself is the stuff of dreams. It is not reliable; it is here this moment and the next moment it is gone.

You want to be secure for the coming moment, for your whole future. Right now you are young, soon you will be old and you would like your wife, your husband, to be with you in your old age, in your sickness. But for that, a few compromises have to be made, and whenever there is compromise there is always trouble.

Marriage created suspicion. The husband was always suspicious about whether the child born to them was his own or not. And the problem is, the father had no way to determine that a child was his own. Only the mother knew. Because the father had no way of being certain, he created more and more walls around the woman—that was the only possibility, the only alternative— to disconnect her from the larger humanity. Not to educate her, because education gives wings to people, thoughts, makes people capable of revolt, so there was no education for women. No religious education for women, because religion creates holy people, and it has been a male-dominated society for centuries and man cannot conceive a woman to be higher and holier than himself.

Man started cutting from the very roots any possibility of woman's growth. She was just a factory to manufacture children. She was not accepted by any culture in the world as equal to man. All over the world the woman has been suppressed. The more she has been suppressed, the more her whole energy has turned sour. And because she has no freedom and the man has every freedom, all her repressed emotions, feelings, thoughts—her whole individuality—turns into a jealous phenomenon. She is continuously afraid that her husband might leave her, might go to some other woman, might become interested in some other woman. He might abandon her, and she is not educated, she is not financially capable of standing on her own feet. She has been brought up in such a way that she cannot go out into the world; she has been told from the very beginning that she is weak.

Indian scriptures say that in childhood the father should protect the girl; in youth the husband should protect the girl; in old age the son should protect the woman. She has to be protected from the very childhood to the grave. She cannot revolt against this male chauvinist society; all she can do is go on finding faults, which are bound to be there. Mostly she is not wrong; she is mostly right.

Whenever a man falls in love with another woman, something in him toward the first woman changes. Now they are again strangers, there is no bridge. She has been crippled, enslaved, and now she has been abandoned. Her whole life is a life of agony and out of this agony arises jealousy.

Jealousy is the anger of the weak—of one who cannot do anything but is boiling within, who would like to burn the whole world but cannot do anything except cry and scream and throw tantrums. This situation will continue until marriage becomes a museum piece.

Now there is no need for marriage. Perhaps it was useful in the past, perhaps it was not useful, but it was only an excuse to enslave women. Things could have been worked out in a different way, but there is no point in going into the past. Right or wrong, one thing is good about the past—it is no more!

As far as the present and the future are concerned, marriage is absolutely irrelevant, inconsistent with human evolution and contradictory to all the values we love: freedom, love, joy.

Because man wanted the woman to be completely imprisoned, he wrote religious scriptures making her afraid of hell, making her greedy for heaven—if she follows the rules. Those rules exist for women, not for men. Now it is so clear that to let women live any longer in this poisonous situation of jealousy is against their psychological health. And women's psychological health influences the psychological health of the whole of humanity. The woman has to become an independent individual.

The dissolution of marriage will be a great, festive event on the earth, and nobody is preventing you. If you love your wife or your husband you can live together for your whole life, nobody is preventing you. Withdrawing marriage is simply giving you your individuality back. Now nobody possesses you. You are not to make love to a man just because he is your husband and he has the right to demand it. In my vision, when a woman makes love to a man because she *has* to make love, it is prostitution—not retail, but wholesale!

Retail is better, you have a chance to change. This wholesale prostitution of marriage is dangerous, you don't have a chance to change. And especially when you have married for the first time you should be given chances because you are an amateur. A few marriages at least will help you to become mature; perhaps then you can find the right partner. And by right partner I don't mean the person who is "made for you."

No woman is made for a certain man, and no man is made for a certain woman. By the right partner I mean that if you have understood a few relationships, if you have been in a few relationships, you will understand which things create miserable situations between you and which situations create a loving, peaceful, happy life. Living with different people is an absolutely necessary education for a right life as far as love is concerned.

You should first graduate from a few relationships. In your college, in your university, you should pass through a few relationships. And you should not be in a hurry to decide—there is no need, the world is big, and each individual has some unique quality and beauty.

As you go through a few relationships you start becoming aware of what kind of woman, what kind of man is going to be a friend to you: not a master, not a slave. And friendship needs no marriage because friendship is far higher.

When you are feeling jealous it is because you have received that jealousy as an inheritance. You will have to change many things, not because I say to change them but because you understand that a drastic change is needed.

For example, the idea has been spread all over the world that if a husband sometimes goes to some other woman, or a wife goes to some other man, then this is going to destroy the marriage. It is absolutely wrong. On the contrary, if every marriage has the weekend free it will cement your relationship more strongly, because your marriage is not disturbing your freedom, because your partner understands the need for variety. These are human needs.

The priests and the moralists and the puritans first decide on an ideal. They make beautiful ideals and then they force the ideals on you. They want to make you all idealists. For ten thousand years we have lived under a dark and dismal shadow of idealism. I am a realist. I don't have any ideal. To me, to understand reality and to go with reality is the only right way for any intelligent man or woman.

My understanding is that if marriage is not such a tight thing, not rigid, but is flexible, just a friendship . . . so that a woman can tell you she has met a beautiful young man and she is going this weekend to be with him—"And if you are interested I can bring him back with me; you will also love the person." And if the husband can say, not as a hypocrite but as an authentic human being, "Your joy, your happiness is my happiness. You enjoy, because I know whenever you come back, enjoying a fresh love will make you fresh also. A fresh love will bring fresh youth to you. You go this week, and next week I may have my own program."

This is friendship. And when they come home they can talk about what kind of man she met, how he turned out, that it was not that great. . . . He can tell her about the new woman he has met. . . . You have a shelter in the home. You can go once in a while into the sky, wild and free, and come back and always your partner is there waiting for you, not to fight but to share your adventures.

It simply needs a little understanding. It has nothing to do with morality, but just a little more intelligent behavior.

You know perfectly well that however beautiful a man or woman might be, it starts becoming heavy on your nerves sooner or later. The same geography, the same topography, the same landscape. . . . The human mind is not made for monotony; neither is it made for monogamy. It is absolutely natural to ask for variety. And it is not against your love. In fact, the more you know other women, the more you will praise your own woman; your understanding will deepen. Your experience will be enriching. The more you have known a few men, the more accurately you will be able to understand your own husband. The idea of jealousy will disappear—you are both free, and you are not hiding anything.

With friends we share everything, particularly those moments that are beautiful—moments of love, moments of poetry, moments of music. And they should be shared. In this way your life will become more and more rich. You may become so attuned to each other that you live your whole life together, but there is no marriage.

Jealousy will persist as long as marriage remains the basic foundation of society.

Just give the man, with your full heart, absolute freedom. And tell him he need not hide anything: "To hide anything is insulting. That means you don't trust me." And the same has to happen with the man, that he can say to his wife, "You are as independent as I am. We are together to be happy, we are together to grow into more blissfulness. And we will do everything for each other, but we are not going to be jailers to each other."

Giving freedom is a joy, having freedom is a joy. You can have so much joy, but you are turning that whole energy into misery, into jealousy, into fighting, into a continuous effort to keep the other under your thumb.

And it is easy: if you understand yourself, you will be able to understand your partner, too. Don't you have other people in your dreams? In fact, to see your own husband or wife in a dream is a rare phenomenon. People never see their marriage partners in their dreams; they have seen enough of them! Now even in the night, even in the dream, there is no freedom?

No, in your dreams you have the wives of your neighbors, the husbands of your neighbors. You should understand that somehow we created a wrong society, a society that is not according to human nature. The desire for variety is an essential quality in anyone who is intelligent. The more intelligent you are the more variety you would like—there is some relationship between intelligence and variety. A cow is satisfied with one kind of grass; for her whole life she will not touch another kind of grass. She does not have the mind to change, to know new things, to discover new territories, to venture into new spaces.

The poets, the painters, the dancers, the musicians, the actors: you will find these people more loving, but their love is not focused on individuals. They are more loving, but to as many individuals as they come in contact with. They are the intelligent people, they represent our creative part. Idiots don't want to change anything. They are afraid of change because any change means they will have to learn something again. The idiot wants to learn something once and remain with it his whole life. It may be a machine, it may be a wife, it may be a husband, it does not matter. You have known one woman, you know her nagging, you have become accustomed to it. Sometimes not only accustomed, you have become addicted, too. If suddenly your woman does not nag you, you will not be able to sleep that night—what happened? What has gone wrong?

One of my friends was continually complaining to me about his wife: "She is always sad, long-faced, and I am so worried to enter the house. I try to waste my time in this club and that club but finally I have to go back home and there she is."

I said to him, "Do one thing just as an experiment. Because she has been so serious and she has been nagging, I cannot imagine that you enter the house smiling."

He said, "Do you think I can manage that? The moment I see her something freezes inside me—smile?"

I said, "Just as an experiment, today you do one thing: take beautiful roses, and the best ice cream available in the city. And go into the house smiling, singing a song!"

He said, "I will do it, but I don't think it is going to make any difference."

I said, "I will come behind you, and see whether there is any difference or not."

The poor fellow tried hard. Many times on the way to his house he started laughing. I asked him, "Why are you laughing?"

He said, "I am laughing at what I am doing! I wanted you to tell me to divorce her and you have suggested I act as if I am going on a honeymoon!"

I said, "Just imagine it is a honeymoon . . . try your best."

He opened the door and his wife was standing there. He smiled and then he laughed at himself because to smile . . . And that woman was standing almost like a stone. He presented the flowers and the ice cream, and then I entered.

The woman could not believe what was happening. When the man had gone to the bathroom she asked me, "What is the matter? He has never brought anything, he has never smiled, he has never taken me out, he has never made me feel that I am loved, that I am respected. What magic has happened?"

I said, "Nothing; both of you have just been doing wrong. Now when he comes out of the bathroom you give him a good hug."

She said, "A hug?"

I said, "Give him one! You have given him so many things, now give him a good hug. He is your husband, you have decided to live together. Either live joyously or say good-bye joyously. There is no reason . . . it is such a small life. Why waste two persons' lives unnecessarily?"

At that very moment the man came from the bathroom. The woman hesitated a little but I pushed her, so she hugged the man and the man was so shocked, he fell on the floor! He had never imagined that she was going to hug him.

I had to help him up. I said, "What happened?"

He said, "It's just that I have never imagined that this woman can hug and kiss—but she can! And when she smiled she looked so beautiful."

Two persons living together in love should make it a point that their relationship is continuously growing, bringing more flowers every season, creating more joys. Even just sitting together silently is enough. But all this is possible only if we drop the old idea of marriage. More than friendship is unnatural, and if marriage is stamped by the court it is killed under that stamp. You cannot bring love under the rule of law.

Love is the ultimate law. You just have to discover its beauties, its treasures. You have not just to repeat, parrot-like, all the great values that make human beings the highest expression of consciousness on this planet. You should exercise them in your relationship.

And this has been my observation, that if one partner starts moving along the right lines, the other follows sooner or later. Because they are both hungry for love, but they don't know how to approach it.

No university teaches that love is an art and that life is not already given to you, that you have to learn from scratch. But it is good that we have to discover with our own hands every treasure that is hidden in life. And love is one of the greatest treasures in existence.

But instead of becoming fellow travelers in search of love, beauty, and truth, people are wasting their time in fighting, in jealousy.

Just become a little alert and start the change from your side; don't expect it from the other side. It will begin from the other side, too. And it costs nothing to smile, it costs nothing to love, it costs nothing to share your happiness with somebody you love.

> It seems to me that jealousy arises not only in romantic relationships, but in all sorts of interactions with other people. Maybe "envy" is the right word for it, but it still means I'm resentful when somebody has something I want, but don't have. Can you talk about this kind of jealousy?

We have been taught to compare, we have been conditioned to always compare. Somebody has a better house, somebody has a more beautiful body, somebody has more money, somebody else has a more charismatic personality. Compare, go on comparing yourself with everybody else you pass by, and a great jealousy will be the outcome. It is the by-product of the conditioning for comparison.

Otherwise, if you drop comparing, jealousy disappears. Then you simply know you are you, and you are nobody else, and there is no need. It is good that you don't compare yourself with trees, otherwise you will start feeling very jealous: why are you not green? And why has existence been so hard on you, such that you don't have the capacity to bear flowers? It is good that you don't compare yourself with birds, with rivers, with mountains; otherwise you will suffer. You only compare yourself with human beings, because you have been conditioned to compare yourself only with human beings. You don't compare yourself with peacocks and with parrots. Otherwise, your jealousy would be greater and greater; you would be so burdened by jealousy that you would not be able to live at all.

Comparison is a very foolish attitude, because each person is unique and incomparable. Once this understanding settles in you, jealousy disappears. Each is unique and incomparable—you are just yourself; nobody has ever been like you and nobody will ever be like you. And you need not be like anybody else, either. Existence creates only originals; it does not believe in carbon copies.

> A bunch of chickens were in the yard when a football
> flew over the fence and landed in their midst. A rooster
> waddled over, studied it, then said, "I'm not complaining,
> girls, but look at the work they are turning out next door."

Next door, great things are happening. The grass is greener, the roses are rosier, everybody seems to be so happy—except you. You are continually comparing. And the same is the case with others, they are comparing too. Maybe they think the grass in your lawn is greener—it always looks greener from a distance—and that you have a more beautiful wife. You are tired of her, you cannot imagine why you allowed yourself to be trapped by this woman, you don't know how to get rid of her—and the neighbor may be jealous that you have such a beautiful wife! You may be jealous of him for the same reason, and he may be feeling the same about his wife.

Everybody is jealous of everybody else. And out of jealousy we create such hell, and we become very mean.

> An elderly farmer was moodily regarding the ravages
> of the flood. "Hiram!" yelled a neighbor. "Your pigs were
> all washed down the creek."
> "How about Thompson's pigs?" asked the farmer.
> "They're gone too."
> "And Larsen's?"
> "Yes."
> "Humphf!" grunted the farmer, cheering up. "It ain't
> as bad as I thought."

If everybody else is in misery, it feels better. If everybody else is losing it feels good, and if everybody else is happy and succeeding it tastes bitter. But why does the idea of the other enter in your head in the first place? Again, let me remind you: it is because you have not allowed your own juices to flow.

You have not allowed your own blissfulness to grow, you have not allowed your own being to bloom; hence, you feel empty inside. But you look at each and everybody's outside, because only the outside can be seen. You know your inside, and you know the others' outside—that creates jealousy. They know your outside, and they know their inside—that creates jealousy.

Nobody else knows your inside. There, you know you are nothing, worthless. And the others on the outside look so happy. Their smiles may be phony, but how can you know they are phony? Maybe their hearts are also smiling. You know your smile is phony, because your heart is not smiling at all; it may be crying and weeping.

You know your interiority—and only you know it, nobody else. You know everybody else's exterior, and people have made their exteriors beautiful, just as you have. Exteriors are showpieces and they are very deceptive.

There is an ancient Sufi story:

A man was very much burdened by his suffering. He used to pray every day to God, "Why me? Everybody seems to be so happy, why am only I in such suffering?" One day, out of great desperation, he prayed to God, "You can give me anybody else's suffering and I am ready to accept it. But take mine, I cannot bear it anymore."

That night he had a beautiful dream—beautiful and very revealing. He had a dream that God appeared in the sky and he said to everybody, "Bring all your sufferings into the temple." Everybody was tired of his suffering; in fact, everybody has prayed sometime or other, "I am ready to accept anybody else's suffering, but take mine away; this is too much, it is unbearable."

So everybody gathered his own sufferings into bags, and they reached the temple, and they were all looking very happy. The day has come, their prayer has been heard! And this man also rushed to the temple.

Then God said, "Put your bags by the walls." All the bags were put by the walls, and then God declared: "Now you can choose. Anybody can take any bag."

And the most surprising thing was this: this man, who had been praying always, rushed to get his own bag before anybody else could choose it! And he was in for a surprise, because everybody else also rushed to his own bag, and everybody was happy to choose it again.

What was the reason? For the first time, everybody had seen others' miseries, others' sufferings—the others' bags were just as big, or even bigger!

And the second reason was that everybody had become accustomed to their own sufferings. Now to choose somebody else's: Who knows what kind of sufferings will be inside the bag? Why bother? At least you are familiar with your own sufferings, and you have become accustomed to them. And they *are* tolerable; for so many years you have tolerated them, why choose the unknown?

Everybody went home happy. Nothing had changed, they were bringing the same suffering back, but everybody was happy and smiling and joyous that he could get his own bag back.

In the morning the man prayed to God and said, "Thank you for the dream; I will never ask again. Whatever you have given me is good for me, must be good for me; that's why you have given it to me."

Because of jealousy you are in constant suffering and you become mean to others. Because of jealousy you start becoming phony, you start pretending. You start pretending things that you don't have, you start pretending things that you *can't* have, which are not natural to you. You become more and more artificial. Imitating others, competing with others, what else can you do? If somebody has something and you don't have it, and you don't have a natural possibility of having it, the only way is to have some cheap substitute for it.

> *Jim and Nancy Smith had a great time in Europe this summer; they went everywhere and did everything. Paris, Rome . . . you name it, they saw it and they did it. But it was so embarrassing coming back home and going through customs. You know how customs officers pry into all your personal belongings. They opened up a bag and took out three wigs, silk underwear, perfume, hair coloring . . . really embarrassing. And that was just Jim's bag!*

Just look inside your bag and you will find so many artificial, phony, pseudo things—for what? Why can't you be natural and spontaneous? It is because of jealousy.

The jealous person lives in hell. Drop comparing, and jealousy disappears, meanness disappears, phoniness disappears.

But you can drop it only if you start growing your inner treasures; there is no other way. Grow up, become a more and more authentic individual. Love yourself and respect yourself the way existence has made you, and then immediately the doors of heaven open for you. They were always open; you simply had not looked at them.

I am very suspicious of my wife, although I know she is innocent. What can I do to drop my suspicions?

There must be something in you that you are really suspicious of. Unless you can trust yourself you cannot trust your wife or anybody else. If you mistrust yourself you will project your mistrust on people around you. The thief thinks that everybody is a thief. It is natural, because he knows himself, and that is his only way of knowing others.

What you think about others is basically a declaration of what you think about yourself. You know that if your wife is not constantly watching you, you will do something. You will start flirting with some woman—you know it! Hence the fear: "If I am in the office, who knows, the wife may be flirting with the neighbors." You know perfectly well what you are doing with the secretary; that's what is creating the problem.

That's why you say, "Though I know my wife is innocent, still I am suspicious." You will remain suspicious till something in you drops. It is not a question about the wife; all questions when they arise are really about you.

> A traveling man went on the road for a short trip, but kept staying away. Every few weeks he'd send his wife a wire saying, "Can't come home, still buying." Every wire was the same: "Can't come home, still buying." This went on for three or four months, when his wife finally sent him a wire that said, "Better come home, I'm selling what you're buying!"

That's how things happen in life.

> The hungover couple talked about the wild party they held the night before.
>
> "Darling, this is rather embarrassing," said the husband, "but was it you I made love to in the library last night?"
>
> His wife looked at him reflectively and asked, "About what time?"

The basic mistrust must be about yourself. You are suspicious of yourself: maybe you are repressing too much, and whenever somebody represses something he starts projecting it onto others. It almost always happens that the man who has a murderous instinct is always afraid that others are thinking to murder him; he becomes paranoid. The person who is very violent is always afraid: "Other people are so violent and I have to be constantly on guard."

Because people don't trust themselves, hence they can't trust anybody else—wife, friend, father, mother, son, daughter. People are living in chronic suspicion. But the basic cause is that you have not been able to accept your facticity.

Accept whatsoever you are. In that very acceptance you will accept others, too. And yes, there is a possibility—if you sometimes become interested in some woman, nothing is impossible; your wife may become interested in some man. But if you understand yourself and accept yourself, you will accept your wife, too.

If you can accept this, that "sometimes I become attracted to other women," then nothing is wrong. Then your wife can also become attracted to some man. But if you reject it in your own being, if you condemn it in your own being, you will condemn it in others' beings too.

My criterion of a saint is one who is able to forgive all and everybody, because he knows himself. But your saints are incapable of forgiving. Your saints go on inventing more and more technologically perfect hells. Why? They have not yet been able to accept themselves.

They tell the story about the young, good-looking attorney who claimed there never was a woman with whom he couldn't make it. One day the office hired a very good-looking secretary whom for weeks every male tried to make and failed in the attempt.

The young attorney boasted that if enough money was bet, he would succeed with her. When they questioned how he would prove it, he said he would record the entire action on his tape recorder, which he would hide under the bed.

When all the bets were made, he proceeded to make a date with her and by the end of the evening, not only was she in his apartment but eventually in his bed—whereupon he reached under and turned on the tape.

In a few moments, in support of his reputation, the secretary was in a state of violent lovemaking, and at its height cried out loudly, "Keep kissing it, honey, keep kissing it!"

Whereupon the attorney in his best courtroom manner leaned under the bed and dictated into the recorder, "Let the record reflect the lady indicated her left breast."

The mind of an attorney, constantly suspicious and assuming the worst. Now he must have become worried: "Keep kissing it, honey, keep kissing it!" Keep kissing what? The record will not say anything and there may be suspicions.

But this is the mind of everybody. The mind is cunning, calculating, suspicious. The mind lives constantly in a kind of distrust, in doubt. The mind's whole climate is that of doubt.

So it is not a question of how to trust your wife, it is a question of how to trust. Mind lives in the climate of doubt; it feeds on doubt. And unless you know how to put the mind off when it is not needed and descend into the heart, you will not know how to trust.

The climate of the heart is trust. Mind cannot trust; mind is incapable of trusting and we have all become hung up in the head. Hence, even though we say that we trust, we don't trust. We insist that we trust, but our very insistence shows that we don't trust. We want to trust, we pretend to trust, we want the other to *believe* that we trust, be we don't trust. The head is impotent as far as trust is concerned. The head is the mechanism for doubt; the head is constantly a question mark.

You will have to know how to come down to the heart, which has been bypassed by the society. The society does not teach you the ways of the heart, it only teaches you the ways of the mind. It teaches you mathematics and logic and it teaches you science, et cetera, et cetera—but they are all the cultivation of doubt.

Science has grown through doubt; doubt has been a blessing as far as science is concerned. But as science has grown more and more, man has shrunk. Humanity has disappeared, love has almost become a myth. Love is no more a reality on the earth. How can it be a reality? The heart itself has stopped beating.

Even when you love, you only *think* that you love; it comes through the head. And the head is not the faculty for love.

Start meditating. Start putting off the constant chattering of the head. Slowly, the mind becomes quiet. Get into things where the mind is not needed—for example, dancing. Dance, and dance to abandon, because in dance the mind is not needed. You can lose yourself in a dance. In losing yourself in a dance, the heart will start functioning again.

Drown yourself in music. And slowly you will see that there is a totally different world of the heart. And in the heart there is always trust. The heart does not know how to doubt, just as the mind does not know how to trust.

FROM FEAR TO LOVE

Just look at the absurdity of people's questions: How to love, how to dance, how to meditate? How to live? Absurd questions . . . but they show the poverty, the inner poverty, of man. He has been postponing everything, and by and by he has forgotten.

Every child knows how to love, and every child knows how to dance, and every child knows how to live. Every child comes complete, with everything ready. One just has to start living.

Have you seen? If you are crying and a small child is watching, he will come near you. He cannot say much, he cannot argue you out of your crying, but he puts his hand on your hand. Have you felt the touch? Never again will anybody touch you like that, like a child can touch—he knows how to touch. Later on, people are simply cold, hard. They touch, but nothing flows from their hands. When a child touches you—the tenderness of it, the softness of it, the message—he pours his whole being in it.

Everybody is born with everything they need to live. And the more you live the more capable you become of life. That is the reward. The less you live, the less capable you are. That is the punishment.

The wholeness you have to seek is within you. You have to watch your life moment to moment, and drop all that seems to be momentary, fragmentary. It may be very exciting, but futile in the end. Drop it! Look deep into those moments that may not be so exciting. The eternal cannot be very exciting, because that which has to be forever and ever has to be very silent, peaceful. Blissful, of course, but not exciting. Deeply blissful, but with no noise around it. More like a silence than like sound. You will have to grow in awareness so you can sort it out.

Fear is part of your intelligence; nothing is wrong in it. Fear simply shows there is death, and we human beings are here only for a few moments. That trembling says that we are not going to be permanently here, we are not eternally here, a few days more and you will be gone.

In fact it is because of fear that human beings have been in deep search of what it means to be religious; otherwise there would have been no point. No animal is religious because no animal is in fear. No animal can be religious because no animal can be aware of death. Human beings are aware of death. Every moment death is there, surrounds you from everywhere—any moment you will be gone. That gives you a trembling. Why be embarrassed, tremble! But again the ego says, "No—you, and afraid? No, this is not for you, this is for cowards. You are a brave man."

It is not for cowards, allow it: allow fear. Only one thing is to be understood, and that is when you allow fear and you tremble, watch it, enjoy it. In that watching you will transcend it. You will see the body is trembling, you will see the mind is trembling, but you will come to feel a point within you, a deep center, that remains unaffected. The storm passes by, but somewhere deep within you is a center that is untouched, the center of the cyclone.

Allow fear, don't fight with it. Watch what is happening. Go on watching. As your watching eye becomes more penetrating and intense, the body will be trembling, the mind will be trembling, but deep within you will be a consciousness that is simply a witness, that only watches. It remains untouched, like a lotus flower in water. Only when you attain to that will you attain to fearlessness.

But that fearlessness is not being unafraid, that fearlessness is not bravery. That fearlessness is a realization that you are two: a part of you will die, and a part of you is eternal. That part that is going to die is going to remain always afraid, and the part that is not going to die, which is immortal, for it there is no point in being afraid. Then a deep harmony exists. You can use fear for meditation. Use all that you have for meditation, so that you go beyond.

? **The strongest emotion that I have is hating death. I want to kill it, once and for all!**

To hate death is to hate life. They are not separate and they cannot be separated. Death and life exist together, there is no way to separate them. The separation is just an abstraction in the mind; it is utterly false. Life implies death, death implies life. They are polar opposites, but complementary to each other.

Death is the pinnacle of life. If you hate death, how can you love life? And it is a great misunderstanding: people who think they love life always hate death, and by hating death they become incapable of living. The capacity to live, the capacity to live at the maximum, comes only when you are ready to die, and ready to die at the maximum. It is always proportionate. If you live in a lukewarm way you will die in a lukewarm way. If you live intensely, totally, dangerously, you will also die in a deep orgasm. Death is the crescendo; life comes to its peak in death. The orgasm that you know through love is nothing compared to the orgasm that death makes available. All the joys of life simply are pale compared to the joy that death brings.

What exactly is death? Death is the disappearance of a false entity in you, the ego. Death also happens in love on a smaller scale, in a partial way; hence, the beauty of love. For a moment you die, for a moment you disappear. For a moment you are no more, and the whole possesses you. You disappear as a part, you become rhythmic with the whole. You don't exist as a ripple in the ocean, you exist as the ocean itself.

That's why all orgasmic experiences are oceanic experiences. The same happens in deep sleep: the ego disappears, the mind functions no more, you relapse into the original joy. But these are nothing compared to death. These are partial things. Sleep is a very tiny death; each morning you will be awake again. Still, if you have slept deeply, the joy lingers on the whole day, a certain quality of tranquility continues deep in your heart. You live differently that day when you have slept well. If you have not been able to sleep well, the day is disturbed. You feel annoyed, irritated, for no reason at all. Small things become great disturbances. You are angry—not at somebody in particular, you are simply angry. Your energy is not at home, it is distracted. You feel uprooted.

Death is a great sleep. The whole turmoil of life . . . seventy, eighty, or ninety years' turmoil, and all the miseries of life, and all the excitements and the distractions and the anxieties simply disappear, are no longer relevant. You fall back into the original unity of existence. You become part of the earth. Your body disappears into the earth, your breath disappears into the air, your fire goes back to the sun, your water to the oceans, and your inner sky has a meeting with the outer sky. This is death. How can one hate death?

You must be carrying a misunderstanding. You must have been carrying the idea that death is the enemy. Death is not the enemy, death is the greatest friend. Death has to be welcomed, death has to be waited for with a loving heart. If you think of death as the enemy, you will die—everybody has to die, your thinking will not make any difference—but you will die in agony because you will be resisting, you will be fighting. In resistance, in fight, you will destroy all the joys that death and only death can deliver to you. The death that could have been a great ecstasy will be just an agony.

And when something is too much of an agony one falls unconscious. There is a limit to tolerance, one can bear only so much. Hence ninety-nine out of a hundred die in a state of unconsciousness. They struggle, they fight to the very end. And when it becomes impossible to fight anymore—they have put all their energies at stake—they fall into a kind of swoon. They die an unconscious death.

And to die an unconscious death is a great calamity, because you will not remember what has happened. You will not remember that death was a door into the divine. You will be carried through the door, but on a stretcher, unconscious. You have missed a great opportunity again.

That's why we go on forgetting about our past lives. If you die consciously you will not forget, because there will be no gap, there will be a continuity. You will remember your past life—and to remember the past life is of great import. If you can remember your past life you will not commit the same mistakes again. Otherwise you will go on moving in a vicious circle: the same cycle, the same wheel will move again and again. You will cherish the same ambitions again and you will commit the same foolishnesses again, because you will think this is the first time you are doing them. You have done them millions of times, but each time you died a gap appeared because you were unconscious. You became discontinuous with your past. Then life starts from ABC again.

That's why you cannot evolve into buddhas. Evolution needs a continuous awareness of the past, so that the same mistakes are no longer committed. Slowly, mistakes disappear. Slowly, you become aware of the vicious circle; slowly, you become capable of getting out of it, too.

If you die unconsciously you will be born unconsciously, because death is one side of the door and birth is the other side of the same door. From one side the door says "Death" and the other side it says "Birth." It is the entrance, it is the exit—it is the same door.

That's why you were born but don't remember it. You don't remember those nine months in the womb, you don't remember passing through the birth canal, you don't remember the agony that you went through, you don't remember your birth trauma. And that birth trauma goes on affecting you; your whole life will remain affected by your birth trauma.

That trauma has to be understood, but the only way to understand it is to remember it. And how to remember it? You are so afraid of death, you are so afraid of birth, that the very fear prevents you from going into it.

You say, "The strongest emotion that I have is hating death." It is your hating life. Love life, and then a natural love for death arises too, because it is life that brings death. Death is not against life, death is the flowering of all that life contains in it as a seed. Death does not come from the blue; it grows in you, it is your flowering, your bloom.

Have you ever seen a real man dying? It is very rare to see a real man dying, but if you have, you will be surprised that death makes the person so beautiful. He has never been so beautiful before—neither in his childhood, because then he was ignorant, nor in his youth, because then passion was too much of a fever. But when death comes, all is relaxed. The foolishness of childhood is no longer there, and the madness of youth is also gone. The miseries of old age, the illnesses and the limitations of old age, are also gone. One is being freed from the body. A great joy arises from the innermost core, and spreads all over.

In the eyes of the real man dying you can see a flame that is not of this world. And in his face you can see a grandeur that is of the beyond. And you can feel the silence, the nonstruggling silence, the nonresistant silence of the man who is slipping slowly, slowly, into death . . . with a deep gratitude and acceptance for all that life has given to him and for all that existence has been so generous with. A gratitude surrounds him.

You will find a totally different space around him. He will die as one should die. And he will release such freedom that those who are close by will be simply stoned on that freedom, will be transported.

In the East, it has always been a great point: whenever a master dies, thousands, sometimes millions of people gather to watch that great phenomenon. Just to be there in the vicinity, to be close by, to see the ultimate fragrance being released, to see the last song that the man is going to sing, and to see the light that comes when the body and soul separate. It is dazzling; it is a great illumination.

Now scientists know perfectly well that if you divide the atom, great energy is released by the division, by the split. Much greater energy is released when the body and soul are divided. They have been together for millions of lives—now suddenly the moment has come when they will be divided. In that division, great energy is released. That energy release can become a tidal wave for those who want to ride on it. They will have great ecstatic experiences.

Don't hate death. And I know, it is not only the questioner who hates death, it is almost everybody, because we have been taught a very wrong philosophy. We have been told that death is against life; it is not. We have been told that death comes and destroys life. That is utter nonsense. Death comes and fulfills life.

If your life has been beautiful, death beautifies it to its ultimate. If your life has been a life of love, then death gives you the maximum experience of love. If your life has been a life of meditation, then death will bring you to the ultimate consciousness. Death only enhances—of course, if your life has been a wrong life, then death enhances that, too. Death is a great magnifier. If you have lived only in anger, then in death you will see just hell inside you, just fire. If you have lived in hatred, then death will magnify hatred. What can death do? Death magnifies, it mirrors—but you are the culprit. Death is just a mirroring phenomenon.

Don't hate death. Otherwise you will miss death and you will miss life too.

You say, "The strongest emotion that I have is hating death." You are wasting your strongest emotion unnecessarily.

Love life. Never be negative, negatives lead nowhere. Don't hate darkness, love light. Put your total energy into loving and you will be surprised, you will be taken aback. If you love light, one day you will suddenly recognize that darkness is nothing but a phase of light, a resting phase of light.

Don't hate the world, as you have been told to again and again in the past by your so-called saints. Love life, love this world, because when your love comes to its total intensity you will discover godliness here and now. It is hidden. It is hidden in the trees, in the mountains, in the rivers, in people—in your wife, in your husband, in your children. If you hate life, if you hate the world and you escape from it, you are going away from godliness.

Affirm life, let your energies be focused on the positive. The negative is not the way to live; nobody can live in the negative. In the negative, people only commit suicide. All negatives are suicidal. Only affirmation, total affirmation, brings you to reality.

You say, "The strongest emotion that I have is hating death. I want to kill it once and for all!"

You cannot do it. Nobody can do it, it is impossible; it is not in the nature of things. The day you were born, death became absolutely certain. Now there is no avoiding it. Death can be dissolved only when you dissolve birth. You have already died! The day you were born, you died—because in the very birth, death is determined. If you really want not to die again, then you will have to do something so that you are not born again.

That is the whole Eastern approach: how not to be born again. There are ways not to be born again. If desire disappears you will not be coming again. It is desire that brings you into the body; desire is the glue that keeps you glued to the body. One body disappears and desire creates another body, and so on and so forth. Dissolve desire, so you will not need any birth. If birth disappears, death disappears of its own accord. Then there is life eternal: no birth, no death.

This is the greatest medicine—the medicine of no birth, no death. This is the taste of the whole Eastern approach, Eastern realization, Eastern insight. But remember, you cannot fight death. You can dissolve birth, and then death is dissolved. But what happens is that ordinarily we love birth, we love life, and that's why we hate death. Now you are going into an impossibility and you will drive yourself crazy.

You say, "I want to kill it!" If you really want to kill death, accept it. Accept it totally—and in that very acceptance, death disappears. Because you never really die, only the ego dies. And if you accept death totally, you have renounced the ego on your own. Then there is nothing left for death to do; you have done its work on your own. What can death take from you? It will take your money, it will take your wife, your husband, it will take your relationships, it will take your world. Don't be attached to these things—then what is left for death to take from you? It will take your ego, your self-identity. The idea that "I exist as a separate being": death will take it away.

You can dissolve it. That's what meditation is all about. It is a conscious, voluntary decision: "I will dissolve this ego, I will not cling to it." If you don't cling to the ego, what is left? You have died already. And only those who have died already conquer death and attain life abundant.

Every time I feel strongly attracted to someone, and feel that I might actually be falling in love, fear comes up. It happens even when the other person is clearly attracted to me, too, so I don't think it's just a fear of rejection. It's more like some strange, existential terror. Can you help me understand what this is?

Love always makes one nervous, and there are reasons why it makes one nervous. It comes from the unconscious, and all your capacities are in the conscious; all your skill, all your knowledge, is in the conscious. Love comes from the unconscious and you don't know how to cope with it, what to do with it, and it is too much.

The unconscious is nine times bigger than the conscious, so whatsoever comes from the unconscious is overwhelming. That's why people are afraid of emotions, feelings. They hold them back, they are afraid they will create chaos—they do, but chaos is beautiful!

There is a need for order and there is a need for chaos too. When order is needed, use order, use the conscious mind; when chaos is needed, use the unconscious and let chaos be. A whole person, a total person, is one who is capable of using both—who does not allow any interference of the conscious into the unconscious, or of the unconscious into the conscious. There are things that you can only do consciously. For example, if you are doing arithmetic, you can do it only from the conscious. But love is not like that, poetry is not like that; they come from the unconscious. So you have to put your conscious aside.

It is the conscious that tries to hold things, because it is afraid. It seems that something so big is coming, a tidal wave; will it be able to survive? It tries to avoid it, it tries to remain away from it; it wants to escape, hide somewhere. But that is not right. That's why people have become dull and dead. All springs of life are in the unconscious. The conscious is only utilitarian; it is a utility, but it is not life's joy, it is not celebration. The conscious is good if you are thinking of livelihood, but not of life. Life comes from the unconscious, from the unknown, and the unknown is always scary.

Allow it. That's my whole work here, to help you to allow the unconscious. And once you start enjoying it your nervousness will disappear. There is no need to control it; one need not be in harness twenty-four hours.

Once it happened that a Chinese emperor went to see a great Zen master. The Zen master was rolling on the floor and laughing, and his disciples were laughing, too; he must have told a joke or something. The emperor was embarrassed. He could not believe his eyes because the behavior was so unmannerly. He could not prevent himself from saying something. He told the master, "This is un-mannerly! It is not expected of a man like you; some decorum has to be there. You are rolling on the floor, laughing like a madman."

The master looked at the emperor. He was carrying a bow; in those days the emperors were warriors, and they carried bows and arrows. The master said, "Tell me one thing: Do you keep this bow always stretched tight, or do you allow it to relax, too?"

The emperor said, "If we keep a bow stretched continuously it will lose elasticity, it will not be of any use then. It has to be left relaxed so that whenever we need it, it has elasticity." And the master said, "That's what I'm doing."

There are moments when people should be so relaxed, so wildly relaxed, that they don't have any formality to follow. And love is that relaxation. One need not be in harness for twenty-four hours. While working, be in the conscious mind; be alert, be calculative. Be intelligent, be skillful, be efficient. But that is only the utilitarian part of life. Out of the office relax and be overflooded by the unconscious; be possessed by it and go wild.

Otherwise it is a vicious circle. You feel nervous, you repress energy. You repress energy and that repressed energy creates more trembling inside you, so you feel more nervous; you feel more nervous, you repress more, and so on and so forth, it goes on and on. The more you repress, the more nervous you will feel; the more nervous you feel, the more you will repress. You have to break through, out of this vicious circle. Just take a jump.

> Can you say something about how guilt and fear are related? Sometimes I find it hard to separate the two.

Fear is natural; guilt is a creation of the priests. Guilt is man-made. Fear is in-built, and it is very essential. Without fear you will not be able to survive at all. Fear is normal. It is because of fear that you will not put your hand in the fire. It is because of fear that you will walk to the right or to the left, whatever is the law of the country. It is because of fear that you will avoid poison. It is because of fear that when the truck driver sounds his horn, you run out of the way.

If the child has no fear there is no possibility that he will ever survive. His fear is a life-protective measure. But because of this natural tendency to protect oneself . . . and nothing is wrong in it, you have the right to protect yourself. You have such a precious life to protect, and fear simply helps you. Fear is intelligence. Only idiots don't have fear, imbeciles don't have fear; hence you have to protect these people, otherwise they will burn themselves, or they will jump out of a building, or they will go into the sea without knowing how to swim—anything they can do.

Fear is intelligence; when you see a snake crossing the path, you jump out of the way. It is not cowardly, it is simply intelligent. But there are two possibilities out of this natural phenomenon. Fear can become abnormal, it can become pathological. Then you are afraid of things of which there is no need to be afraid, although you can find arguments even for your abnormal fear.

For example, somebody is afraid of going inside a house. Logically, you cannot prove that he is wrong. He says, "What is the guarantee that the house will not fall?" Now, houses are known to fall, so this house can also fall. People have been crushed by houses falling. Nobody can give an absolute guarantee that this house is not going to fall; an earthquake can happen, anything is possible. Another man is afraid and he cannot travel because there are train accidents. Somebody else is afraid and cannot get into a car, there are car accidents. Somebody else is afraid of an airplane. If you become afraid in this way, this is not intelligent. Then you should be afraid of your bed too, because almost ninety-seven percent of people die in their beds—so that is the most dangerous place to be! Logically, you should remain as far away from the bed as possible, never go close to it. But then you will make your life impossible.

Fear can become abnormal; then it is pathology. And because of this possibility the priests have used it, politicians have used it, all kinds of oppressors have used it. They make it pathological, and then it becomes very simple to exploit you. The priest makes you afraid of hell. Just look in the scriptures, with what joy they depict all the tortures, with really great relish! Adolf Hitler must have been reading these scriptures; he must have found such great ideas from these scriptures describing hell. He himself was not such a creative genius as to be able to invent the concentration camps and all kinds of atrocities. He must have found them in religious scriptures—they were already there, priests had already done the work. He only practiced what priests have been preaching. He was really a religious man! Priests were only talking about the hell that was waiting for you after death. Hitler said, "Why wait so long? I will create a hell here and now so you can have a taste of it."

The priests became aware very early that the fear instinct in man can be exploited. He can be made so afraid that he will fall at the feet of the priests and beg them, "Save us! Only you can save us." And the priest will agree to save them only if they follow him. If they follow the rituals prescribed by the priest, he will save them. And out of fear people have been following all kinds of stupidities, superstitions.

The politician also became aware that people can be made very much afraid. And if you make them afraid, you can dominate them. It is out of fear that nations exist. Indians are afraid of the Pakistanis, and the Pakistanis are afraid of the Indians, and so on all over the world. It is so stupid! We are afraid of each other, and because of our fear the politician becomes important. The politician says he will save you here, in this world, and the priest says he will save you in the other world. And they conspire together.

It is fear that creates guilt, but not the fear itself. Fear creates guilt via the priests and politicians. The priests and the politicians create in you a pathology, a trembling. And naturally, the human being is so delicate and so fragile, he becomes afraid. Then you can tell him to do anything and he will do it, knowing perfectly well that it is stupid, knowing perfectly well deep down that it is all nonsense—but who knows? Out of fear a man can be forced to do anything just to save himself. And because the pathology that has been created in you is unnatural, your nature rebels against it. Then once in a while you do something natural, which goes against this unnatural fear, and guilt arises.

Guilt means you have an unnatural idea in your mind about how life should be, what should be done. Then one day you find yourself following nature and you do the natural thing, you go against the ideology you are carrying. Because you go against the ideology, guilt arises and you are ashamed. You feel inferior, unworthy.

But by giving people unnatural ideas you cannot transform them. Hence the priests have been able to exploit people, but they have not been able to transform them. They are not interested in transforming you either; their whole idea is to keep you always enslaved. They create a conscience in you. Your conscience is not really your conscience, it is created by your religions. They say, "This is wrong." You may know from the deepest core of your being that there seems to be nothing wrong in it, but they say it is wrong and they go on hypnotizing you from your very childhood. The hypnosis goes deep, sinks deep in you, becomes almost part of your being. It holds you back.

They have told you sex is wrong, but sex is such a natural phenomenon that you are attracted toward it. And nothing is wrong in being attracted toward a woman or a man. It is just part of nature. But your conscience says, "This is wrong." So you hold yourself back. Half of you goes toward the other and half of you is pulling you back. You can't make any decision; you are always divided, split. If you decide to go with the woman or the man, your conscience will torture you: "You have committed a sin." If you don't go, your nature will torture you: "You are starving me!" Now you are in a double bind. Whatever you do you will suffer, and the more you suffer, the more you go to the priest for his advice. The more you suffer, the more you seek salvation.

Bertrand Russell is absolutely right that if a man is given total, natural freedom from this so-called conscience and morality, and if he is helped to become an integrated, natural being—intelligent, understanding, living his life according to his own light and not according to somebody else's advice—the so-called religions will disappear from the world.

I perfectly agree with him. The so-called religions will certainly disappear from the world. If people are not in suffering, they won't seek salvation. But Bertrand Russell goes on and he says religion itself will disappear from the earth. There I don't agree with him. The so-called religions will disappear, and because the so-called religions will disappear there will be, for the first time in the world, an opportunity for an authentic religiousness to exist. Christians will not be there, Hindus will not be there, Mohammedans will not be there: only then will a new kind of religiousness spread over the earth. People will be living according to their own consciousness. There will be no guilt, no repentance, because these things never change people. People remain the same; they just go on changing their outer garb, their form. Substantially, nothing changes through guilt, through fear, through heaven, through hell. All these ideas have utterly failed. We have lived in a very wrong kind of world; we have created a wrong kind of situation. People only go on changing superficially: the Hindu becomes a Christian, the Christian becomes a Hindu, and nothing ever changes. All remains the same.

The reformed prostitute is giving testimony with the Salvation Army on a street corner on a Saturday night, punctuating her discourse by beating on a big brass drum.

"I used to be a sinner!" she shouts (boom!) "Used to be a bad woman (boom!) I used to drink! (boom!) Gamble! (boom!) Whore! (boom! boom!) Used to go out Saturday nights and raise hell! (boom! boom! boom!) Now what do I do Saturday nights? I stand on this street corner, beating on this motherfucking drum!"

PART III

Watchfulness:
The Key to
Transformation

Disidentifying from your thoughts is easier
than disidentifying from your feelings because thoughts
are more superficial. Disidentifying from the feelings is a
little difficult because they are deeper, and they are rooted
more in your biology, in your chemistry, in your hormones.
Thoughts are just floating clouds. They are not rooted in
your chemistry, in your biology, in your physiology, in your
hormones; they are just floating clouds without any roots.
But feelings have roots, so it is difficult to uproot them.

It is easy to become watchful about the theory of
relativity; it is difficult to be a witness of your anger,
your love, your greed, your ambition. The reason is they are
rooted more deeply in the body. But witnessing is such
a sharp sword: it cuts thoughts, feelings, emotions, in a
single blow. And you will know it by experience as you go
deeper in your meditation. The body is left far behind, the
emotions, the thoughts . . . only the witnessing remains.
That is your authentic nature.

CREATE A LITTLE DISTANCE

If you can meditate, if you can create a little distance between your mind and your being, if you can see and feel and experience that you are not your mind, a tremendous revolution happens within you. If you are not your mind, then you cannot be your jealousy, you cannot be your sadness, you cannot be your anger.

Then they are just there, unrelated to you; you don't give any energy to them. They are really parasites who have been living on your blood, because you were identified with the mind. Meditation means disidentification with the mind.

It is a simple method, not something complex that only a few people can do. Just sit silently at any time, any moment, and watch. Close your eyes and watch what is going on. Just be a watcher. Don't judge what is good, what is bad, this should not be, this should be . . .

No judgment, you are simply a watcher.

It takes a little time to attain pure watchfulness. And the moment you are a pure watcher, you will be surprised that the mind has disappeared.

There is a proportion: if you are only one percent a watcher, then ninety-nine percent is mind. If you are ten percent a watcher, then ninety percent is mind. If you are ninety percent a watcher, then only ten percent of the mind is left.

If you are one hundred percent a watcher, then there is no mind—no sadness, no anger, no jealousy—just a clarity, a silence, a benediction.

One has to start watching the body: walking, sitting, going to bed, eating. One should start from the most solid, because it is easier, and then one should move to subtler experiences. One should start watching thoughts, and when one becomes an expert in watching thoughts, then one should start watching feelings. After you feel that you can watch your feelings, then you should start watching your moods, which are even more subtle than your feelings, and more vague.

The miracle of watching is that as you are watching the body, your watcher is becoming stronger; as you are watching the thoughts, your watcher is becoming stronger; as you are watching the feelings, the watcher is becoming even more strong. When you are watching your moods the watcher is so strong that it can remain itself—watching itself, just as a candle in the dark night not only lights everything around it, it also lights itself.

To find the watcher in its purity is the greatest achievement in spirituality, because the watcher in you is your very soul; the watcher in you is your immortality. But never for a single moment think, "I've got it," because that is the moment when you miss.

Watching is an eternal process; you always go on becoming deeper and deeper, but you never come to the end where you can say, "I have got it." In fact, the deeper you go the more you become aware that you have entered into a process that is eternal, without any beginning and without any end.

But people are watching only others; they never bother to watch themselves. Everybody is watching what the other person is doing, what the other person is wearing, how he looks—that is the most superficial watching. Everybody is watching; it is not something new to be introduced into your life. It has only to be deepened, moved away from others and arrowed toward your own inner feelings, thoughts, moods—and finally, the watcher itself.

> *A Jew is sitting in a train opposite a priest. "Tell me, Your Worship," the Jew asks, "why do you wear your collar back to front?"*
>
> *"Because I am a father," answers the priest.*
>
> *"I am also a father, and I don't wear my collar like that," says the Jew.*
>
> *"Oh," says the priest, "but I am a father to thousands."*
>
> *"Then maybe," replies the Jew, "it is your trousers you should wear back to front."*

People are very watchful about everybody else. You can laugh very easily about the ridiculous acts of other people, but have you ever laughed about yourself? Have you ever caught yourself doing something ridiculous? No, you keep yourself completely unwatched; your whole watching is directed to others, and that is not of any help.

Use this energy of watchfulness for a transformation of your being. It can bring you so much bliss and so much benediction that you cannot even dream about it. A simple process, but once you start using it on yourself it becomes a meditation.

One can make meditations out of anything. Anything that leads you to yourself is meditation. And it is immensely significant to find your own meditation, because in the very finding you will find great joy. And because it is your own finding, not some ritual imposed upon you, you will love going deeper into it. The deeper you go into it the happier you will feel—peaceful, more silent, more together, more dignified, more graceful.

You all know watching, so there is no question of learning it. It is just a question of changing the object of watching. Bring it closer. Watch your body and you will be surprised. I can move my hand without watching, and I can move my hand with watching. You will not see the difference, but I can feel the difference. When I move it with watchfulness there is a grace and beauty in it, a peacefulness, and a silence. You can walk, watching each step; it will give you all the benefit that walking can give you as an exercise, plus it will give you the benefit of a great, simple meditation.

The temple in Bodhgaya where Gautam Buddha became enlightened has been made in memory of two things: One is a bodhi tree under which Buddha used to sit. And just by the side of the tree there are small stones for taking a slow walk. He was meditating, sitting, and when he would feel that sitting had been too much—a little exercise was needed for the body—he would walk on those stones. That was his walking meditation.

When I was in Bodhgaya having a meditation camp there, I went to the temple. I saw Buddhist lamas from Tibet, from Japan, from China. They were all paying their respect to the tree, and I saw not a single one paying his respect to those stones on which Buddha had walked miles and miles. I told them, "This is not right. You should not forget those stones. They have been touched by Gautam Buddha's feet millions of times." But I know why they were not paying any attention to them, because they had forgotten completely that Buddha was emphasizing that you should watch every act of your body: walking, sitting, lying down. You should not let a single moment go by unconsciously.

Watchfulness will sharpen your consciousness. This is the essential of religiousness; all else is simply talk. And if you can manage watchfulness, nothing else is needed.

My effort here is to make the journey as simple as possible. All the religions have done just the opposite, they have made things very complex—so complex that people have never tried them. For example, in the Buddhist scriptures there are 33,000 principles to be followed by a Buddhist monk; even to remember them is impossible! Just the very number 33,000 is enough to freak you out: "I am finished! My whole life will be disturbed and destroyed." Just find a single principle that suits you, that feels in tune with you, and that is enough.

I often find myself being in very dramatic and miserable moods, but every once in a while I see myself walking around with a long, long face and with thoughts like "I am a failure." And then suddenly an overwhelming giggling comes up inside me, which sometimes explodes into laughter and the feeling of being absolutely happy. It is so strong I can't even hold on to my dramatic mood anymore! Is this related to what you call the watcher?

There is certainly a relationship between the watcher and the laughter arising in you, because the watcher can see not only the stupidities of other people, but the stupidities of oneself.

The watcher could see your dramatic mood. Before the watcher came in, you were identified with the dramatic mood; you had forgotten that it was just a dramatic mood.

Just watch people. Everybody is carrying a face that is a role, repeating some dialogue inside, preparing. What he is going to say to the wife, because he is late . . . and he knows perfectly well that not even once in his whole life has he been able to deceive her, but still he goes on doing the same stupidity.

If the watcher comes in, if suddenly you remember to witness, you will start giggling at yourself that you are such a fool. You go on falling in the same ditch every day, deciding every day never to fall again in the same ditch. But when you come near the ditch, the attraction, the fascination with falling in the ditch is so great that you forget all your decisions. You console yourself "Just once more. From tomorrow, I'm going to keep the promise I've given to myself." But this has happened so many times. And you will do it your whole life, unless you allow the watcher to see the ridiculous acts that you are doing.

And there is certainly a deep relationship. As you watch you will start giggling about why you unnecessarily have a serious face. In fact, nobody is even looking at you; you can relax! And even if they are looking at you, a serious face is not so beautiful. A joyous face, a face full of smiles, radiant, may be worth having. If you are going to be an actor, then at least choose a good role!

Everybody has chosen such ugly roles to play; their faces are dull and sad, their vibe is that of a corpse. Still they want everybody to love them, respect them. Even dogs don't bark at them, even they tolerate; they just don't look, they just say, "Let him go on in his misery." Dogs have their own fundamental ideology; they bark at people who wear uniforms—policemen, postmen, they are absolutely against uniforms. They are certainly very rebellious people. The whole army, the whole brigade is going past, and all the people are in the same uniform? Dogs cannot resist the temptation to protest. But when you pass by with your long face, even the dog does not protest. But if you could see yourself, you would giggle at yourself, "Why you are carrying such a face?" And you will be surprised, if you are really watching, the dog is also giggling at you.

Perhaps you have not noted the fact. Next time you have a full-hearted laugh, try to see a very fundamental fact: watching is easiest while you are laughing, because laughing is not a serious act, and it is natural. Laughing creates an atmosphere of silence in you. If your laughter is really total, the mind stops: "Let this fool first laugh." Those are the moments when you can bring in the watcher very easily.

Just to support your giggling . . . and remember to watch while you are giggling:

The first grade class gathered around the teacher for a game of Guess the Animal. The first picture the teacher held up was a cat. "Okay, boys and girls," she said brightly, "can anyone tell me what this is?"

"I know! I know! It is a cat," yelled a little boy.

"Very good, Eddy. Now who knows what this animal is called?"

"That's a dog," piped up the same little boy.

"Right again. And what about this animal?" she asked, holding up a picture of a deer.

Silence fell over the class. After a minute or two the teacher said, "I will give you a hint, children, listen. It is something that your mother calls your father around the house."

"I know! I know!" screamed Eddy. "It is a horny bastard!"

A sailor was stranded on a desert island and managed to survive by making friends with the local natives—such good friends, in fact, that one day the chief offered him his daughter for an evening's entertainment. Late that night, while they made love, the chief's daughter kept shouting, "Oga, boga! Oga, boga!" The arrogant sailor assumed this must be how the natives express their appreciation when something is fantastic.

A few days later the chief invites the sailor for a game of golf. On his first stroke, the chief hit a hole in one. Eager to try out his new vocabulary, the sailor enthusiastically shouted "Oga boga! Oga boga!"

The chief turned around with a puzzled look on his face and asked, "What you mean, 'wrong hole'?"

> When you talk about love and passion, intensity and authenticity, I feel a warm glow of recognition inside—I feel the truth of it as I have sometimes glimpsed it at my peaks. But when you talk of detachment, aloofness, watching, I feel cold fear and deadness inside. I cannot grasp this paradox. How can I fall in love and remain aloof? How can I lose myself in a beautiful view and remain detached?
>
> I recognize that what you say about oscillating helplessly between heaven and hell, ecstasy and despair, is true of my life. I see that this helplessness is unsatisfactory and painful. But if the alternative is a cold, detached aloofness, then I feel I would rather keep my heaven and hell, my joy and my sorrow, and forget all about watching.

The most important thing to understand in life is that life is a paradox; life exists through being paradoxical. Life is not logical, it is paradoxical. It exists between birth and death, it exists between night and day, it exists between hate and love, it exists between man and woman. It exists between the positive electricity and the negative electricity, it exists between yin and yang, between Shiva and Shakti. Just look around, look in, look out, and you will find the paradox everywhere.

If life were logical, then there would have been no paradox. But life is not logical, and cannot be! Just think of a world where only love exists and no hate—then love will not be possible; it will disappear with the hate. Think of a world where only darkness exists and no light, or light exists and no darkness . . . it is impossible. Where only birth exists and no death—it would have been very logical, but it would have been very boring, too.

Life is dialectical, not logical. It is a movement between polarities. Those polarities are not really opposite, although they look opposite; they are complementaries also. Hate and love are not two things; in fact it is one thing, lovehate. It is one thing, birthdeath; it is one thing, daynight; it is one thing, manwoman. It is like the peaks of the Himalayas and the valleys. The peaks cannot exist without the valleys, and the valleys cannot exist without the peaks—they are together. And this paradox will be found on every plane, everywhere.

Now, you say, "I would rather keep my heaven and hell, my joy and my sorrow, and forget all about enlightenment, if the alternative is a cold, detached aloofness." I am not saying that you have to choose a cold, detached life. I am saying that passionate love and cool aloofness is the paradox. The same paradox that exists between birth and death, love and hate; it is the same paradox. Only the passionately involved person knows what cool aloofness is. You will be surprised, because you have been told just the opposite up to now.

You have been told that the Buddha is cool, detached, far away. That the worldly person is passionate and the saintly person is dispassionate, that the worldly man lives a hot life and the monk moves into a monastery and lives a cold life. That has been so up to now, but both have remained lopsided. The worldly man knows only one part of the polarity. That is his misery. He knows only heat; he does not know the soothing coolness of being a buddha. And the monk knows only coldness, he does not know the euphoria, the ecstasy, the excitement, the tremendous celebration of being in a hot passion.

There is Zorba the Greek, who knows what hot passion is, and there is our idea of the Buddha—note that I call it our *idea* of the Buddha—who knows only cool silence. We have created the division, and because of this division the worldly man is not rich because he is only half. The religious man is not whole either, and without being whole he can never be holy, he knows only the other end of the polarity. Both are miserable.

Go into the marketplace and see, and go into a monastery and see. You will find in the monastery immense misery, dullness, deadness, and you will see in the eyes of your monks stupidity and nothing else. Because when you live at just one pole you lose sharpness, you lose variety, you lose richness.

My way of looking at things is that there is no need to choose. Remain choiceless and you will see the play of polarities. Both ends of the spectrum are yours, and both have to be lived. Yes, you have to be deeply, intensely, authentically passionate—just as you have to become cool, silent, quiet. You have to love and you have to meditate. Meditation and love should not be divided, they should be like the valley and the peak together. The peak has beauties, the sunlit peak and the virgin snow, and in the morning it is all gold and in the full moon it is all silver, and the purity of the air, and the closeness of the stars—you can almost whisper to them. But the valley is also beautiful: the darkness and its velvety texture, darkness and its infinity, darkness and its mystery, and the shade of the trees, and the sound of running water. Both are beautiful.

I teach you not to choose but to accept both, and both will help each other to become more and more sharp. On one side is Zorba the Greek, on the other side is Gautam the Buddha— I teach you Zorba the Buddha. That's why Zorbas are against me, because they cannot think of the Buddha. Materialists are against me because they ask why I bring religiousness in. And the so-called religious people are against me because they ask how I could bring love into the life of a religious person, how I can dare to talk about the body and its joys. Both are angry with me because I say the path is from sex to superconsciousness. One would like to stop at sex, and the other would like not to talk about sex but only about superconsciousness. But I accept life in its whole spectrum, I accept life in its totality.

You can accept only when you accept in totality; if you reject something, that means you are trying to be wiser than life itself, existence itself. Existence has not rejected anything. Your mahatmas are trying to be wiser than life itself.

Life exists in polar opposites, and exists beautifully. If you love, you will be surprised that soon a great desire arises to be alone—out of love. Each lover feels it. And if you have not felt it then you have not loved, then your love is lukewarm; it has not been really passionate. If it has been passionate, a great desire will arise to be alone: to have one's own space, to move inward, to fall in, to disappear inward, because love when it is so passionate, tires you, exhausts, empties you. And it is beautiful to empty yourself, but then you start feeling that you need nourishment.

And from where will you get nourishment? You simply move inward, you escape in, you close your eyes to the world and you simply forget all about others. . . . In those moments of inwardness your energies accumulate; you are again feeling full. And then too full, and out of that too-fullness, overflowing arises and you have to seek and search for somebody who is ready to share your energy, who is ready to share your song, who is ready to

dance with you. Out of aloneness, a great desire arises to be together. This is the rhythm.

I am not telling you to become cold, I am not telling you to
choose aloofness and a detached life. I am telling you these are two
aspects. If you want to live your life in its multidimensionality—
as matter, as spirit, as body, as soul, as love, as meditation, as outward exploration and inward journey— if you want to live life in
its totality, the ingoing breath and the outgoing breath, you need
not choose. If you choose you will die.

That's why in the marketplace and in the monasteries both
you will find people who are dead. A few have chosen only to
exhale, and a few have chosen only to inhale. The breath
needs both; the breath becomes a perfect circle when you exhale
deeply and out of that exhalation comes a deep inhalation; and
when you inhale deeply, out of that inhalation comes a deep
exhalation.

And remember: if your exhalation is not deep, your inhalation cannot be deep. If your inhalation is poor, your exhalation
will be poor. They keep balancing each other. The deeper you go
out, the deeper you will go in, and vice versa. I teach this unity.

You need not be worried. But you became worried because
sometimes I am teaching love and that feels good to you . . . But
let me tell you, let me be frank with you. You have not really
known love yet. If you had known love, you would have understood the other pole also. From your own experience you would
have understood that love creates a great need to be alone, and
aloneness creates a great need to be together. This is a truth that
has to be taught to everybody. Lovers don't know it, so they feel
guilty if they want to be alone. And if one person wants to be
alone, the other feels rejected. This is an utter misunderstanding.
If the husband says, "Leave me alone tonight," the wife feels rejected, she feels angry. It seems as if she is no longer needed. That
is not the case; they are misunderstanding the whole thing. And

if one day the wife says, "Leave me alone," the husband is hurt very much; his male ego is hurt very much.

The moment you say to your lover or beloved, "I want to be alone for a few days. I would like to go to the mountains for a few weeks, alone," the other cannot understand because they have never been told the fundamental fact that love creates the desire to be alone. And if you don't go into aloneness, your love will become flat. It will slowly become only a phony thing; it will lose all authenticity.

Accept life in its totality. To be in hot passion is good, and to be in cool compassion is also good. Let them both be your wings; don't cut one wing, otherwise you will never be able to go on that eternal flight—the flight from the alone to the alone.

That's what Plotinus has called it: the flight of the individual to the universal soul. You will need both wings.

I teach you love, I teach you meditation—and I teach you a tremendous synthesis of both. And it is not that you have to create the synthesis. The synthesis is natural; you have only not to disrupt it. Watch your own experiences, and what I am saying will be proved valid, because I am not talking ideology here, I am simply talking about facts.

> A much-decorated Russian hero returned from duty on the Finnish front where he had performed valorous service. He had been up in the mountains for months on end in the dead of winter. This was his first furlough in a full year.
>
> A reporter came to see him. With a twinkle in his eye, the reporter asked, "Tell me, Captain Ivan Petrovich, what was the second thing you did after being away from your wife for a full year?"
>
> Ivan answered without hesitation, "The second thing? Why, the second thing I did was take off my skis."

If you have been too long in the mountains, how can you take your skis off first?

> *A ship was coming into harbor after six months at sea. The women of the town had all come down to the quayside to welcome their returning husbands. One woman was waving to her husband perched forward in the bow of the ship and shouting to him, "E.F! E.F!"*
>
> *He was shouting, "F.F! F.F!"*
>
> *"E.F! E.F!"*
>
> *"F.F! F.F!"*
>
> *A bystander turned to the woman and asked, "What is all this E.F. F.F. business?"*
>
> *She replied, "I am saying we should eat first."*

SUPPRESSION OR TRANSFORMATION

The Freedom of Being Human

Man is the only being who can suppress his energies—or who can transform them. No other being can do either. Suppression and transformation exist as two aspects of one phenomenon, which is that man can do something about himself.

The trees exist, the animals exist, the birds exist, but they cannot do anything about their existence; they are part of it. They cannot stand aside from it, they cannot be "doers." They are so merged with their energy, they cannot separate themselves.

Man can do things. He can do something about himself. He can observe himself from a distance; he can look at his own energies as if they are separate from him. And then either he can suppress them, or he can transform them.

Suppression means only trying to hide certain energies that are there, not allowing them to have their being, not allowing them to have their manifestation. Transformation means changing energies, moving them toward a new dimension.

There is fear, because you feel that control will be lost, and once control is lost you cannot do anything. I teach a new control—the control of the witnessing self. Not the control of a manipulating mind, but the control of a witnessing self. That control is the highest form possible, and that control is so natural that you never feel you are controlling. It is a kind of control that happens spontaneously with witnessing.

If you follow suppression you can become so-called human beings: bogus, superficial, hollow within, just dummies, not authentic, not real. If you don't follow suppression but follow indulgence, you will become like animals: beautiful, more beautiful than so-called civilized man, but just animals. Not alert, not aware, not conscious of the possibility of growth, of your human potential.

If you transform the energy, then you become divine. And remember, when I say divine, both things are implied in it. The wild animal with its total beauty of being is there. That wild animal is not rejected and denied, he is there—richer, because he is more alert. So all the wildness is there and the beauty of it, and all that civilization has been trying to force is there, but it is spontaneous, not forced. Once the energy is transformed, nature and godliness meet in you—nature with its beauty, godliness with total grace.

This is what being a sage means. A sage is a meeting of nature and the divine, a meeting of body and soul, a meeting of that which is below and of that which is above, a meeting of the earth and the sky.

? You say that we should neither suppress nor indulge in emotions like anger, but that we should remain passively alert and meditative. Obviously, it will need a sort of inner effort to avoid suppression or indulgence—but then is this not also a sort of suppression?

No! It is an effort, but not "a sort of suppression." Not every effort is suppression.

There are three types of effort. One is the effort involved in expression; when you express your anger, it is an effort. Then the second type of effort is when you suppress it. When you express what you are doing, you are forcing your energy outward to the person, to the object. You are throwing out your energy, and the other is the target. Energy moves to the other; it is an effort on your part. When you suppress, you pull the energy back to the original source, to your own heart. You force it back; it is an effort, but the direction is different. In expression it moves away from you, in suppression it moves back to you.

The third option—alertness, passive alertness—is also an effort but the dimension is different. The energy moves upward. In the beginning it is an effort. When I say be passively alert, in the beginning even passivity is bound to be an effort. Only by and by, as you become more acquainted with it, will it not be an effort. And when it is not an effort, it becomes even more passive—and the more passive, the more magnetic. It pulls the energy upward.

But in the beginning, everything is going to be an effort, so don't become a victim of words. It creates problems. Mystics have always been talking about effortlessness; they say don't make any effort. But in the beginning even this is going to be an effort. When we say "Be effortless" we only mean don't force the effort. Allow it to come through awareness. If you force it, you will become tense. If you become tense, the energy of anger cannot move upward and be transformed. Tension is horizontal; only a non-tense mind can be above, hovering like a cloud.

Look at the clouds floating with no effort—in the same way, just bring your witnessing in, like a floating cloud. In the beginning it is going to be an effort, but remember only that it is going to become effortless. You will be reinforcing the alertness and allowing it more and more.

This is difficult because language creates the difficulty. If I tell you to relax, what will you do? You will make a sort of effort. But then I tell you not to make any effort, because if you make any effort, that will create tension and you will not be able to relax. I tell you to simply relax. Then you are at a loss, and you are bound to ask, "Then what do you mean? If I am not going to make any effort, then what am I supposed to do?"

You are not supposed to do anything, but in the beginning that nondoing will look like a doing. So I will say, "Okay! Make a little effort, but remember that the effort is to be left behind. Use it as a starter just in the beginning. You cannot understand nondoing; you can only understand doing. So use the language of doing and action; start, but use effort only as a starter. And remember, the sooner you leave it behind the better."

I have heard that when Mulla Nasruddin became very old, he became a victim of insomnia, he couldn't sleep. Everything was tried—hot baths, pills, tranquilizers, syrups—but nothing was of any help. And the whole family was disturbed, because Mulla could not sleep and he would not allow anyone in the house to sleep. The whole night had become a nightmare for everybody.

They searched desperately for any method, any medicine that would help Mulla to sleep, because the whole family was going crazy. Finally they brought a hypnotist. The family came to old Mulla very happily, and they told him, "Now you need not be worried, Papa. This is a miracle man. He creates sleep within minutes.

He knows the very magic of it, so don't be worried. Now there is no fear, and you will be able to sleep."

The hypnotist showed a watch with a chain to Nasruddin and said, "Only very little faith will do the miracle. You need a little trust in me. Just trust me, and you will fall like a small babe into deep sleep. Look at this watch."

He started moving that watch left and right. Nasruddin looked at it, and the hypnotist said, "Left-right, left-right. Your eyes are becoming tired, tired, tired. You are falling asleep, asleep, asleep, asleep."

Everyone was in joy—happy. Mulla's eyes closed, his head moved down, and he looked like a small babe going into deep sleep. A very rhythmic breathing came. The hypnotist took his fee, and he put his finger on his lips, just to indicate to the family not to worry, they would not be disturbed now. Then he sneaked out. The moment he was out, Mulla opened one eye and said, "That nut! Has he gone yet?"

He was making an effort to relax, so he relaxed "like a babe." He had started breathing rhythmically and closed his eyes, but it was all an effort. He was helping the hypnotist. He thought that he was helping the hypnotist. But it was an effort on his part, so nothing happened. Nothing *could* happen; he was awake. If he could have just been passive, if he could have simply heard what was being said, looked at what was being shown, the sleep would have happened. No effort on his part was necessary; only a passive acceptance was necessary. But even for you to bring your mind to that passive acceptance, in the beginning you will need effort.

So don't be afraid of effort. Start with effort, and just remember that you have to move beyond effort. Only when you have moved beyond will you be passive, and that passive awareness brings the miracle.

With passive awareness, the mind is no longer there. For the first time your inner center of being is revealed, and there is a reason. Effort is needed for anything that is to be done in the world. If you want to do anything in the outer world, effort is needed. But if you want to do something in the inner, no effort is needed. Just relaxation is needed. Nondoing is the art there, just as doing is the art in the outside world.

This passive alertness is the key. But don't become disturbed by language. Start with effort. Just keep in mind that you have to leave it, and go on leaving it. Even leaving will be an effort; but a moment comes when everything has gone. Then you are there, simply there not doing anything—just there, being. That "being-ness" is what is meant by enlightenment, and all that is worth knowing, worth having, worth being, happens to you in that state.

> *?* You have also said to ignore negative mind contents and not give energy to them. I find it difficult to stay on the razor's edge of ignoring without falling into suppressing and thus putting things back into the unconscious. Can you please tell me how to discriminate between these two?

You already know it, your question contains the discrimination. You know perfectly well when you are ignoring and when you are suppressing. Ignoring simply means not paying attention to it. Something is there; let it be there. You are unconcerned this way or that, whether it should remain or go. You have no judgment. You have simply accepted that it is there, and it is none of your business whether it should be there or not.

In suppressing you are taking an active part. You are wrestling with that energy, you are forcing it into the unconscious.

You are trying not to be able to see it anywhere. You want to know that it is no longer there.

For example, anger is there; just sit silently and watch that the anger is there. Let it remain. How long can it remain? Do you think it is something immortal, eternal? Just as it has come, it will be gone. You simply wait. You don't do anything about it, for or against. If you do something for, you are expressing it, and when you are expressing it you are getting into a mess because the other person may not be a meditator—most probably he will not be. He will also react, and with greater rage. Now you are in a vicious circle. You are angry, you made the other angry, and you go on becoming angry with each other more and more. Sooner or later your anger will become almost a solid rock of hatred, violence. And while you are moving in this vicious circle you are losing consciousness. You may do something for which you will repent later on. You may murder, you may kill, or at least you may attempt to. And after the episode is over you may wonder: "I never thought that I could murder somebody!" But you created the energy, and energy can do anything. Energy is neutral. It can create, it can destroy; it can light your house or it can set your house on fire.

Ignoring means you are not doing anything about it. The anger is there. Just take note of it, that anger is there, just the way you see a tree is there outside. Do you have to do something about it? A cloud is moving in the sky; do you have to do something about it? Anger is also a cloud moving on the screen of your mind. So watch; let it move.

And it is not a question of being on a razor's edge. Don't make small things into big things. This is a very small thing and can be done very simply; you just have to accept that it is there. Don't try to remove it, don't try to act upon it, and don't feel ashamed that you are angry. Even if you feel ashamed, you have started acting— can't you be a nondoer?

Sadness is there, anger is there. Just watch. And be ready for a surprise; if you can watch, and your watchfulness is uncontaminated, is pure—you are really not doing anything, but simply looking—the anger will slowly pass by. The sadness will disappear, and you will be left with such a clean consciousness. You were not so clean before, because the possibility of anger was there. Now that possibility has become actual, and the possibility is gone with the anger. You are far cleaner. You were not so silent, so peaceful; now you are. Sadness had taken up some energy; it would not have allowed you a deep sense of happiness, it would have clouded your consciousness. Anger, sadness, and all the other negative emotions are eating your energy. They are all there because you have repressed them, and because they are repressed you don't let them out. You have closed the door and you have put them in the basement; they cannot escape. Even if they want to escape, you won't let them out. And they will disturb your whole life. In the night they will become nightmares, ugly dreams. In the day they will affect your actions.

And there is always a possibility that some emotion may become too big to control. You have been repressing and repressing and repressing, and the cloud is becoming bigger. A point comes when you cannot control it anymore. Then something happens, which the world will see as you doing, but those who know can see that you are not doing it, you are under a great impulsive force. You are behaving like a robot; you are helpless.

You are murdering, you are raping, you are doing something ugly—but in fact you are not doing it. You have collected all that material, which has become so powerful that now it can force you to do things: things in spite of you, things against you. Even while you are doing it you know it is not right. You know, "I should not be doing it. Why am I doing it?" But still you will do it.

Many murderers in many courts of the world have said very honestly that they have not murdered. But the court cannot believe it, the law cannot believe it. I can believe it, but the courts and the law are all primitive, they have not come to maturity. They are not yet psychologically based. They are simply the revenge of the society—put into beautiful words, but it is really nothing but the same thing the man has done. He has murdered, now the society wants to murder him. He was alone, but the society has the law, the court, the police, the jail. And it will go through a long ritual to prove to itself, "We are not murdering the man, we are simply trying to prevent crime." But this is not the fact.

If you want to prevent crime, then your law should be based more on psychology, psychoanalysis, meditation. Then you will be able to see that no individual has ever done anything wrong, just your whole society is wrong. The society is wrong because it teaches people to repress, and when they repress there comes a point when what they have repressed starts overflowing and they are simply helpless. They are victims. All your criminals are victims, and your judges and politicians and priests are criminals. But this has been going on for centuries, so it has become accepted.

Don't do anything, just ignore . . . and it is not difficult, it is a very simple phenomenon. For example, there is a chair in your room. Can't you ignore it? Do you have to do something about it? There is no need to do anything about it. Just take a look at the contents of your mind from a distance, just a little distance so that you can see, "This is anger, this is sadness, this is anguish, this is anxiety, this is worry," and so on and so forth. Let them be there. "I am unconcerned. I am not going to do anything for or against." And they will start disappearing.

If you can learn a simple thing, of letting these things disappear, you will have such a clarity of consciousness: your vision will be so penetrating, your insight so far-reaching that not only will it change your individuality, it will allow the repressed contents in the unconscious to surface. Seeing that you have learned not to repress, things will start moving out. They want to go out into the world. Nobody wants to live in your basement in the darkness! Seeing that you are allowing things to move out, and they need not wait for the night when you are asleep, they will start coming up. You will see them coming up from the basement of your being and moving out from your consciousness. Slowly your unconscious will be empty.

And this is the miracle, the magic: if the unconscious is empty, the wall between the conscious and unconscious collapses. It all becomes consciousness. First you had only one-tenth of your mind conscious; now you have all ten parts together, conscious. You are ten times more conscious. And the process can go deeper; it can release the collective unconscious. The key is the same. It can release the cosmic unconscious. And if you can clean all the unconscious parts below your consciousness, you will have such a beautiful awareness that to enter into the superconscious will be as easy as a bird taking wing.

It is your open sky. It is just that you were so loaded . . . so much weight that you could not fly. Now there is no weight. You are so light that gravitation loses its force over your mind; you can fly to the superconscious, to the collective conscious, to the cosmic conscious.

Godliness is within your reach. You just have to release the devils you have been forcing into unconsciousness. Release those devils and godliness is within your reach. And both things can happen together. As the lower part is cleaned, the upper world becomes available to you. Remember, again I say, it is a simple process.

What is the relationship between mastery over the self and control?

They are contraries. Mastery over the self has no self in it; it is utterly selfless. Mastery is there, but there is no self to master; there is nothing to master or to be mastered, there is only pure consciousness. In that purity you are part of the whole; in that purity you are godliness itself. But there is no self.

When we say "self-mastery" we are using wrong language. But nothing can be done, because all language is wrong at those heights; in those moments of plenitude no word is adequate. In control there is self; in control there is more self than ever. The uncontrolled person has not that much self, that much ego—how can he have? He knows his weaknesses.

That's why you will come across the strange phenomenon that your so-called saints are more egoistic than sinners. The sinners are more human, more humble. The saints are almost inhuman because of their control: they think they are supra-human because they can control their instincts, they can go on long fasts, they can remain sexually starved for years or for their whole life. They can remain awake for days together, not a single moment's sleep because they can have such control over the body, over the mind, it naturally gives them a great ego. It feeds their idea that "I am somebody special." It nourishes their disease.

The sinner is more humble. He has to be; he knows he cannot control anything. When anger comes he becomes angry. When love comes he becomes loving. When sadness comes he becomes sad. He has no control over his emotions. When he is hungry he is ready to do anything to get food; even if he has to steal he will do it. He will find every possible way.

A famous Sufi story:

Mulla Nasruddin and two other saints went for a pilgrimage to Mecca. They were passing through a village, it was the last phase of their journey. Their money was almost finished; just a little bit was left. They purchased a certain sweet called halva, but it was not enough for all the three and they were so hungry. What to do? And they were not even ready to divide it because then it would not fulfill anybody's hunger. So everybody started bragging about himself that "I am more important to existence, so my life has to be saved."

The first saint said, "I have been fasting, I have been praying for so many years; nobody here present is more religious and holy than I am. And God wants me to be saved, so the halva has to be given to me."

The second saint said, "Yes, I know, you are a man of great austerities, but I am a great scholar. I have studied all the scriptures, my whole life I have devoted in service of knowledge. The world does not need people who can fast. What can you do? You can only fast. You can fast in heaven! The world needs knowledge. The world is so ignorant that it cannot afford to miss me. The halva has to be given to me."

Mulla Nasruddin said, "I am not an ascetic, so I cannot claim any self-control. I am not a very knowledgeable person either, so I cannot claim that either. I am an ordinary sinner, and I have heard that God is always compassionate to the sinners. The halva belongs to me."

They could not come to any conclusion. Finally they decided that all three should sleep without eating the halva: "Let God himself decide: whoever is given the best dream by God, in the morning that dream will be decisive."

In the morning the saint said, "Nobody can compete with me anymore, now it is certain. Give me the halva, because in the dream I kissed God's feet. That is the ultimate that one can hope for—what greater experience can there be?"

The scholar, the knowledgeable man, laughed and he said, "That is nothing—because God hugged me and kissed me! You kissed his feet? He kissed *me* and hugged me! Where is the halva? It belongs to me."

They looked at Nasruddin and asked, "What dream did you have?"

Nasruddin said, "I am a poor sinner, my dream was very ordinary—so ordinary it is not even worth telling. But because you insist and because we have agreed, I will tell you. In my sleep, God appeared and he said, 'You fool! What are you doing? Eat the halva!' And how could I disobey his order? So there is no halva left now, I have eaten it."

Self-control gives you the subtlest ego. Self-control has more "self" in it than anything else. But self-mastery is a totally different phenomenon; it has no self in it. Control is cultivated, practiced; with great effort you have to manage it. It is a long struggle, then you arrive at it. Mastery is not a cultivated thing, it is not to be practiced. Mastery is nothing but understanding. It is not control at all.

For example, you can control anger, you can repress it, you can sit on top of it. Nobody will know what you have done, and you will be praised by people that in such a situation where anybody would have become angry, you remained so calm and collected and cool. But you know that all that calmness and coolness was on the surface and that deep down you were boiling. Deep down there was fire, but you repressed it in the unconscious, you forced it deep into your unconscious and you sat upon it like a volcano, and you are still sitting on it.

The man of control is the man of repression. He goes on repressing, and because he goes on repressing, he goes on accumulating all that is wrong. His whole life becomes a junkyard. Sooner or later, and it is going to be sooner than later, the volcano explodes—because there is only a certain limit you can contain. You repress anger, you repress sex, you repress all kinds of desires, longings—how long can you go on repressing? You can contain only so much, then one day it is more than you can control. It explodes.

Your so-called saints, men of self-control, can be provoked very easily. Just scratch a little, and you will be surprised; the animal comes up immediately. Their saintliness is not even skin-deep; they are carrying many demons in themselves that they are somehow managing. And their life is a life of misery, because it is a life of constant struggle. They are neurotic people and they are on the verge of insanity, always on the verge. Any small thing can just prove the last straw on the camel. They are not religious in my vision of life.

The truly religious person controls nothing, represses nothing. If you are a truly religious person you try to understand, not to control. You become more meditative, you watch your anger, your sex, your greed, your jealousy, your possessiveness. You watch all these poisonous things that surround you, simply watch, try to understand what anger is, and in that very understanding you transcend. You become a witness, and in that witnessing the anger melts as if the sun has risen and the snow has started melting.

Understanding brings a certain warmth; it is a sunrise inside you and the ice starts melting around you. It is like a flame inside you and darkness starts disappearing.

The man of understanding, meditation, is not a man of control—just the opposite. He is a watcher. And if you want to watch, you have to be absolutely nonjudgmental. The man who controls is judgmental, continuously condemning: "This is wrong." Continuously appraising: "This is good, this is evil, this will lead to hell, this will lead to heaven." He is constantly judging, condemning, praising, choosing. The man of control lives in choice, and the man of understanding lives in choicelessness.

It is choiceless awareness that brings real transformation. And because nothing is repressed, no ego arises. No "self" arises. And because understanding is a subjective, interior phenomenon, nobody knows about it. Nobody can see it except you. And the ego comes from the outside, from other people, what they say about you. It is others' opinion about you that creates the ego. They say you are intelligent, they say you are so saintly, they say you are so pious—and naturally you feel great! Ego is derived from the outside, it is given by others to you. Of course, they say one thing in front of you and they say something else, just the opposite, behind your back.

Sigmund Freud used to say that even if for twenty-four hours we decide that every person on the earth will say only the truth, and only the truth, then all friendship will disappear. All love affairs will dissolve, all marriages will go down the drain. If a decision is taken that the whole of humanity will practice only what is truthful and nothing else only for twenty-four hours . . . When a guest knocks on your door you will not say, "Come in, welcome, I was just waiting for you. How long it has been that I have not seen you! How long I have suffered, where have you been? You make my heart throb with joy." You will say the truth that you are feeling. You will say, "So this son-of-a-bitch has come again! Now, how to get rid of this bastard?" That is deep inside, that is what you are controlling. You will say it to somebody else behind the person's back.

Watch yourself, what you say to people to their face and what you say behind their backs. What you say behind a person's back is far truer, closer to your feeling, than what you say to his face. But the ego depends on what people say to you, and it is very fragile—so fragile that on each ego it is written "Handle with Care."

Pieracki, a Pole, Odum, a black man, and Alvarez, a Mexican, were out of work and living together. Pieracki came home one night and announced he had got a job. "Hey, fellas, wake me up tomorrow at six," he said. "I have to be at work by six-thirty!"

While Pieracki slept, Odum said to Alvarez, "He got a job because he is white. We can't get one because I am black and you are brown." So during the night they put

shoeblack all over Pieracki, and they agreed on a plan to
wake him late so that he would have to rush out right
away to make it to work on time.

Next morning when Pieracki arrived at work, the fore-
man said, "Who are you?"

"You hired me yesterday," he replied. "You told me to
be here at six-thirty!"

"I hired a white man—you're black!"

"I'm not!"

"Yes, you are! Go and look in the mirror!"

The Pole rushed over to the mirror, looked at himself
and exclaimed, "My God! They woke up the wrong man!"

Your ego depends on mirrors. And every relationship functions as a mirror, every person you meet functions as a mirror,
and this ego goes on controlling you.

And why does it control in the first place? It controls because
the society appreciates control, because the society gives you even
more ego if you control. If you follow the ideas of the society, its
morality, its puritanism, its ideas of holiness, it praises you more
and more. More and more people pay respect to you; your ego goes
higher and higher, soars higher.

But remember, ego will never bring any transformation to
you. Ego is the most unconscious phenomenon that is happening
in you; it will make you more and more unconscious. And the person who lives through the ego is almost drunk with it; he is not in
his senses.

Fernando was getting married. There was a big wed-
ding feast and the wine flowed like water. Things were
going fine until Fernando couldn't find his beautiful bride.
After looking over the guests he found that his pal, Luis,
was also missing.

> Fernando started searching the premises. He looked
> into the bridal chamber and discovered Luis making love
> to his bride. Fernando closed the door softly, and crept
> down the stairs to his guests.
>
> "Queek! Queek! Everybody come look!" he shouted.
> "Luis ees so drunk he theenk he ees me!"

The ego keeps you almost in a drunken state. You don't know who you are because you believe what others say about you. And you don't know who others are because you believe what others say about others. This is the make-believe, illusory world in which we live.

Wake up, become more conscious. By becoming conscious you will become a master of your own being. Mastery knows nothing of self, and the self knows nothing of mastery. Let that be absolutely clear to you.

My teaching is not for self-control, self-discipline. My teaching is for self-awareness, self-transformation. I would like you to become as vast as the sky—because that's what you really are.

THOUGHT, FEELING, ACTION

Understanding Your "Type"

Thoughts are a preoccupation. People who are too much in thoughts remain in a private kind of world. They have their own world of thoughts and dreams and projections and desires. They go on rushing here and there, but they don't look at the trees, the greenery, the flowers, the birds, the people, the children; they can't see anything.

I have heard a very old joke, but one of tremendous importance:

Michelangelo was working on his famous ceiling in the Sistine Chapel. For seven years he worked on a high scaffolding, and he was lying there the whole day on his back working on the ceiling. Many times he had noticed that in the afternoons, when there was nobody else in the church, an old blind woman would come to pray. Somebody would bring her in and leave her there, and for hours she would sit and pray.

One day, one hot afternoon, Michelangelo was not feeling like working so he sat up on his scaffolding and looked down. Only the old woman was there, the rest of the church was utterly empty. And she was doing her usual prayer and tears were coming to her eyes . . . Michelangelo was in a joking mood.

He shouted down, "I am Jesus Christ. What do you want? Just tell me and I will fulfill it." He was expecting that the woman would say what she wanted. But the woman raised her face, with her blind eyes, and said, "You shut up! I am not talking to you, I am talking to your mother!"

This is preoccupation. Who bothers about Jesus Christ? When you are in a certain thought or in a certain thought process you become closed. Only that much of a tunnel remains open. You move in that tunnel, and that tunnel of your thoughts has nothing to do with reality. It is your *thought*, it is just a vibe in your mind, just a vibration. That's why it is said that if you are too much in your thoughts you cannot know the truth.

All kinds of meditations presuppose one thing, and that is thoughtlessness. And just as there are thoughts in the mind, so there are emotions in the heart. Thoughts have to go if you want knowing to arise, and if you want loving to arise in your heart, then your sentimentality and your emotions have to go.

People are ready to accept that thoughts have to go and then your intelligence is pure, but they have not contemplated the second thing—that your heart is pure only when your emotions and your so-called sentiments have gone. Many people think sentimentality to be feeling; it is not. Thoughts are not intelligence and sentimentality is not love. And there are only two ways.

All the mystics talk about two ways: the way of knowing, of intelligence, and the way of feelings, of love. But both need the same essential thing. If you are searching through intelligence, then drop thinking so that intelligence can function unhindered. And if you are working through the path of love, then drop emotionality, sentimentality, so that your love can function unhindered. Either you will see the truth through the heart, the mirror of the heart, or you will see it through the mirror of your intelligence. Both are perfectly good; whatever you choose or whatever you feel is more in accord with you.

The path of the heart is the feminine path and the path of intelligence, meditation, knowing, is the male path. But remember one thing: you may be a male biologically but you may not be a male psychologically. You may be a female biologically but you may not be a female psychologically. You have to look into yourself psychologically. The physiology does not decide, the psychology does. Many women will find through knowing, and many men will find through loving.

So don't just take it for granted that because physiologically you have a male body the path of knowledge is your path, no. A man is both man and woman, and a woman is both woman and man. In many ways these two points meet. The only difference is of emphasis. And if you are a male in one way you will be a female in another way, to compensate. If you are a woman in one way you will be a man in another way to compensate, because the total unity has to be absolutely in equilibrium. All your feminine and masculine aspects—biological, physiological, psychological—have to come to a synthesis; otherwise you cannot exist. They all have to be absolutely balanced.

So look into your own self. Find out who you are. What gives you enthusiasm, knowing, or loving? What makes you ecstatic, knowing, or loving? What gives you a song in your being?

Now Albert Einstein cannot go through the path of love; his joy is his intelligence. And you can offer existence only your joy, nothing else. That is the offering, the only offering; you cannot offer flowers from trees, you can offer only *your* flowering. Einstein has flowered as an absolutely beautiful intelligence—that is the flower that he has to offer to existence. That is *his* flower; in his own tree that flower has bloomed. A Chaitanya or a Jesus are a different kind of people. Their heart has opened, they have flowered in love. They can offer *their* flower. You can only offer your own flowering, and to flower you will have to remove the hindrances.

A real intelligence is free from any preoccupation with thoughts. That's why all the great scientists say that whenever they have discovered something, they have discovered it not while they were thinking but when the thinking stopped and there was an interval, a gap. In that gap was the insight: the intuitive flash, like lightning.

When thought stops, your thinking is pure. It will look paradoxical. When thought stops—let me repeat it—your thinking is pure, your capacity to reflect reality is pure. When emotions disappear, sentimentality disappears, then your love energy is pure.

Every seeker has to find it. Even though sometimes it will be very confusing for you to decide. There are marginal cases who are forty-nine percent feminine and fifty-one percent male, or visa versa, and it is very difficult for them to decide who they are. In the morning the proportion may be forty-nine percent man, fifty-one percent woman; in the evening the proportion may change. You are a flux. In the morning you may decide that you are on the path of love and by the evening you decide that you are on the path of knowing.

Sometimes it happens that on the surface you are one thing and potentially you are another. Sometimes it happens that a man looks very manly, and deep inside he has a very soft heart. Maybe it is just because of the soft heart that he has created an armor around himself of strength, of aggression—because he is afraid of his own softness. He is afraid that that softness will make him vulnerable, that if he opens his heart he will be exploited and cheated by everybody, he will be nowhere in this competitive world. Being afraid of his softness he has become closed, he has put a Great Wall of China around his heart. He has become aggressive in the same proportion that he feels he is soft and vulnerable. So if he thinks about himself in terms of the surface he will think he is a very hard man, a warrior type, a very calculative man. He may be misguided by his own armor, he may be deceived by his own deception. He had created that deception for others, but one thing to be understood is that when you dig a ditch for others, finally you fall into it yourself.

Or there may be somebody who looks very, very feminine— soft, graceful, elegant—and deep down he may be a very dangerous man, an Adolf Hitler or a Benito Mussolini or a Genghis Khan. That too is possible, that too happens. When a person becomes so afraid of his own aggression and violence, he creates a softness around himself; otherwise, nobody will relate to him. He is afraid that nobody will relate to him so he becomes very polite, he learns etiquette, he is always bowing to people, always smiling so that nobody can see the violence that he is carrying like a poison, like a dagger. If you have a dagger you have to hide it; otherwise, who is going to relate to you? You cannot carry it in the open, you have to hide it somewhere. And once you have hidden it somewhere, by and by you yourself forget about it.

One of the functions of a master is to help you to look into your real potentiality, because that is decisive: not your armor, not your character, not who you appear to be on the surface, but you in the deepest core of your being. You as existence has created you, not you as the society or you yourself have created you. Only from that point do things start growing.

If you start working on yourself still carrying your armor, you will never grow, because armor can't grow, it is a dead thing. Only your being can grow. Structures don't grow, they are not alive. Only the life in you can grow: the life that is a gift from nature.

And meditation can happen in two ways. One is that all

movement disappears—then you sit like a Buddha, utterly still, like a statue. When all movement disappears the mover disappears, because the mover cannot exist without the movement. Then there is meditation.

Or, two, you dance. You go on dancing and dancing and dancing and a moment comes of such ecstasy, of such extreme movement of energy, that in that movement the rock-like ego cannot exist. It becomes a whirlwind. The rock disappears and there is only dance. The movement is there but the mover is no more there. Again, meditation has happened.

Those who are following the path of love, for them dance will suit perfectly. Those who are following the path of knowing, for them sitting Buddha-like, unmoving, will be helpful.

> **Can you say more about the different types? Many people seem to fluctuate between the emotional and the intellectual—so how can one come to a final decision about which type one belongs to?**

It is difficult. Psychology recognizes three basic types of functioning. The first is intellectual, or cognitive. The second is emotional, or emotive, and the third is active. "Intellectual" means one whose authentic urge is to know. He can stake his life for knowing. Someone working on poison can take poison just to know what happens. We cannot conceive of it. He looks stupid—because he will die! What is the meaning of knowing a thing if you are going to die? What will you do with this knowledge? But then the intellectual type puts knowing above living, above life. To know is life for him, not to know is death for him. To know is his love, not to know is just to be useless.

A Socrates, a Buddha, a Nietzsche, they are in search of knowing what being is, what we are; to them this is basic. Socrates says an uncomprehended life is not worth living. If you don't know what life is, then it is meaningless. For us it may not look at all meaningful, the statement may not look meaningful at all, because we go on living and we don't feel the need to know what life is. But this is the type who lives to know. Knowledge is his love. This type developed philosophy. *Philosophy* means "love of knowledge, to know."

The second type is emotive, to feel. For this type, knowledge is meaningless unless one feels it. Something becomes meaningful to them only when one feels it—one must feel it! Feeling is through a deeper center, the heart. Knowing is through the intellect. Poets belong to this category of feeling—painters, dancers, musicians. Knowing is not enough. It is just dry, it is without heart, heartless. Feeling is the thing! So an intellectual type can dissect a flower in order to know what it is, but a poet cannot dissect it. He can love it, and how can love dissect a flower? He can feel it, and he knows that only through feeling is the real knowing.

So it may be that a scientist knows more about a flower but still, a poet will never be convinced that the scientist knows more. A poet knows that *he* knows more, and he knows deeply. A scientist is only acquainted; the poet knows from heart to heart, he has a talk with the flower heart to heart. He has not dissected it, he doesn't know what the chemistry of it is. He may not even know the name, to what species this flower belongs, but he says, "I know the very spirit."

Hui-Hai, a Zen painter, was ordered by the Chinese Emperor to paint some flowers for his palace. Hui-Hai said, "Then I will have to live with flowers."

But the Emperor said, "There is no need. In my garden every flower is there. You go and paint!"

Hui Hai said, "Unless I feel the flowers, how can I paint? I must know the spirit. And by eyes how can the spirit be known, and by hands how can the spirit be touched? So I will have to live in intimacy with them. Sometimes with closed eyes, just sitting by their side, just feeling the breeze that communicates, just feeling the scent that comes, I can be just in a silent communion with them. Sometimes the flower is just a bud, sometimes the flower flowers. Sometimes the flower is young and the mood is different, and sometimes the flower becomes old and death lingers nearby. And sometimes the flower is happy and celebrating, and sometimes the flower is sad. So how can I just go and paint? I will have to live with the flowers. And each flower that is born, one day will die—I must know the whole biography, I must live with a flower from its birth to death, and I must feel it in its so many moods.

"I must know how it feels in the night when darkness is there, and how it feels in the morning when the sun has come up, and how, when a bird flies and a bird sings, how the flower feels then. How, when storm winds come, and how when everything is silent . . . I must know it in its multiplicity of being—intimately—as a friend, as a participant, as a witness, as a lover. I must be related to it! Only then can I paint it, and then too I cannot promise, because the flower may prove such a vastness that I may not be capable of painting it. So I cannot promise, I can only try."

Six months passed, and the Emperor became impatient. Then he said, "Where is that Hui-Hai? Is he still trying to commune with the flowers?"

The gardener said, "We cannot disturb him. He has become so intimate with the garden that sometimes we pass just nearby and we cannot feel that a man is there—he has become just a tree! He goes on contemplating."

Six months had passed. The Emperor went to Hui-Hai and he said, "What are you doing? When will you paint?"

Hui-Hai said, "Don't disturb me. If I am to paint, I must forget about painting completely. So don't make me remember again, and don't disturb me! How can I live intimately with the flowers if there is some purpose? How is intimacy possible if I am just here as a painter and only trying to be intimate because I have to paint? What nonsense! No business deal is possible here—and don't come again. When the right time comes I will come to you myself, but I cannot promise. The right time may come or it may not come."

For three years the Emperor waited. Then Hui-Hai came. He came into his royal court, and the Emperor looked at him. He said, "Now don't paint . . . because you have become just like a flower. I see in you all the flowers I have seen! In your eyes, in your gestures, in your movements you have become just a flower."

Hui-Hai said, "I have come just to say that I cannot paint, because the man who was thinking to paint is no more."

This is a different way, that of the emotive type who knows by feeling. For the intellectual type, even in order to feel he has to know first. He knows first, and only then can he feel. His feeling also comes through knowing.

Then there is a third type, active—a creative type. He cannot remain with knowing or feeling, he has to create. He can know only through creation. Unless he creates something, he cannot know it. Only through being a creator does he become a knower.

This third type lives in action. Now what do I mean by "action"? Many dimensions are possible, but this third type is always action-oriented. He will not ask what life means, or what life is. He will ask, "What is life to do? What is it for? What to create?" If he can create, then he is at ease. His creations may differ. He may be a creator of human beings, he may be a creator of a society, he may be a creator of a painting—but creativity is there. For example, this Hui-Hai: he was not an active type, so he dissolved himself into feeling totally. Had he been an active type, he would have painted. Only through painting would he have been fulfilled. So these are three types of functioning.

Many things have to be understood.

One, I said that Buddha and Nietzsche both belong to the first type—but Buddha belongs rightly and Nietzsche belongs wrongly. If an intellectual type really develops, then he will become a buddha. But if he goes on a wrong path, if he goes berserk and misses the point, he will become a Nietzsche, he will go mad. Through knowing he will not be a realized soul, through knowing he will become mad. Through knowing he will not come to a deep trust. He will go on creating doubts, doubts, doubts, and ultimately, trapped in his own doubts, he will just be insane. Buddha and Nietzsche both belong to the same type, but they are two extremes. Nietzsche can become a buddha, and Buddha can become a Nietzsche. If a buddha goes wrong, he will be mad. If a Nietzsche goes right, he will be a realized soul.

For the feeling type I will name the Indian mystic Meera and the Marquis de Sade. Meera belongs to the right kind of feeling type. If feeling goes right, it develops into a love of the divine — but if it goes wrong, then it becomes sexual perversity. De Sade belongs to the same type as Meera, but his feeling energies go wrongly, and then he becomes just a perverted man, just abnormally insane.

If the feeling type goes wrong, he becomes sexually perverted. If the intellectual type goes wrong, he becomes skeptically mad.

And the third type of action: Hitler and Gandhi both belong to the third type. If it goes right, then a Gandhi is there. If it goes wrong, then a Hitler. Both belong to action. They cannot live without *doing* something. But doing can be just insane, and a Hitler is insane. He was doing, but the doing became destructive. If the active type goes right, then he is creative; if wrong, then he becomes destructive.

These are three basic, pure types. But no one is a pure type; that is the difficulty. These are just categories — no one is a pure type, everyone is mixed, all the three types are in everyone. So really, it is not a question of which type you belong to; the real question is which type is predominant in you. Just to explain it to you: it can be divided, but no one is a pure type, no one can be, because all the three are in you. If all three are in a balance, then you have a harmony; if all the three are unbalanced, then you go berserk, insane. That is the difficulty in deciding. So decide which is predominant: that is your type.

How to decide which is predominant? How to know to what type I belong or what type is more significant to me, primary to me? All the three will be there, but one will be secondary. So there are two criteria to be remembered. One, if you are a knowing type then all your experiences basically will begin with knowing, never with anything else. For example, if a knowing type falls in love with someone, he cannot fall at first sight. He cannot! It is impossible. First he must know, be acquainted, and it will be a long process. Decision can come only through a long knowing process. That's why this type of person will always miss many opportunities, because a moment's decision is needed and this type cannot decide in the moment. And that's why this type is ordinarily never active. He cannot be, because by the time he can conclude, the moment has passed. While he is thinking, the moment is passing. By the time he comes to a conclusion, the conclusion is meaningless. When the moment was there to conclude, he could not do it. So he cannot be active, really. And this is one of the calamities in the world: that those who can think cannot be active, and those who can be active cannot think. This is one of the basic calamities, but it is so.

And always remember: the knowing type consists of very few. The percentage is very small, two or three percent at the most. For them everything will begin by knowing. Only then will feeling follow and only then action. This will be the sequence with this type—knowing, feeling, action. He may miss, but he cannot do otherwise. He will always think first.

The second thing to remember is that this knowing type will begin with knowing, will never conclude before knowing, and will not take any standpoint unless both pro and con have been known. This type becomes a scientist. This type can become an absolutely impartial philosopher, scientist, observer.

So whatever your reaction or action is in situations, find out where it begins. The beginning point will decide the predominance. One who belongs to emotion will begin to feel first, and then will gather all the reasons. Reasoning will be secondary. He will begin to feel first. He sees you and he decides in his heart that you are good or you are bad. This decision is a feeling decision. He doesn't know about you, but at first sight he will decide. He will feel whether you are good or you are bad, and then he will go on accumulating reasons for whatever he has already decided beforehand.

The feeling type decides first—then reasoning follows, then he rationalizes. So look to see in yourself whether you decide first, upon just seeing a person, whether you become convinced that he is good, bad, loving, nonloving, and then you create reasons, then you try to convince yourself about your own feeling: "Yes, I was right, he is good, and these are the reasons. I knew it all along, and now I have found out I was right. I have talked with others. Now I can say he is good." But the conclusion came first that "he is good."

So with a feeling type the syllogism of logic is just operating in reverse. The conclusion comes first, then the process. With the reasoning type, the conclusion never comes first. First the process, then he concludes in the end.

So go on finding out about yourself. What is your way of deciding things? With the active type, action is first. He decides in the moment to act, then he begins to feel, then in the end he creates reasons.

I told you that Gandhi is an active type. He decides first; that's why he will say, "This is not my decision, God decided in me." Action comes to him so immediately, with no process, how can he say, "I have decided"? A thinking type will always say, "I have decided." A feeling type will always say, "I feel like that." But an active type—a Mohammed, a Gandhi—they will always say, "Neither have I felt, nor have I thought. This decision has come to me." From where? From nowhere! If he doesn't believe in God, then he will say, "From nowhere! This decision has bubbled up in me. I don't know from where."

If he believes in God, then God becomes the decision maker. Then God initiates everything, and Gandhi goes on doing his part. Gandhi can say, "I erred, but the decision was not mine." He can say, "I may not have followed rightly, I may not have understood the message rightly, I may not have gone as far as I should, but the decision was God's. I had just to fall in behind it, I had just to surrender and follow." For Mohammed, for Gandhi, that is the way.

I said that Hitler is a wrong type, but he also talks in these terms. He also says, "This is not Adolf Hitler who is speaking, this is the very spirit of history. This is the whole Aryan mind! This is a racial mind speaking through me." And, really, many of those who heard Hitler felt that when he was speaking he was not Adolf Hitler at all. It was as if he was just a vehicle of a greater force.

The active man always looks like that. Because he acts so immediately, you cannot say that he decides, he thinks, he feels. No, he acts! And the action is so spontaneous, how can you imagine from where the action comes? Either it comes from God or it comes from the Devil, but it comes from somewhere else. And then Hitler and Gandhi will both go on reasoning about it; but they will decide first.

So these are the three types. If action comes to you first and then feeling and then thinking, then you can determine your predominant characteristic. And to determine that predominant factor is very helpful, because then you can proceed straight; otherwise your progress will always be zigzag. When you don't know what type you are, you go on unnecessarily into dimensions and directions that are not suited to you. When you know your type, you know what is to be done with yourself, how to do it, from where to begin.

The first thing is to note what comes first and what second. And the second might look very strange. For example, the active type can do the opposite very easily; that is, he can relax very easily. Gandhi's relaxation was miraculous, he could relax anywhere. So it seems very paradoxical. One would think that an active type must be so tense that he could not relax, but this is not the case. Only an active type can relax so easily. A thinking type cannot relax easily, a feeling type finds it even more difficult to relax, but an active can relax very easily.

So the second criterion is that whatever the type to which you belong, you can move to the opposite very easily. In other words, if you can move to the opposite, that is an indication of your predominant type. If you can relax very easily, you belong to the active type. If you can go into nonthinking, no-thought, very easily, then you belong to the thinking type. If you can go into no-feeling very easily, you belong to the feeling type.

This seems strange because ordinarily we think, "A feeling type—how can he go into nonfeeling? A thinking type, how can he go into nonthinking? An active type, how can he go into non-action?" But it only appears paradoxical; it is not. It is one of the basic laws that opposites belong together, two extremes belong together. Just like the pendulum of a big clock goes to the extreme left, then to the extreme right. And when it has reached the peak at the right, it begins to move toward the left. When it is going to the right, it is accumulating momentum for going left. When it is going left, it is getting ready to go right. So the opposite is easy.

Remember, if you can relax easily, you belong to the active type. If you can meditate easily, you belong to the thinking type. That's why a Buddha can go into meditation so easily, and that's why a Gandhi can relax so easily. Whenever he would find time, Gandhi would sleep. Sleep was so easy for him.

A Buddha can go into nonthinking, a Socrates can go into non-thinking, very easily. Ordinarily, it looks odd. A person who can think so much, how can he just dissolve thinking? How can he just go into no-thought? Buddha's whole message is of no-thought, and he was a thinking type. He has thought so much, re-ally, that he is still contemporary. Twenty-five centuries have passed but Buddha still belongs to the contemporary mind. No one belongs to the contemporary mind as much as Buddha does. Even a present-day thinker cannot say that Buddha is out of date. He has thought much, centuries ahead of his time, and he still has an appeal. So whoever is a thinker anywhere, Buddha has an appeal for him because he is the purest type. But his message is "Go into nonthinking." Those who have thought deeply have al-ways said to go into nonthinking.

And the feeling type can go into nonfeeling. For example, Meera is a feeling type; Chaitanya is a feeling type. Their feeling is so great that they cannot remain loving just toward a few per-sons or a few things. They must love the whole world. This is their type. They cannot be satisfied with limited love. Love must be unlimited; it must spread to the infinite.

One day Chaitanya went to a teacher. He had become enlight-ened in his own right; his name was known all over Bengal. He went to a teacher of Vedanta and put his head at the teacher's feet. The teacher was taken aback, because he respected Chaitanya so much. He said, "Why have you come to me? What do you want? You have realized yourself, I cannot teach you anything." Chaitanya said, "Now I want to move into *vairagya*, nonattachment. I have lived the life of feeling and now I want to move into no-feeling. So help me."

A feeling type can move to nonattachment, and Chaitanya moved that way. Ramakrishna was the feeling type, and in the end he moved to Vedanta. His whole life he was a devotee of the Mother Goddess Kali, and then in the end he became a disciple of a Vedanta teacher, Totapuri, and was initiated into a nonfeeling world. Many people said to Totapuri, "How can you initiate this man Ramakrishna? He is a feeling type! For him love is the only thing. He can pray, he can worship, he can dance, he can go into ecstasy. He cannot move to nonattachment, he cannot move to the realm beyond feelings."

Totapuri said, "That's why he *can* move, and I will initiate him. You cannot move; he will move."

So the second criterion to decide is if you can move to the opposite. See what the beginning is, and then whether the movement is toward the opposite. These are the two things. And search within yourself constantly. For twenty-one days, continuously note these two things. First, how you react to a situation—what the beginning is, the seed, the start—and then to what opposite you can move easily. To nonthinking? To nonfeeling? To nonaction? And within twenty-one days you can come to an understanding of your type—the predominant one, of course.

The other two will be there like shadows, because pure types never exist. They cannot. All the three are within you; only one is more significant than the others. And once you know what type you are, your path becomes very easy and smooth. Then you don't waste your energy. Then you don't dissipate your energy unnecessarily on paths that don't belong to you.

Otherwise, you can go on doing many things, and you create only confusion, you create only a disintegration. Even to fail according to your own nature is good, because even that failure will enrich you. You will be matured through it, you will know much through it, you will become much through it. So even failure is good if it is according to one's own type.

Find out to which type you belong, or which type is predominant. Then, according to that type, begin to work. Then the work will be easy.

? Can you say something about what kinds of
meditation techniques or approaches are
most appropriate for each type of person?
I feel like I'm more a "heart" or "feeling"
type, but I'm not sure.

The heart has a different way of communication. It is an energy communication, which, it is said, many saints in the world have had. St. Francis of Assisi is the most famous. Now it has become a matter of scientific truth; now many researchers all over the world say that plants have very deep sensitivity, deeper than human beings, because human sensitivity is disturbed by the mind, the intellect. Man has completely forgotten how to feel; even when he says "I feel," in fact he *thinks* he feels.

People come to me and they say, "We are in love." And if I insist: "*Really*, are you in love?" they shrug their shoulders and they say, "Well, we *think* we are in love." The feeling is not direct, it comes through the head. And when feeling comes through the head it is confused. It is not bubbling up from the heart.

But scientific researchers have come to know that not only birds but plants, and not only plants, even metals, have a sensitivity. They feel—and they feel tremendously. They give messages that you may not be able to catch, but now scientists have created instruments that can detect the messages given by them. If they are in fear they start trembling. You may not be able to see the trembling; it is very subtle. Even with no wind blowing, the detectors show that the plant inside is trembling very much. When they are happy, they are ecstatic; the instruments show that the plants are ecstatic. When they are in pain, afraid, filled with anger, rage—all sorts of feelings can now be detected.

Something very deep has happened to man: a wound, an accident. He has lost touch with his feelings.

If you talk long enough to trees, to birds, to animals—and if you don't feel foolish, because the mind will interfere and say that this is foolish—if you don't listen to the mind, but you bypass it and connect directly, a tremendous energy of feeling will be released in you. You will become totally a new sort of being. You had never known it was possible to be this way. You will become sensitive—sensitive to pain and pleasure.

That's why humanity has stopped the functioning of feeling: because when you become sensitive to pleasure, you also become sensitive to pain. The more you can feel happy the more you can feel unhappy also.

That fear, that one can become very unhappy, has closed you, has helped the human mind to create barriers so that you cannot feel. When you cannot feel, then doorways are closed. You cannot become unhappy, and you cannot become happy either.

But try it; it is a kind of prayerfulness, because it is heart to heart. First try with human beings—just with your own child, sit silently with the child and allow feeling. Don't bring the mind in. Sit with your wife, or with your friend, or your husband, holding hands together in a dark room, not doing anything, just trying to feel each other. In the beginning it will be difficult, but by and by you will have a different mechanism functioning within you and you will start *feeling*.

Some people can revive their heartfulness very easily. It is not dead in them. For others it may be difficult. Some people are body oriented, some are heart oriented, some are head oriented. Those who are heart oriented can revive this kind of feeling very easily.

Those who are head oriented, it will be difficult for them to have any feeling. For them, prayer does not exist. Gautam Buddha, and Mahavira, the Jain mystic who lived around the same time, were head-oriented people. That's why prayer was not a part of their teachings. They were intelligent people, well trained intellectually, logically. They developed meditation but they have not talked about prayer. Nothing like prayer exists in Jainism; it cannot exist. It exists in Islam—Mohammed is a heart-oriented person, he has a different quality. It exists in Christianity—Jesus is a heart-oriented person. It exists in Hinduism, but not in Buddhism or Jainism. There is nothing like prayer in those approaches.

And some people are body oriented. They are the potential hedonists. For them there is no prayer, no meditation—only indulgence in the body. That is their primary way of being happy, their primary way of being.

So if you are a heart-oriented person—if you feel more than you think, if music gives you deep stirrings, if poetry touches you, if beauty surrounds you and you can feel—then the more prayerful approaches are for you. Then start talking to birds and trees—and the sky, it will be helpful. But don't make it a mind thing, let it be heart to heart. Be related.

That's why people of the heart think about God as a father or as a beloved, some energy with which they are deeply related. The head-oriented people are always laughing: What nonsense are you talking? God, the father? Then where is the mother? They always make a joke out of it because they cannot understand. For them, God is truth. For the people of the heart, God is love. And for the people of the body, the world is God—their money, their house, their car, their power, their prestige.

A person who is body oriented needs a different type of approach. In fact only recently in the West, particularly in America, a new sort of work has arisen that is for the body-oriented man. That work is based in body sensitivity. A new sort of spirituality is being born.

In the past there have been two types of spiritual approaches: meditation oriented and prayer oriented. There has never been a body-oriented approach to spirituality. There have been body-oriented people but they have always said that there is no religion, because they denied prayer, they denied meditation. These are the epicureans, hedonists, the atheists who say there is no God, that we have only this body and this life is all. But they never created a religion.

But now a new approach toward entering into the innermost core of life is gaining hold for body-oriented people, and it is beautiful, because these people, they need a different type of methodology. They need an approach that allows their body to function in a religious way. For these people Tantra can be very helpful. Prayer and meditation will not be helpful. But there must be a way from the body also toward one's innermost core.

So if you are body oriented, don't be discouraged; there are ways you can reach through the body, because the body also belongs to nature and existence. If you feel you are heart-oriented, then try the prayerful, artistic expressions and approaches. If you feel you are intellect oriented, then try meditation.

> **You have developed new kinds of meditations for contemporary people—what type of person will find your meditations to be helpful?**

My meditations are different in a way. I have tried to devise methods that can be used by all three types. Much of the body is used in them, much of the heart, and much intelligence. All the three are joined together, and they work on different people in different ways.

A body-oriented person immediately loves the methods—but he loves the active parts, and he comes to see me and he says, "Wonderful, the active parts are wonderful but when I have to stand silently—then there is nothing." He feels very healthy through them; he feels more rooted in the body. For a heart-oriented person the cathartic part is more important; the heart is released, relieved of burdens, and it starts functioning in a new way. And when a third type, the type who belongs to intelligence, comes, he loves the last parts when he is just sitting or standing silently, when it becomes meditation.

Body, heart, mind—all my meditations move in the same way. They start from the body, they move through the heart, they reach to the mind and then they go beyond.

Through the body you can relate to existence. You can go to the sea and enjoy swimming in it, but then just become the body, without getting into feelings, with no thinking, just being "of the body." Lie down on the beach and let the body feel the sand, the coolness, the texture.

Run—just now I was reading a very beautiful book called *The Zen of Running*: that is for body-oriented people. The author has discovered that by running there is no need to meditate, just by running meditation happens. He must be absolutely body oriented. Nobody has ever thought that meditation is possible by running—but I know, I used to love running myself. It happens. If you go on running, if you run fast, thinking stops, because thinking cannot possibly continue when you are running very fast. For thinking an easy chair is needed; that's why we call thinkers "armchair philosophers." They sit and relax in a chair, the body completely relaxed, then the whole energy moves into the mind.

If you are running, then the whole energy moves into the body, there is no possibility for the mind to think. And when you run fast, you breathe deep, you exhale deep, you become just the body. A moment comes when you *are* the body and nothing else. In that moment you become one with the universe, because there is no division. The air flowing past you and your body become one. A deep rhythm happens.

That's why games have always been so attractive to people, and athletics. And that's why children so much love dancing, running, jumping: they are bodies! The mind has not yet developed.

If you feel you are the body type, then running can be very beautiful for you: take a four- or five-mile run every day and make it a meditation. It will transform you completely.

But if you feel you are a heart-oriented person, then talk to birds, try to have a communion. Watch! Just wait, sit silently with a deep trust and welcoming that they should come to you, and they will start coming by and by. By and by they will be sitting on your shoulders. Accept them. Talk to trees, to rocks, but let it be a heart talk, emotional. Cry and weep and laugh. Tears can be more prayerful than words, and laughter can be more prayerful than words, because they come deep down from the heart. No need to verbalize—just feel. Embrace the tree and feel it, as if you are becoming one with it. And soon you will feel that the sap is not running only in the tree, it has started to run in you. Your heart is not beating only in you; deep down in the tree there is a response. One has to do it to feel it.

But if you feel that you are a third type, then meditation is for you. Running won't help. Then you will have to sit like Buddha, silently, just sitting doing nothing. Sitting so deeply that even thinking looks like a doing and you drop it. For a few days the thoughts will continue, but if you go on sitting, just watching them, without any judgment for or against, they stop visiting you. They stop by and by, gaps come, intervals happen. In those intervals you will have the glimpses of your being.

Those glimpses can be had from the body, they can be had from the heart, they can be had from the head. All the possibilities are there because your being is in all the three, and yet beyond the three.

CLOUD-WATCHING

Observer and Observed

Don't judge, because the moment you start judging you will forget watching. And the reason is that the moment you start judging—"This is a good thought"—for that much space you were not watching. You started thinking, you became involved. You could not remain aloof, standing by the side of the road and just seeing the traffic.

Don't become a participant by appraising, valuing, condemning; no attitude should be taken about what is passing in your mind. You should watch your thoughts just as if clouds are passing in the sky. You don't make judgments about the clouds—this black cloud is evil, this white cloud looks like a sage. Clouds are clouds, they are neither evil nor good.

So are thoughts—just a small wave passing through your mind. Watch without any judgment and you are in for a great surprise. As your watching becomes settled, thoughts will come less and less. The proportion is exactly the same; if you are fifty percent settled in your witnessing, then fifty percent of your thoughts will disappear. If you are sixty percent settled in your witnessing, then only forty percent of thoughts will be there. When you are ninety-nine percent a pure witness, only once in a while will there be a lonely thought—one percent passing on the road, otherwise the traffic is gone. That rush-hour traffic is no longer there.

When you are one hundred percent nonjudgmental, just a witness, it means you have become just a mirror—because a mirror never makes any judgments. An ugly woman looks into it, the mirror has no judgment. A beautiful woman looks into the mirror, it makes no difference. Nobody looks into it, and the mirror is as pure as when somebody is being reflected in it. Neither reflection stirs it, nor no-reflection.

Witnessing becomes a mirror. This is a great achievement in meditation. Then you have moved halfway, and this was the hardest part. Now you know the secret, and the same secret has just to be applied to different objects.

From thoughts you have to move to the more subtle experiences of emotions, feelings, moods. From the mind to the heart, with the same condition: no judgment, just witnessing. And the surprise will be that most of your emotions, feelings, and moods that possess you will start to dissipate. Now, when you are feeling sad you become really sad, you are possessed by sadness. When you are feeling angry, it is not something partial. You become full of anger; every fiber of your being is throbbing with anger.

Watching the heart, the experience will be that now nothing possesses you. Sadness comes and goes, you don't become sad; happiness comes and goes, you don't become happy either. Whatever moves in the deeper layers of your heart does not affect you at all. For the first time you taste something of mastery. You are no longer a slave to be pushed and pulled this way and that way, where any emotion, any feeling, anybody can disturb you for any trivia.

> You speak about watching the clouds of moods passing by, but you have also talked about being total, going totally into whatever is happening. I like to watch the clouds of anger, sadness, jealousy, etc. But when moods like happiness and joy arise, I like to become identified with them and go totally into them and express them. Should I watch every mood or should I go totally into every mood? I can't seem to bring these things together. Would you please comment?

No one can bring these two things together. You will have to choose one. My suggestion is to watch everything with equal distance, with equal aloofness. Sadness, anger, jealousy, happiness, joy, love—remain aloof from all of them, and just be total in your watching.

Your watchfulness should be total. You can be identified with your watching because that is your nature, that's what you are. There is no question of disidentifying from it; even if you try you cannot succeed. Your intrinsic nature is simply that of a witness. A single quality of awareness makes your whole being. So watch everything as if it is a cloud passing by.

I can see your difficulty. You would like to be identified with love, you would like to be identified with happiness and not to be identified with sadness. You would not like to be identified with misery. But this kind of choice is not allowed by existence. If you really want to get beyond the mind and all its experiences—sadness and joy, anger and peace, hate and love; if you want to get beyond all these dualities—you have to watch them equally, you cannot choose. If you choose, you will not be able to watch even those things you want to watch. So the first thing is, just be a watcher.

It will be a little difficult in the beginning to watch things that are so sweet, so beautiful . . . because watching makes you distant from every experience that is passing by like a cloud. You cannot cling. Up to now that's what you have been doing: clinging to what you think is good, and trying to get away from what you think is ugly and miserable. But you have created only a mess of yourself. You have not been successful.

The best way is to be totally a watcher. If you find it difficult there is an alternative. But that alternative is harder, it is more difficult than this one—and that is to get identified with every cloud that moves. If there is misery, then become absolutely miserable. Then don't hold anything back, just go with it to the very end. If you are angry, then be angry and do whatever stupidity it suggests to you to do. If some crazy cloud passes by, be crazy. But then don't miss anything. Whatever comes to you, be totally with it in that moment, and when it is gone it is gone.

This also will liberate you, but it is a more difficult path. If you want something really dangerous to play with, you can get identified with everything. Then don't make any differentiation—this is good to get identified with and this is bad to get identified with. Then there is no question: without any discrimination, get identified, and within a week you will be finished with it. Just one week will be enough, because so many things are passing by. You will be so tired, so exhausted. If you survive, we will meet again . . . and if you don't survive, good-bye!

But this is a dangerous path. I have never heard of anybody surviving. And you know perfectly well what kind of things come to your mind. Sometimes you feel like barking—then get into it, bark like a dog, and whatever the world thinks, let them think. You have chosen your path, you will get free . . . perhaps totally free; enlightenment and freedom from the body will come together! But it is a bit dangerous.

People may try to prevent you, because nobody knows what kinds of things come to your mind. Your own people—your friends, your family, your wife, your husband—may try to prevent you. There are many people all over the world whose families have forced them into insane asylums because they felt that was the only way to protect them. And this happens everywhere.

In my village, the richest family had one person locked inside the basement of their house for his whole life. Everybody knew that something had happened to the person because he suddenly disappeared. But so many years passed that by and by, people had forgotten. I came to know just by chance, because one of my students was the son of the man who was kept in chains. Because he was from my village he used to come to see me often, and one day I just asked him about it. I said, "I have never seen your father."

He became very sad and he said, "I cannot lie to you, but what is happening to my father is such a heavy weight on my heart. Because my family is the richest family of the village, they don't want anybody to know what they are doing with my father. They beat him; he has been caged in the basement almost like a wild animal. He cries, shouts, screams, but nobody listens, nobody goes near him. Just from an opening at the top of the cellar, food is dropped to him. Everything that he needs is dropped down from the top; nobody wants to look at him."

"But," I said, "what has he done?"

He said, "Nothing special, he was just crazy. He used to do things that are not normal." For example, he might go naked into the market. Now, there was no harm . . . he had not done any harm to anybody, he had just been walking naked in the market-place, but that was enough for the family to lock him up. And they made him more and more insane. This was not going to help, this was not a cure, not a treatment.

So if you get identified with all your ideas then you should think, before you start the practice, what people will think about it and how they will behave with you—although it is possible to get free of all those emotions if you get identified with all of them, without any choice.

Either be choicelessly identified or be choicelessly unidenti-fied. The real thing is choicelessness. But if you go the first way you will be on safer ground. Be a choiceless watcher. Don't choose something good and don't throw away something bad. Nothing is good, nothing is bad; only witnessing is good and nonwitnessing is bad.

> Doctor," said the housewife, "I have come to see you about my husband. We have been married for over twenty-five years. He has been a good husband, happy, contented and very devoted to me, but since he came to see you about his headaches he has been a different man. Now he never comes home at night, he never takes me out anymore, he never buys me anything nor gives me any money. Hell, he never even looks at me. Your treatment seems to have changed his entire personality."
>
> "Treatment?" said the doctor. "All I did was give him a prescription for a pair of glasses."

Even a pair of glasses can make a dramatic change to your whole personality, your whole behavior. And this will not be such a small thing as a pair of glasses. If you start getting identified with everything you will be in difficulty from every corner. It is better to choose the safer way; all awakened people have chosen that way. It is without exception the sanest path.

> Sometimes after moments of clarity and lightness, it seems old intimates like violent feelings, jealousy, feeling furious, et cetera, come back even stronger than before, as if they were just waiting around the corner to have their chance again. Can you say something?

I can say something, but those feelings of violence and jealousy and furiousness will still be waiting around the corner. Just by my saying something, they are not going to disappear—because without knowing, you are nourishing them. Without knowing, your desire to get free of them is very superficial.

You are not doing what I have been emphasizing continually; you are doing just the opposite. You are fighting with the darkness, and you are not bringing the light in. You can go on fighting with the darkness as long as you want but you are not going to be victorious. That does not mean that you are weaker than darkness, it simply means that what you are doing has no effect on darkness.

Darkness is only an absence, you cannot do anything directly to it. Just bring light in. And it is not that when you bring light in, darkness will rush outside through all the doors. Darkness is an absence; light comes, and there is no question of absence anymore. Darkness does not go anywhere, it has no existence of its own.

I will read your question: "Sometimes after moments of clarity and lightness, it seems old intimates like violent feelings, jealousy, feeling furious, et cetera, come back even stronger than before, as if they were just waiting around the corner to have their chance again."

Your clarity and your lightness are only momentary. If you bring in the light for a moment and then blow out the candle, the darkness will be back again—not that it was waiting around the corner, but you have again created the absence of light. Your torch of consciousness should be burning continuously; then there will not be any darkness.

These feelings that you think are very dangerous are almost impotent. Violence is there because you have not grown your potential for love; it is the absence of love. And people go on doing stupid things. They try to be nonviolent by repressing the violence, they make tremendous efforts to be nonviolent. But there is no need for anybody to be nonviolent. You are moving in a wrong direction. Violence is a negative thing, and you are trying to destroy violence and become nonviolent. I would say forget about violence. It is the absence of love—be more loving. All the energy that you are putting into repressing violence and becoming nonviolent, pour it into being love.

It was unfortunate that Mahavira and Gautam Buddha both used the word *nonviolence*. I can understand their difficulty. Their difficulty was that by "love" people understand biological love; to avoid that misunderstanding they used a negative term, "nonviolence." But it supports the idea that violence is the positive thing and nonviolence is the negative thing. In fact, violence is the negative thing and love is the positive thing. But they were afraid of using the word "love," and because of their fear that "love" may create the idea of ordinary love in people's minds, they used an unfortunate word: *nonviolence*. And for twenty-five centuries, that nonviolence has been practiced. But you will find most of these people shrunken and dead. Their intelligence does not seem to have blossomed, their consciousness does not seem to have blossomed. Just the mistake of using a wrong word has created twenty-five centuries of immense torture, in thousands of people.

I want you to know that love is the positive thing, and love does not mean only biological love. And you also understand it: you love your mother, you love your brother, you love your friend, and there is no biology involved. These are ordinarily available experiences of nonbiological love. You love a rose flower; is there any biology involved? You love a beautiful moon, you love music, you love poetry, you love sculpture; is there any biology involved? I am taking these examples from ordinary life, just to show you that love has many, many dimensions.

So rather than having just moments of clarity and lightness, be more loving—loving to the trees, loving to the flowers, loving to music, loving to people. Let all kinds of love enrich your life and violence will disappear. A person of love cannot hurt anybody. Love cannot hurt, and cannot be violent.

These violent feelings will not disappear unless their energy is transformed into love. And the true love knows nothing of jealousy. Any love that is followed by jealousy is certainly not the true love, it is biological instinct.

The higher you move—from body to mind, from heart to being—all these crude feelings disappear. Love that happens from being to being knows no jealousy.

And how are you going to find such love?

It is a radiation of your silence, of your peace, of your inner well-being, of your blissfulness. You are so blissful that you want to share it; that sharing is love. Love is not a beggar. It never says, "Give me love." Love is always an emperor, it only knows to give. It never even imagines or expects anything in return.

Be more meditative, become more conscious of your being. Let your inner world become more silent, and love will be flowing through you.

People have all these problems. The problems are different— violence, jealousy, misery, anxiety—but the medicine for all these illnesses is only one, and it is meditation.

And I would like you to be reminded that the word *medicine* and the word *meditation* come from the same root. *Medicine* means something that can cure your body, and *meditation* means something that can cure your soul. Meditation is meditation only because it is a medicine for your innermost illnesses.

A man selling Vaseline petroleum jelly had gone around a number of houses in town a week before and had left some samples, asking people to see if they could find an ingenious use for it. Now he went around to the same houses, asking people what uses they had found for Vaseline.

The man in the first house, a wealthy city gent, said, "I used it for medicinal purposes. Whenever my children scraped their elbows or knees, I would rub it on."

The man in the second house said, "I used it for mechanical purposes, such as greasing the bearings of my bicycle and lawnmower."

The man in the third house, a scruffy, unshaven, working-class fellow, said, "I used it for sexual purposes."

In a shocked voice, the salesman asked, "What do you mean?"

"Well," said the scruffy man, "I put a whole lot of it on the handle of my bedroom door to keep the kids out!"

You can give the same thing to different people and they will come out with different uses, according to their own unconsciousness. But if they are conscious they will find only one use.

A man, a Christian missionary in Japan, went to one very great master, Nan-In, with the New Testament. He was certain that by listening to the beautiful statements of Jesus, particularly the Sermon on the Mount, Nan-In would be converted to Christianity.

The missionary was received with great love and he said, "I have come with my holy book and I want to read a few sentences . . . perhaps they will change your whole life."

Nan-In said, "You have come a little late, because I am changed completely, the transformation has happened. But still, you have come a long way—you can at least read a few sentences."

So the missionary started reading, and just after two or three sentences Nan-In said, "That's enough. Whoever has written these sentences will become a buddha in some future life."

The missionary was shocked: this man was saying, "This man shows some potential, he will become a buddha?!" He said to Nan-In, "But he is the only son of God!"

Nan-In laughed and he said, "That is the trouble. That's what is preventing him from becoming a buddha. Unless he drops such nonsensical ideas, he will not blossom to his full potential. He has beautiful ideas but alongside them he has some stupid ideas, too. There is no God, so the question of being the only begotten son does not arise. In some future life, don't be worried—he will drop them. He seems to be a man of intelligence, and he has suffered enough for his stupid ideas. He got crucified; that was enough punishment. But you should not cling to the stupid part of his statements."

The missionary said, "But it is the very foundation of our religion that Jesus is the only begotten son of God, that there is a God who created the world and that Jesus was born of a virgin."

Nan-In laughed and said, "This poor fellow, if he could drop these small fictitious things, he would have already become a buddha. If you find him somewhere, bring him here, and I will put him right. There was no need to crucify him; all that he needed was someone who could have introduced him into the mysteries of meditation."

Meditation is perhaps the master key for all our problems. Fighting with problems separately will take lives, and still you will not be out of their grip. They will stand around the corner, waiting for their chance—and naturally, if they had to wait too long, they will take as much revenge as possible.

Meditation is not doing anything directly to your violence, not doing anything to your jealousy, to your hate. It is simply bringing light into your house, and the darkness disappears.

? I find I can occasionally watch anger, hurt, frustration; but laughter has always come upon me before I realize it and can watch it. Would you please talk to us about witnessing in this respect?

Laughter is in a way unique. Anger, frustration, worrying, and sadness are all negative and they are never total. You cannot be totally sad, there is no way. Any negative emotion cannot be total because it is negative. Totality needs positivity. Laughter is a positive phenomenon and that's why it is unique. It is a little difficult to be aware of laughter, for two reasons. One, it comes suddenly. In fact, you become aware only when it has come. Unless you are born in England . . . there it never comes suddenly. It is said that if you tell a joke to an Englishman, he laughs twice— first, just to be polite. He does not understand why he is laughing but because you have told a joke he is expected to laugh, and he does not want to hurt you so he laughs. And then in the middle of the night when he gets the joke . . . then he really laughs.

Different races behave differently. Germans laugh only once, when they see that all others are laughing. They join in not to be left alone, because otherwise people will think that they have not understood. And they will never ask anybody what the meaning is either, because that will make them appear ignorant. One man has been with me for many, many years, but every day he would ask somebody or other, "What was the matter? Why were people laughing?"—and he was laughing, too, just not to be left out, but he could never manage to understand a joke. Germans are too serious and it is because of their seriousness that they can't understand.

If you tell a joke to a Jew, he won't laugh, but he will say, "It is an old joke, and moreover you are telling it all wrong." They are the most proficient people about jokes. There are very few jokes that don't have a Jewish origin. So never tell a joke to a Jew, because he is certainly going to tell you, "It is very ancient—don't bother me with it. Secondly, you are telling it all wrong. First learn to tell a joke; it is an art." But he will not laugh.

Laughter naturally comes as thunder comes: suddenly. That is the very mechanism of a joke, any simple joke. Why does it make people laugh? What is the psychology of it? It builds up a certain energy in you; your mind starts thinking in a certain way as you are listening to the joke, and you are excited to know the punch line, how it ends. You start expecting some logical end—because the mind cannot manage anything else but logic—and a joke is not logical. So when the end comes it is so illogical and so ridiculous, but so fitting . . . the energy you were holding, waiting for the end, suddenly bursts forth into laughter. Whether the joke is great or small does not matter, the psychology is the same.

In a small church school the teacher had a beautiful statue, and she was going to give it as a reward to the boy or the girl who gave the right answer to a question. After one hour of teaching she was going to ask a single question, and anybody who gave the right answer would have the statue.

For one hour the teacher told the boys and the girls about Jesus Christ, telling stories about him, his philosophy, his crucifixion, his religion, that he has the greatest following in the world; everything was condensed into an hour's teaching. Then in the end she asked, "I would like to know, who is the greatest man in the world?"

A little American boy stood up and said, "Abraham Lincoln."

The teacher said, "That is good, but not good enough. Sit down."

A little girl from India put her hand up when the teacher asked again, "Who is the greatest man in the world?" The girl answered, "Mahatma Gandhi." The teacher was feeling very frustrated. A whole hour's effort! She said, "That is good, but still not good enough."

Then a very small boy started waving his hand frantically. The teacher said, "Yes, you tell me who is the greatest man in the world."

He said, "There is no question . . . Jesus Christ."

The teacher was puzzled because the boy was a Jew. He won the prize, and when everybody was leaving she took him aside and asked, "Aren't you a Jew?"

He said, "Yes, I am a Jew."

"Then why did you say Jesus Christ?"

He said, "In my heart of hearts I know it is Moses, but business is business!"

Any joke ends with a turn that you were not expecting logically. Then suddenly the whole energy that was building up in you explodes in laughter.

In the beginning it is difficult to be aware in laughter, but it is not impossible. Because it is a positive phenomenon it will take a little more time, but don't try too hard; otherwise you will miss the laughter! That is the trouble. If you try hard to remain aware, you will miss the laughter. Just remain relaxed and when the laughter comes, just like a wave coming in the ocean, silently watch it. But don't let your watcher disturb the laughter. Both have to be allowed.

Laughter is a beautiful phenomenon, it is not to be dropped. But it has never been thought of this way. You don't have any picture of Jesus Christ laughing, or Gautam Buddha laughing, or Socrates; they are all very serious. To me, seriousness is a sickness. A sense of humor makes you more human, more humble. The sense of humor, according to me, is one of the most essential parts of religiousness. A religious person who cannot laugh fully is not fully religious; something is still missing. So you have to walk almost on a razor's edge. Laughter has to be allowed completely.

So first take care of the laughter; that laughter is allowed completely. And watch. Perhaps at first it will be difficult: laughter will come first, and then suddenly you will become aware. No harm. Slowly, slowly, the gap will be smaller. Just time is needed, and soon you will be able to be perfectly aware and totally in laughter.

But it is a unique phenomenon. You shouldn't forget that no animal laughs, no bird laughs—only man, and then too only intelligent people. It is part of intelligence to see immediately the ridiculousness of some situation. And there are so many ridiculous situations all around. The whole of life is hilarious; you just have to sharpen your sense of humor.

So remember to go slowly; there is no hurry and your laughter should not be disturbed. Awareness with total laughter is a great achievement.

Other things—sadness, frustration, disappointment—they are just worthless, they have to be thrown out. There is no need to be very careful about them. Don't handle them carefully; just be fully aware and let them disappear. But laughter has to be saved.

Remember why Gautam Buddha and Jesus and Socrates are not laughing: they forgot, they treated laughter the same way as negative emotions. They were so insistent on awareness that even laughter disappeared. Laughter is a very fine phenomenon and very valuable. As sadness, misery, and suffering disappeared with awareness, they became more and more rooted in awareness and forgot completely that there may be something that has to be saved—and that is laughter.

My feeling is that if Jesus had been able to laugh, Christianity would not have been such a calamity as it proved to be. If Gautam Buddha had been able to laugh, then the millions of Buddhist monks after him would not have been so sad, so dull, so without juice, so lifeless. Buddhism spread all over Asia and it turned the whole of Asia pale.

It is not incidental that Buddhism has chosen a pale color as the color of the clothes of their monks, because paleness is the color of death. When fall comes and trees become nude, their leaves become pale and they start falling, and there are only branches. That paleness is like when a man is dying, and his face becomes pale. He is dying; already the process of death has set in, and within minutes he will be dead. In fact, we and the trees are not different; we behave the same way.

Buddhism made the whole of Asia sad. I have been searching for jokes that have their origin in India and I have not found a single one. Serious people . . . always talking about God and heaven and hell and reincarnation and the philosophy of karma. The joke does not fit in anywhere! When I started speaking in public—I was talking about meditation—I might tell a joke. Once in a while some Jaina monk, or a Buddhist monk, a Hindu preacher, would come to me and say, "You were talking so beautifully about meditation, but why did you bring in that joke? It destroyed everything. People started laughing. They were just starting to get serious and you destroyed all your effort. You did something for half an hour to make them serious, and then you told a joke and you destroyed the whole thing! Why in the world should you tell jokes? Buddha never told a joke, Krishna never told a joke."

I am neither Buddha nor Krishna, and I am not interested in seriousness. In fact, *because* they were becoming serious, I had to bring in that joke. I don't want anybody to become serious, I want everybody to be playful. And life has to become, more and more, closer to laughter than seriousness.

MEDITATIONS AND EXERCISES
FOR TRANSFORMATION

EDITOR'S NOTE: *Osho suggests that with any meditation technique or exercise you experiment for three days and see if it "clicks" with you. If you don't feel any changes happening in you, or if the technique doesn't seem to fit with your type, then try another. Often we cannot see ourselves very clearly at first, and an exercise or meditation might appeal to the mind but turn out not to be very useful for us at all. Or, we might bring in all kinds of rationalizations to try to avoid experimenting with a technique or exercise, precisely because it would be the most helpful of all!*

All the methods in this chapter are offered as possible experiments; it is up to you to try them in a playful way, and discover what feels right for you.

Several references have been made in the main body of this book to meditation. The Osho Active Meditations are techniques that Osho has developed specifically for contemporary men and women living in a fast-paced, stressful environment. These meditations are scientifically designed to help the individual become aware of and then dissolve the emotional and physical blocks and tensions that prevent him from experiencing meditation. A list of the four most fundamental of these techniques appears at the end of this section, with information about each technique and where to learn more. Osho says this about the understanding that underlies the meditation techniques he has developed:

My techniques basically start with catharsis. Whatever is hidden must be released. You must not go on repressing;
rather, choose expression as the path. Do not condemn yourself. Accept what you are because every condemnation creates
division. . . .

This may seem paradoxical, but those who repress their neuro-
sis become more and more neurotic, while those who express it
consciously throw it out. So unless you become consciously insane,
you can never become sane. R.D. Laing is right. He is one of the
most sensitive men in the West. He says, "Allow yourself to be insane." You are insane, so something has to be done about it. What
I say is to become conscious of it. What do old traditions say? They
say "Repress it; do not allow it to come out, otherwise you will become insane." I say allow it to come out; that is the only way
toward sanity. Release it! Inside, it will become poisonous. Throw
it out, remove it from your system totally. Expression is what is
moral. And to do this catharsis, you have to approach it in a very
systematic, methodical way because it is becoming mad with a
method—consciously mad.

You have to do two things: remain conscious of what you are
doing, and then do not suppress anything. This is the discipline
and this has to be learned: to be conscious and nonsuppressive; in
other words, to be conscious and expressive.

THE ABC OF WATCHING

There are three difficulties in becoming aware. These are very
essential for each seeker to understand. In fact, everybody becomes aware, but only when an act is finished. You have been
angry: you slapped your wife, or you threw a pillow at your husband. Later on when the heat is cooled, the moment has passed,

you become aware. But now it is pointless, now nothing can be done. What has been done cannot be undone; it is too late.

Three things are to be remembered. One is becoming aware while the act is happening. That is the first difficulty for the person who wants to become aware—becoming aware in the act itself. Anger is there like smoke inside you. Becoming aware in the very thick of it, that is the first difficulty, but it is not impossible. Just a little effort and you will be able to catch hold of it. In the beginning you will see that you become aware when the anger has gone and everything has cooled; you become aware after fifteen minutes. Try, and you will become aware after five minutes. Try a little more and you will become aware almost immediately, after just one minute. Try a little more and you will become aware just when the anger is evaporating. Try a little more and you will become aware exactly in the middle of it. And that is the first step: to be aware in the act.

Then the second step, which is even more difficult because now you are going into deeper waters. The second step, or the second difficulty, is remembering *before* the act, when the act has not yet happened but is still a thought in you. It has not been actualized but it has become a thought in your mind. It is there potentially, there like a seed; it can become the act any moment.

Now you will need a little more subtle awareness. The act is gross—you hit a person. You can become aware while you are hitting, but the *idea* of hitting is far more subtle. Thousands of ideas go on passing in the mind; who takes note of them? They go on and on, the traffic continues, and most of those ideas never become acts. This is the difference between "sin" and "crime." A crime is when some idea becomes an act. No court can punish you for a thought. You can think of murdering somebody, but no law can punish you for it. You can enjoy the idea, you can dream about it, but you are not subject to any law unless you act, unless you do something and the thought is transformed into actuality. Then it becomes a crime. But religion goes deeper than the law. It says when you think it, it is already a sin. Whether you actualize it or not does not matter; you have committed murder in your inner world and you are affected by it, you are contaminated by it, you are blemished by it.

The second difficulty is to catch hold when the thought is arising in you. It can be done, but it can be done only when you have crossed the first barrier, because thought is not as solid as action. But still, it is solid enough to be seen; you have to just practice a little bit. Sitting silently, just watch your thoughts. Just see all the nuances of a thought—how it arises, how it takes form, how it remains, abides, and how then it leaves you. It becomes a guest and then when the time comes it leaves you. And many thoughts come and go; you are a host where many thoughts come and go. Just watch.

Don't try from the very beginning with the difficult thoughts, try with simple thoughts. That will make it easier, because the process is the same. Just sit in the garden, close your eyes, and see whatever thought is passing—and they are always passing. The dog barks in the neighborhood, and immediately a process of thought starts in you. You suddenly remember a dog you had in your childhood and how much you had loved that dog, and then the dog died, and how you suffered. Then comes the idea of death, and the dog is forgotten and you remember the death of your mother . . . and with the idea of the mother suddenly you remember your father . . . and things go on and on. And the whole thing was triggered by a foolish dog who is not even aware that you are sitting in your garden, who is simply barking because he knows nothing else to keep himself occupied. He was not aware of you, he has not barked for you especially, but a chain was triggered.

Watch these simple chains, and then slowly try them with more emotionally involved things. You are angry, you are greedy, you are jealous—just catch hold of yourself in the middle of the thought. That is the second step.

And the third is to catch hold of this process, which ultimately results in an act, before it becomes a thought. That is the most difficult; right now you cannot even conceive of it. Before anything becomes a thought, it is a feeling.

These are the three things: feeling comes first, then comes thought, then comes the act. You may not be aware at all that each thought is produced by a certain feeling. If the feeling is not there, the thought will not come. Feeling becomes actualized in thought, thought becomes actualized in the act.

Now you have to do the almost impossible thing: to catch hold of a certain feeling. Have you not watched sometimes? You don't really know why you are feeling a little disturbed; there is no real thought that can be identified as the cause, but you are disturbed, you feel disturbed. Something is getting ready underground, some feeling is gathering force. Sometimes you feel sad. There is no reason to feel sad, and there is no thought to provoke it; still, the sadness is there, a generalized feeling. That means a feeling is trying to come above ground; the seed of the feeling is sending its leaves out of the ground.

If you are able to become aware of the thought, then sooner or later you will become aware of the subtle nuances of the feeling. These are the three difficulties. And if you can do these three things, suddenly you will fall into the deepest core of your being.

Action is the farthest from the being, then comes thought, then comes feeling. And behind feeling, just hidden behind feeling, is your being. That being is universal. That being is the goal of all meditators. And these three barriers have to be crossed. These three barriers are like three concentric circles around the center of being.

Find a time and a place to remain unoccupied. That's what meditation is all about. Find at least one hour every day to sit silently doing nothing, utterly unoccupied, just watching whatever passes by inside. In the beginning you will be very sad, looking at things inside you. You will feel only darkness and nothing else, and ugly things and all kinds of black holes appearing. You will feel agony, no ecstasy at all. But if you persist, persevere, the day comes when all these agonies disappear, and behind the agonies is the ecstasy.

Start with small things and you will understand. When you go for a morning walk, enjoy the walk—the birds in the trees and the sunrays and the clouds and the wind. Enjoy, and still remember that you are a mirror; you are reflecting the clouds and the trees and the birds and the people. Go on a morning walk and still remember that you are not it. You are not the walker but the watcher. And slowly, slowly you will have the taste of it—it is a taste, it comes slowly. And it is the most delicate phenomenon in the world; you cannot get it in a hurry. Patience is needed.

Eat, taste the food, and still remember that you are the watcher. In the beginning it will create a little trouble in you because you have not done these two things together. In the beginning, I know, if you start watching you will feel like stopping eating, or if you start eating you will forget watching.

Our consciousness is one-way—right now, as it is—it goes only toward the target. But it can become two-way: it can eat and yet watch. You can remain settled in your center and you can see the storm around you; you can become the center of the cyclone.

Transforming Fear

Fear has a beauty of its own, a delicacy and a sensitivity of its own. In fact it is a very subtle aliveness. The word is negative, but the feeling itself is very positive. Only alive processes can be afraid; a dead thing has no fear. Fear is part of being alive, part of being delicate, part of being fragile. So allow the fear. Tremble with it, let it shake your foundations—and enjoy it as a deep experience of being stirred.

Don't take any attitude about fear; in fact, don't call it fear. The moment you have called it fear you have taken an attitude. You have already condemned it; you have already said that it is wrong, that it should not be there. You are already on guard, already escaping, running away. In a very subtle way you have broken yourself away from it. So don't call it fear. This is one of the most essential things: to stop calling things names. Just watch the feeling of it, the way it is. Allow it, and don't give it a label; remain ignorant.

Ignorance is a tremendously meditative state. Insist on being ignorant, and don't allow the mind to manipulate. Don't allow the mind to use language and words, labels and categories, because it has a whole process. One thing is associated with another, and it goes on and on and on. Just simply look—don't call it fear.

Allow the Trembling

Become afraid and tremble—that is beautiful. Hide in a corner, go under a blanket and tremble. Do what an animal will do if he is afraid. What will a small child do if he is afraid? He will cry. Or a primitive tribesman, what will he do? Only primitive people know that when they are possessed by fear, their hairs will stand on end. Civilized people have forgotten the experience; it has become simply a metaphor. We think it is just a saying, and not really true. But it actually happens.

If you allow fear to take possession of you, your hair will stand on end. Then for the first time you will know what a beautiful phenomenon fear is. In that turmoil, in that cyclone, you will come to know that there is still a point somewhere within you that is absolutely untouched. And if fear cannot touch it, then death cannot touch it. There is darkness and fear all around, with just a small center that is absolutely transcendental to it. Not that you try to be transcendental: you simply allow the fear to totally take possession of you, but suddenly you become aware of the contrast, you become aware of the still point. Fear is one of the doors from where one enters into one's being.

Do What You're Afraid to Do

Whenever there is some fear, always remember not to run away, because that is not the way to solve it. Go into it. If you are afraid of the dark night, go into the dark night, because that is the only way to overcome it. That is the only way to transcend the fear. Go into the night; there is nothing more important than that. Wait, sit there alone, and let the night work.

If you feel afraid, tremble. Let the trembling be there but tell the night, "Do whatever you want to do. I am here." After a few minutes you will see that everything has settled. The darkness is no longer dark, it has come to be luminous. You will enjoy it. You can touch it—the velvety silence, the vastness, the music of it. You will be able to enjoy it and you will say, "How foolish I was to be afraid of such a beautiful experience!"

Whenever there is fear, never escape from it. Otherwise that will become a block and your being will never be able to grow in that dimension. In fact, take hints from fear. Those are the directions in which you need to travel. Fear is simply a challenge. It calls you: "Come!" In your life there will be many fearful spaces. Take the challenge and go into them. Never escape and never be a coward. Then one day, hidden behind each fear, you will find treasures. That's how you become multidimensional.

And remember, all that is alive will give you fear. Dead things don't give you fear because there is no challenge in them.

Relax and Watch

Whenever you feel frightened, just relax. Accept the fact that fear is there, but don't do anything about it. Neglect it; don't pay any attention to it.

Watch the body. There should not be any tension in it. If tension doesn't exist in the body, the fear disappears automatically. Fear creates a certain tense state in the body, so that it can get rooted in it. If the body is relaxed, fear is bound to disappear. A relaxed person cannot be scared. You cannot frighten a relaxed person. Even if fear comes, it will come like a wave and go; it will not grow roots.

And fear coming and going like waves, and you remaining untouched by it, is beautiful. When it gets rooted in you and starts growing in you, then it becomes a growth, a cancerous growth. Then it cripples your inner organism.

So whenever you feel frightened, the one thing to look at is that the body should not be tense. Lie down on the floor and relax—relaxation is the antidote to fear—and it will come and go. You simply watch.

That watching should be indifferent. One just accepts that it's okay. The day is hot; what can you do? The body is perspiring; one has to pass through it. The evening is coming close, and a cool breeze will be blowing. So just watch it, and be relaxed.

Once you have the knack of it—and you will have it soon—you will see that if you are relaxed, fear cannot get attached to you.

Fall Asleep Dying

At night before you go to sleep, for just five or ten minutes just lying down on the bed, start feeling that you are dying—every night. Within a week you will be able to enter into that feeling and you will be enjoying it. It will be a surprise to you how much tension in the body will disappear. Let the whole body die, fall asleep dying, and in the morning you will feel so fresh and full of energy. The energy will be flowing harmoniously.

TRANSFORMING ANGER

Remember, we pour our energy into anger; only then does it become vital. It has no energy of its own; it depends on our cooperation. In watching, the cooperation is broken; you are no longer supporting it. It will be there for a few moments, a few minutes, and then it will be gone. Finding no roots in you, finding you unavailable, seeing that you are far away, a watcher on the hills, it will dissipate, it will disappear. And that disappearance is beautiful. That disappearance is a great experience.

Seeing the anger disappear, great serenity arises: the silence that follows the storm. You will be surprised that each time anger arises and if you can watch, you will fall into such tranquility as you have not known before. You will fall into such deep meditation . . . when the anger disappears you will see yourself so fresh, so young, so innocent, as you have never known yourself. Then you will be thankful even to anger; you will not be angry at it— because it has given you a new beautiful space to live in, a new utterly fresh experience to go through. You have used it, you have made a steppingstone out of it.

This is the creative use of the negative emotions.

Just Be Angry

When you feel angry, there is no need to be angry against someone; just be angry. Let it be a meditation. Close the room, sit by yourself, and let the anger come up as much as it can. If you feel like beating, beat a pillow. . . .

Do whatsoever you want to do; the pillow will never object. If you want to kill the pillow, take a knife and kill it. It helps, it helps tremendously. One can never imagine how helpful a pillow can be. Just beat it, bite it, throw it. If you are against somebody in particular, write their name on the pillow or stick a picture on it.

Make your anger a total act in meditation, and then see what happens. You will feel it coming from your whole body. If you allow it, then every cell of your body will be in it. Every pore, every fiber of the body will become violent. Your whole body will be in a mad situation. It will go mad, but allow it, and don't withhold.

You will feel ridiculous, foolish—but anger *is* ridiculous; you cannot do anything about it. So let it be and enjoy it like an energy phenomenon. It is an energy phenomenon. If you are not hurting anybody there is nothing wrong in it. When you try this you will see that any idea of hurting anybody else disappears by and by. You can make it a daily practice, just twenty minutes every morning.

Then watch what happens the whole day. You will be calmer, because the energy that would have become anger has been thrown out; the energy that would have become poison is thrown out of the system. Do this for at least two weeks, and after one week you will be surprised to find that whatever the situation, anger is not coming up.

Getting the Chip Off Your Shoulder

Just go in your room, close the door, and think of the experience of anger when you went mad. Remember it, and re-enact it. That will be easy for you. Re-enact it again, do it again, relive it. Do not just remember it, *relive* it. Remember that someone had insulted you, and what was said and how you reacted to the person. React again, replay it.

Your mind is just a tape-recording device, and this incident is recorded in the same sequence as it happened, just as if it has been placed on a tape-recording in your brain. You can have the same feeling again. Your eyes will go red, your body will start trembling and will become feverish, the whole thing will be re-enacted. So don't just remember, relive it. Start feeling the experience again, and the mind will get the idea. The incident will come back to you and you will relive it. But in reliving it, remain undisturbed.

Start from the past—this is easy because now it is a play, the actual situation is not there. And if you become capable of doing this, then you will be able to do it when a situation for anger is really there, when a real situation is there. This re-enacting something from the past will do much to help you.

Everyone has scars in his mind; unhealed wounds are there. If you re-enact them, you will be unburdened. If you can go to your past and finish something that has remained incomplete, you will be unburdened from your past. Your mind will become fresher; the dust will be thrown away.

That incomplete thing goes on hovering over the mind like a cloud. It influences everything that you are and that you are doing. That cloud has to be dispersed. Move back on the time track and bring back desires that have remained incomplete, and relive the wounds that are still hurting you. They will be healed. You will become more whole, and through this you will have the knack of how to remain undisturbed in a situation that is disturbed.

Taking Notice Thrice

In Buddhism they have a particular method that they call "taking notice thrice." If a problem arises—for example, if somebody suddenly feels jealousy, or greed, or anger—they have to note three times that it is there. If anger is there, the disciple has to say inwardly three times, "Anger . . . Anger . . . Anger." Just to take complete note of it so that it doesn't miss the consciousness, that's all. Then he goes on with whatsoever he was doing. He doesn't do anything with the anger, but simply notes it thrice.

It is tremendously beautiful. Immediately you become aware of the disturbance, you take note of it, and it is gone. It cannot take hold of you because that can only happen when you are unconscious. This taking notice thrice makes you so aware inside that you are separate from the anger. You can objectify it, because it is there and you are here. And Buddha told his disciples to do this with everything.

Running Like a Child

Start running in the morning on the road. Start with half a mile and then one mile and come to at least three miles eventually. While running, use the whole body. Don't run as if you are in a straitjacket. Run like a small child, using the whole body—hands and feet—and run. Breathe deeply and from the belly. Then sit under a tree, rest, perspire, and let the cool breeze come; feel peaceful. This will help very deeply.

The musculature has to be relaxed. If you like swimming, you can go swimming also. That will help. But that too has to be done as totally as possible. Anything in which you can become totally involved will be helpful. It is not a question of anger or any other emotion. The question is to get into anything totally; then you will also be able to get into anger and love. One who knows how to get into anything totally can get into everything totally; what it is, is not the point.

And it is difficult to work with anger directly because it may be deeply repressed. So work indirectly. Running will help much anger and much fear to evaporate. When you are running for a long time and breathing deeply, the mind stops functioning and the body takes over. For a few moments sitting under the shade of the tree, perspiring, enjoying the cool breeze, there are no thoughts. You are simply a throbbing body, an alive body, an organism in tune with the whole, just like an animal.

Within three weeks you will feel things going very deeply. Once anger is relaxed, gone, you will feel free.

Remember You Are the Source

Someone has insulted you—anger suddenly erupts, you are feverish. Anger is flowing toward the person who has insulted you. Now you will project this whole anger onto the other. He has not done anything. If he has insulted you, what has he done? He has just pricked you, he has helped your anger to arise—but the anger is yours.

The other is not the source; the source is always within you. The other is hitting the source, but if there is no anger within you it cannot come out. If you hit a buddha, only compassion will come out because only compassion is there. Anger will not come out because anger is not there. If you throw a bucket into a dry well, nothing comes out. In a water-filled well, you throw a bucket and water comes out, but the water is from the well. The bucket only helps to bring it out. So one who is insulting you is just throwing a bucket in you, and then the bucket will come out filled with the anger, hate, or fire that was within you. You are the source, remember.

For this technique, remember that you are the source of everything that you go on projecting onto others. And whenever there is a mood against or for, immediately move within and go to the source from where this hate is coming. Remain centered there; do not move to the object. Someone has given you a chance to be aware of your own anger; thank him immediately and forget him.

Close your eyes, move within, and now look at the source from where this love or this anger is coming. From where? Go within, move within. You will find the source there because the anger is coming from your source.

Hate or love or anything is coming from your source. And it is easy to go to the source at the moment you are angry, or in love, or in hate, because then you are hot. It is easy to move in then. The wire is hot and you can take it in, you can move inward with that heat. And when you reach a cool point within, you will suddenly realize a different dimension, a different world opening before you. Use anger, use hate, use love to go within.

One of the greatest of Zen masters, Lin Chi, used to say, "While I was young I was fascinated by boating. I had one small boat, and I would go on the lake alone. For hours together I would remain there.

"Once it happened that with closed eyes I was in my boat meditating on the beautiful night. Then a boat came floating downstream and struck my boat. My eyes were closed, so I thought, 'Someone is here with his boat, and he has struck my boat.' Anger arose. I opened my eyes and I was just going to say something to that man in anger; then I realized that the boat was empty! Then there was no way for my anger to move. To whom could I express it? The boat was empty, it was just floating downstream on its own and it had come and struck my boat. So there was nothing to do. There was no possibility to project the anger on an empty boat."

So Lin Chi said, "I closed my eyes. The anger was there—but finding no way out, I closed my eyes and just floated backward with the anger. And that empty boat became my realization. I came to a point within myself in that silent night. That empty boat was my master. And now if someone comes and insults me, I laugh and I say, 'This boat is also empty.' I close my eyes and I go within."

Transforming Sadness and Depression

Editor's Note: *As Osho mentions earlier in the book, much of our sadness and depression is related to suppressed anger, and will naturally be addressed by experimenting with the methods in the previous section. Here are some more methods to try:*

Find the Inner Smile

When you are happy, start doing one thing: Whenever you are sitting and you have nothing to do, just relax your lower jaw and open the mouth just slightly. Start breathing from the mouth but not deeply. Just let the body breathe so it will be shallow and will be more and more shallow. And when you feel that the breathing has become very shallow and the mouth is open and your jaw is relaxed, your whole body will feel very relaxed.

In that moment, start feeling a smile, not on the face but all over your inner being—and you will be able to. It is not a smile that comes on the lips, it is an existential smile that spreads just inside.

Try tonight and you will know what it is, because it cannot be explained. No need to smile with the lips on the face, but just as if you are smiling from the belly; the belly is smiling. And it is a smile, not a laughter, so it is very soft, delicate, fragile—like a small rose flower opening in the belly and the fragrance spreading all over the body.

Once you have known what this smile is you can remain happy for twenty-four hours. And whenever you feel that you are missing that happiness, just close your eyes and catch hold of that smile again and it will be there. And in the daytime, as many times as you want, you can catch hold of it. It is always there.

Decide First Thing

There was a Sufi mystic who remained happy his whole life—no one had ever seen him unhappy—who was always laughing, who was laughter, whose whole being was a perfume of celebration.

In his old age, when he was dying—on his deathbed and still enjoying, laughing hilariously—a disciple asked, "You puzzle us. You are still laughing; how are you managing it?"

The old man said, "It is simple. I asked my master. I went to my master as a young man; I was only seventeen and already miserable, and my master was old, seventy, and he was sitting under a tree, laughing for no reason at all. There was nobody else there, nothing had happened, nobody had cracked a joke or anything, and he was simply laughing, holding his belly. I asked him, 'What is the matter with you? Are you mad or something?'

"He said, 'One day I was also as sad as you are. Then it dawned on me that it is my choice, it is my life.' Since that day, every morning when I get up the first thing I decide is . . . before I open my eyes I say to myself, 'Abdullah'"—that was his name—"'what do you want? Misery? Blissfulness? What you are going to choose today?' And it happens that I always choose blissfulness."

Laughing/Earthing/Dancing

Just sitting silently, create a giggle in the very guts of your being, as if your whole body is giggling, laughing. Start swaying with that laughter; let it spread from the belly to the whole of your body—hands laughing, feet laughing. Go crazily into it. For twenty minutes do the laughing. If it comes uproariously, loudly, allow it. If it comes silently then sometimes silently, sometimes loudly, but spend twenty minutes laughing. Then lie down on the earth or on the floor; spread yourself on the floor, facing the floor. If it is warm and you can do it in your garden in contact with the earth that will be far better. If it can be done naked that will be even better. Make contact with the earth, the whole body lying down there on the earth, and just feel that the earth is the mother and you are the child. Get lost in that feeling.

Twenty minutes of laughter, then twenty minutes of deep contact with the earth. Breathe with the earth, feel one with the earth. We come from the earth and one day we will be going back to it. After those twenty minutes of energizing—because the earth will give so much energy that your dancing will have a different quality to it—dance for twenty minutes. Just any dance, put music on and dance.

If it is difficult, it is cold outside or if you don't have any private space outdoors, then you can do this inside your room. If it is possible, do it outside. If it is cold, cover yourself with a blanket. Find ways and means, but continue to do it, and within six to eight months you will see great changes happening on their own.

Be As Negative As You Can

For forty minutes, just become negative—as negative as you can. Close the doors, put pillows around the room. Unhook the phone, and tell everybody that you are not to be disturbed for one hour. Put a notice on the door saying that for one hour you should be left totally alone. Make things as dim as possible. Put on some gloomy music, and feel dead. Sit there and feel negative. Repeat "No" as a mantra.

Imagine scenes of the past—when you were very dull and dead, and you wanted to commit suicide, and there was no zest to life—and exaggerate them. Create the whole situation around you. Your mind will distract you. It will say, "What are you doing? The night is so beautiful, and the moon is full!" Don't listen to the mind. Tell it that it can come back later on, but for now you are devoting your time completely to negativity. Cry, weep, shout, scream, swear, whatever you feel like, but remember one thing: don't become happy. Don't allow any happiness. If you catch yourself, immediately give yourself a slap! Bring yourself back to negativity and start beating the pillows, fighting with them, jumping. Be nasty! And you will find it very difficult to be negative for these forty minutes.

This is one of the basic laws of the mind: that whatever negative thing you try to do consciously, you cannot do. But *do it*—and when you do it consciously, you will feel a separation. You are doing it but still you are a witness; you are not lost in it. A distance arises, and that distance is tremendously beautiful.

After forty minutes, suddenly jump out of the negativity. Throw the pillows away, turn on the lights, put on some beautiful music and have a dance for twenty minutes. Just say "Yes! yes! yes!"—let it be your mantra. And then take a good shower. It will uproot all the negativity, and it will give you a new glimpse of saying yes.

Move to the Opposite

If you have been angry, then do something that is just the contrary to break the habit. Not only that—when you break a habit, energy is released. If you don't use that energy, again the habit will have to be formed by the mind; otherwise, where will the energy go? So always move to the opposite.

If you have been sad, try to be happy. It is difficult, because the old path is the way of least resistance—it is easier—and to be happy you will have to make an effort. You will have to consciously give a fight to the dead mechanical habits of the mind. So you will have to recondition it. That is, you create a new habit of being happy.

Unless a new habit is created—of being happy—the old habit is bound to persist, because the energy needs some outlet. You cannot simply remain without any outlet. You will die, you will suffocate. If your energy is not becoming love, it is bound to become sour, bitter; anger, sadness. Sadness is not the problem; neither is anger or unhappiness. The problem is how not to get into the old rut.

So live a little more consciously. And when you find yourself getting into the old habit, just do the opposite immediately; don't wait for a single moment. It is easy—once you know the knack of how to do it. You are getting set . . . just do something!

Anything will do. Go for a long walk, start dancing. Let the dance be a little sad in the beginning, mm? It is bound to be: you are sad, how can you suddenly become happy? Start dancing in sadness and the dancing will divert the sadness. You have brought something new into the sadness that has never been there before. You have never danced before when you were unhappy and sad, so you will puzzle the mind. The mind will feel at a loss—what to do?—because the mind can only function with the old. Anything new, and the mind is simply inefficient. . . .

Everybody by and by becomes expert—expert in sadness, expert in unhappiness, expert in anger. Then you become afraid of losing your expertise, because you have become so efficient.

Feeling sad—dance, or go and stand under the shower and see sadness disappearing from your body as the body heat disappears. Feel that with the water showering on you, the sadness is being removed just as perspiration and dust are removed from the body. And see what happens.

TRANSFORMING JEALOUSY

If you suffer from jealousy, just watch how it arises in you—how it grabs you, how it surrounds you, clouds you, how it tries to manipulate you. How it drags you into paths where you never wanted to go in the first place, how finally it creates great frustration in you, how it destroys your energy, dissipates your energy and leaves you very negatively depressed, frustrated. Just watch the whole thing.

Just see the facticity of it—without condemnation, without appreciation, without any judgment for or against. Just watch, aloof, distant, as if you have nothing to do with it. Be very scientific in watching.

One of the most important scientific contributions to the world is nonjudgmental observation. When a scientist is experimenting, he simply experiments without any judgment, without any conclusion. If he has a conclusion already in his mind, that means he is not a scientist; his conclusion will influence the experiment.

Be a scientist in your inner world. Let your mind be your lab, and you observe—with no condemnation, remember. Don't say, "Jealousy is bad." Who knows? Don't say, "Anger is bad." Who knows? Yes, you have heard, you have been told, but that is what others say; this is not your experience. You have to be very existential, experiential—unless your experiment proves it, you are not to say yes or no to anything. You have to be utterly nonjudgmental. And then, watching jealousy is a miracle.

You simply go without any decision, just to see exactly what it is. What is this jealousy? What is this energy called jealousy? And watch it as you watch a rose flower: just look into it. When there is no conclusion your eyes are clear. Clarity is attained only by those who have no conclusions. Watch, look into it, and it will become transparent, and you will come to know that it is stupid. And knowing its stupidity, it drops of its own accord. You don't need to drop it.

Watching Sex

Move into sex; nothing is wrong in it, but remain a watcher. Watch all the movements of the body; watch the energy flowing in and out, watch how the energy is falling downward; watch the orgasm, what is happening—how two bodies move in a rhythm. Watch the heartbeat: faster and faster it goes, a moment comes when it is almost mad. Watch the warmth of the body; the blood circulates more. Watch the breathing; it is going mad and chaotic. Watch the moment when a limit comes to your voluntariness and everything becomes involuntary. Watch the moment from where you could have come back, but beyond that there is no return. The body becomes so automatic, all control is lost. Just a moment before the ejaculation you lose all control, the body takes over.

Watch it: the voluntary processes, the nonvoluntary process. The moment when you were in control and you could have gone back, the return was possible, and the moment when you cannot come back, the return has become impossible; now the body has taken over completely, you are no longer in control. Watch everything—and millions of things are there. Everything is so complex and nothing is as complex as sex, because the whole bodymind is involved; only the witness is not involved, only one thing remains always outside.

The witness is an outsider. By its very nature the witness can never become an insider. Find out this witness and then you are standing on the top of the hill, and everything goes in the valley and you are not concerned. You simply see; what is your concern? It is as if it is happening to somebody else.

From Desire to Love

Whenever you feel sexual desire arising, there are three possibilities. One is to indulge in it; that is the ordinary thing, everybody is doing that. Second is to repress it, to force it down so it goes out of your consciousness into the darkness of the unconscious, to throw it into the basement of your life. That's what your so-called extraordinary people are doing—mahatmas, saints, monks. But both are against nature and both are against the inner science of transformation.

The third—a very rare minority ever tries it—is that when the sexual desire arises, close your eyes. It is a very valuable moment: desire arising is energy arising. It is like the sun rising in the morning. Close your eyes; this is the moment to be meditative. Move downward to the sex center where you are feeling the thrill, the vibration, the kick. Move there and just be a silent onlooker. Witness it, don't condemn it. The moment you condemn it you have gone away from it. And don't enjoy it, because the moment you enjoy you are unconscious. Just be alert, watchful, like a lamp burning in a dark night. You just take your consciousness there, unflickering, unwavering. You see what is happening at the sex center. What is this energy?

Don't call it names, because all words have become contaminated. Even if you say it is "sex," you have immediately started condemning it. The very word has become condemnatory. Or, if you belong to a different generation, then the very word has become something sacred. But the word is always loaded with emotion. Any word that is loaded with emotion becomes a barrier on the path of awareness.

Just don't call it anything, just watch the fact that an energy is arising near the sex center. There is a thrill—watch it. And watching it, you will feel a totally new quality of energy. Watching it, you will see it is rising upward; it is finding a path inside you. And the moment it starts rising upward you will feel a coolness falling on you, a silence surrounding you, a grace, a beatitude, a benediction, a blessing all around you. It is no longer like a thorn, painful. It no longer hurts; it is very soothing, like a balm. And the more you remain aware, the higher it will go. If it can come up to the heart, which is not very difficult—difficult, but not *very* difficult—if you remain alert you will see it has come to the heart, and when it comes to the heart you will know for the first time what love is.

Feel Your Pain

If somebody has hurt you, feel thankful that the person has given you an opportunity to feel a deep wound. He or she has opened a wound in you. The wound may be created by many hurts that you have suffered in your whole life. The other may not be the cause of all the suffering, but a process has been triggered. Just close the door to your room, sit silently, with no anger for the person but with total awareness of the feeling that is arising in you: the hurt feeling that you have been rejected, that you have been insulted. And then you will be surprised that not only is this person there: all the men and all the women and all the people who have ever hurt you will start moving in your memory.

You will start not only remembering them, you will start reliving them. You will be going into a kind of primal. Feel the hurt, feel the pain, don't avoid it. That's why in many therapies the patient is told not to take any drugs before the therapy begins, for the simple reason that drugs are a way to escape from your inner misery.

Whatsoever the pain of it and whatsoever the suffering of it, let it be so. First experience it in its total intensity. It will be difficult, it will be heartrending. You may start crying like a child, you may start rolling on the ground in deep pain, your body may go through contortions. You may suddenly become aware that the pain is not only in the heart, it is all over the body—that it is aching all over, that it is painful all over, that your whole body is nothing but pain.

If you can experience it—this is of tremendous importance— then start absorbing it. Don't throw it away. It is such a valuable energy, don't throw it away. Absorb it, drink it, accept it, welcome it, feel grateful to it. And say to yourself, "This time I'm not going to avoid it, this time I'm not going to reject it, this time I'm not going to throw it away. This time I will drink it and receive it like a guest. This time I will digest it."

It may take a few days for you to be able to digest it, but the day it happens, you have stumbled upon a door that will take you really far, far away. A new journey has started in your life, you are moving into a new kind of being—because immediately, the moment you accept the pain with no rejection anywhere, its energy and its quality change. It is no longer pain. In fact, one is simply surprised; one cannot believe it, it is so incredible. One cannot believe that suffering can be transformed into ecstasy, that pain can become joy.

Uncondition Your Past

Sadness is nothing but the same energy that could have been happiness. When you don't see that your happiness is flowering, you become sad. Whenever you see somebody happy, you become sad; why is it not happening to you? It can happen to you! There is no problem in it. You just have to uncondition your past. You will have to go a little out of the way for it to happen, so just make a few efforts to open yourself.

Start one meditation in the night. Just feel as if you are not a human being at all. You can choose any animal that you like. If you like a cat, good. If you like a dog, good . . . or a tiger—male, female, anything you like. Just choose, but then stick to it. Become that animal. Move on all fours in the room and become that animal. For fifteen minutes enjoy the fantasy as much as you can. Bark if you are a dog and do things a dog is expected to do—and really do them! Enjoy it. And don't control, because a dog cannot control. A dog means absolute freedom, so whatever happens in that moment, do. In that moment don't bring in the human element of control. Be really doggedly a dog. For fifteen minutes roam around the room . . . bark, jump.

Continue this for seven days. It will help. You need a little more animal energy. You are too sophisticated, too civilized, and that is crippling you. Too much civilization is a paralyzing thing. It is good in small doses, but too much of it is dangerous. One should always remain capable of being an animal. If you can learn to be a little wild, your problems will begin to disappear.

So just do one thing for a few days: whenever you feel you are becoming miserable, go slowly into it, don't go fast; make slow movements, T'ai Chi movements.

If you are feeling sad, then close your eyes and let the film move very slowly. Go slowly, slowly into it, having the vision all around, looking, watching what is happening. Go very slowly so that you can see each act separately, each fiber of the whole cloth separately.

For just a few days do slow movements, and in other things also, slow down. For example, if you walk, walk more slowly than you have been walking up to now. From this moment start lagging behind. Eating, eat slowly . . . chew more. If you usually take twenty minutes to have a meal, take forty minutes; slow it down fifty percent. If you open your eyes fast, slow down. Take your shower in double the time that you usually do; slow down everything.

When you slow down everything, automatically your whole mechanism slows down. The mechanism is one: it is the same mechanism you walk with, it is the same mechanism you talk with, it is the same mechanism you become angry with. There are no different mechanisms; it is only one organic mechanism. So if you slow down everything, you will be surprised that your sadness, your misery, all are slowed down.

Buddha used this approach very deeply for his disciples and for himself. He told them to walk slowly, to talk slowly, to go into each movement so slowly . . . as if you have no energy. And that creates a tremendous experience: your thoughts slow down, your desires slow down, your old habits all slow down. Just slow down for three weeks.

OSHO ACTIVE MEDITATIONS

Following is a list of the most widely used Osho Active Meditations, with a brief description of each. Each meditation technique is accompanied by special music, composed with Osho's guidance, to give structure and support to each stage of the process.

Osho Dynamic Meditation   A meditation in five stages beginning with deep, chaotic breathing into the belly, followed by catharsis and energy release, centering, silence, and celebration. This is among the most physically demanding—and emotionally cleansing—of all the Osho Active Meditations, and is best done first thing in the morning.

Osho Kundalini Meditation   Often referred to as the "sister meditation" to Dynamic, this technique is generally done in late afternoon or early evening, at the end of the day's work. It allows the body to shake out and release accumulated tensions and stress in a loose and natural way, followed by dance, and ending with a period of silent watching.

Osho Nataraj Meditation   Dancing totally and freely for forty-five minutes, followed by stillness and silence.

Osho Nadabrahma Meditation   Based on an ancient Tibetan method, this technique begins with humming to gently open all the energy centers in the body, adding slow and graceful hand movements and ending with a silent period. Promotes centering, healing, and relaxation.

For more detailed information and descriptions of the techniques, including video demonstrations of the different stages, go to www.osho.com/meditation.

About the Author

The Osho teachings defy categorization, covering everything from the individual quest for meaning to the most urgent social and political issues facing society today. His books are not written but are transcribed from audio and video recordings of extemporaneous talks given to international audiences over a period of thirty-five years. Osho has been described by the *Sunday Times* of London as one of the "1000 Makers of the 20th Century" and by American author Tom Robbins as "the most dangerous man since Jesus Christ."

About his own work, Osho has said that he is helping to create the conditions for the birth of a new kind of human being. He has often characterized this new human being as "Zorba the Buddha"—capable of enjoying both the earthy pleasures of a Zorba the Greek and the silent serenity of a Gautam Buddha. Running like a thread through all aspects of Osho's work is a vision that encompasses both the timeless wisdom of the East and the highest potential of Western science and technology.

Osho is also known for his revolutionary contribution to the science of inner transformation, with an approach to meditation that acknowledges the accelerated pace of contemporary life. The unique Osho Active Meditations are designed to first release the accumulated stresses of body and mind, so that it is easier to experience the thought-free and relaxed state of meditation.

OSHO International Meditation Resort

The Osho International Meditation Resort is a place where people can have a direct personal experience of a new way of living with more alertness, relaxation, and fun. Located about 100 miles southeast of Mumbai in Pune, India, the resort offers a variety of programs to thousands of people who visit each year from more than 100 countries around the world.

Originally developed as a summer retreat for Maharajas and wealthy British colonialists, Pune is now a thriving modern city that is home to a number of universities and high-tech industries. The Meditation Resort spreads over forty acres in a tree-lined suburb known as Koregaon Park. The resort campus provides accommodation for a limited number of guests, and there is a plentiful variety of nearby hotels and private apartments available for stays of a few days up to several months.

Resort programs are all based in the Osho vision of a qualitatively new kind of human being who is able both to participate creatively in everyday life and to relax into silence and meditation. Most programs take place in modern, air-conditioned facilities and include a variety of individual sessions, courses, and workshops covering everything from creative arts to holistic health treatments, personal transformation and therapy, esoteric sciences, the "Zen" approach to sports and recreation, relationship issues, and significant life transitions for men and women. Individual sessions and group workshops are offered throughout the year, alongside a full daily schedule of meditations.

Outdoor cafes and restaurants within the resort grounds serve both traditional Indian fare and a choice of international dishes, all made with organically grown vegetables from the commune's own farm. The campus has its own private supply of safe, filtered water.

Visit www.osho.com/resort for more information, including travel tips, course schedules, and guest house bookings.

For More Information

about Osho and his work, see:

www.osho.com

a comprehensive Web site in several languages that includes an online tour of the Meditation Resort and a calendar of its course offerings, a catalog of books and tapes, a list of Osho information centers worldwide, and selections from Osho's talks.

Or contact:

Osho International
New York
email: oshointernational@oshointernational.com